PERSPECTIVES ON GALBRAITH

PERSPECTIVES ON GALBRAITH

*Conversations
And Opinions*

FREDERICK J. PRATSON

CBI PUBLISHING COMPANY, INC.
51 Sleeper Street
Boston, Massachusetts 02110

Library of Congress Cataloging in Publication Data

Pratson, Frederick J.
    Perspectives on Galbraith.

    Bibliography: p.
    1. Galbraith, John Kenneth, 1908-   2. Econo-
mists — United States — Biography. I.   Galbraith, John Kenneth, 1908-   II. Title.
HB119.G33P7   330'.092'4   78-8975
ISBN 0-8436-0748-3

Printed in the United States of America

Other books by Frederick J. Pratson

Land of the Four Directions   *Chatham Press*
The Sea in their Blood   *Houghton Mifflin*
A Guide to Atlantic Canada   *Chatham Press*
The Special World of the Artisan   *Houghton Mifflin*
New Hampshire   *Stephen Greene Press*

iv

For my parents,
John and Catherine.

CONTENTS

FOREWORD

John Kenneth Galbraith is probably the closest thing America has had in our generation to a Renaissance Man. As economist, ambassador, philosopher, professor, writer, skier, and public scold, he has had a continuing and extremely influential impact on an entire generation of American life and national economic policy.

In his brilliant, witty, and articulate way, he has been a pioneer of modern economic theory and a hair shirt for traditional economic thought. He has encouraged serious analysis of the deficiencies of economic models, emphasizing the flaws of competition and the misallocation of resources caused by such factors as economic concentration, administered prices, and monopolistic practices. His efforts have done much to close the gap between theory and reality on economic issues.

He has also been a pioneer in trying to lead us safely across the Great Divide between the private and public sectors in American life. *The Affluent Society* is perhaps his greatest monument in blazing this trail. More than any other economist, he sensitized the nation to a long list of urgent social needs — needs that must be met by government, but that cannot be met by policies that foolishly starve the public sector. He dramatized the dilemma of "private affluence and public squalor." He foresaw the decay of the cities and the crises over unemployment, over health and education, over housing and transportation. He tried to warn us that old myths about the size and role of government were jeopardizing our ability to deal with new reality, making all our problems worse.

In these and other ways, Galbraith has been a profound, persuasive, and progressive influence on all who care about the future of this country. His role is secure as a giant in the contemporary intellectual and political history of America.

Edward M. Kennedy
United States Senator

ACKNOWLEDGMENTS

I want to take this opportunity to thank John Kenneth Galbraith for the many hours of his valuable time which he so generously gave me in London, Cambridge (Mass.), and Newfane, Vermont. I believe that the conversations which we had together are what makes this book unique. I had complete freedom to use this original material as I saw fit. Although Ken Galbraith has had a keen interest in this project, and naturally so since is about him and his ideas, in no way did he direct or influence its development and outcome. This project was a most enjoyable, entertaining and educational experience for me, and I feel very fortunate to have such a fine human being as a friend.

I owe a great debt to Andrea Williams for her assistance and warm friendship. Her ability to make things happen, meticulous attention to detail, and many expressions of encouragement made this book possible. And I would like to extend my appreciation to Emy Lou Davis, her associate.

I would like to thank David Otte, my literary agent; Michael Tucker, vice president of CBI Publishing Company, Inc.; Anne Norton, my typist; and Michael Hamilton; all of whom have made substantial contributions to the realization of this project.

I would also like to thank the many outstanding individuals who agreed to participate in this book, and who gave a wide range of insights about one of the most interesting personalities living in the world today. I also want to express my deep appreciation to the many other people who contributed their talents to the evaluation or editing of the manuscript and to the production of the book.

And very special thanks to Patricia Gibson Pratson, my wife, a rare soul on this earth who has a knack for pumping up flagging spirits and making this writer march on with a sense of renewed purpose.

INTRODUCTION

But when I tell him he hates flatterers,
he says he does, being then the most
flattered.
Julius Caesar
William Shakespeare

J ohn Kenneth Galbraith is one of the world's most influential individuals. He is also the most entertaining. He is admired, envied, praised, and hated. He is seldom ignored.

Galbraith is a many-sided international personality. He is an economist, writer, teacher, lecturer, television star. He has been a politician of sorts, a diplomat, and a government official. And it is this many-sided quality that makes it difficult for people to categorize him conveniently.

The difficulty of placing a label on Galbraith does not grow out of obscurity or reticence. He is a very accessible figure. He talks clearly, frankly, and most of the time for the record. He was extremely generous in making himself available to me. I spent many days with Galbraith, walking through London or the Vermont woods, speaking with him in his study and office. His colleagues, friends, and critics expressed themselves with candor.

Yet the paradox remains. Galbraith is highly visible, accessible, candid. But still he is elusive.

Since Galbraith is one of the most influential figures in the world today, I have tried to present the many aspects of his thoughts as a means of better understanding his influence. This book offers a number of facets of Galbraith, through his published works, through interviews with him, and through what other people have to say about him. As an example of my attempt to find out what makes Galbraith tick, I once asked him if he was a seeker of truth.

"The loudest, the most eloquent seekers of truth are the people who least want to discover it," he told me. "The most vehement speeches about the search for truth are made by university presidents who are most uncomfortable with members of the faculty who have come up with it. I would like to think that I'm motivated by some basic and uncontrollable love of truth, but I would be quite wrong. What I relish most is the use of truth as a weapon of embarrassment. I enormously enjoy the embarrassment which comes to the alleged seeker of truth when he or she is faced with it. And this has always given me more pleasure than any moralistic pursuit of truth itself. When I have hit upon something which is obvious, which I know has been swept under the rug, the thought never crosses my mind that it is wrong, immoral to have hidden the truth. The thought that always comes to me is how inconvenient it will be for someone I don't necessarily like to have to face this as a description of reality."

At first, I was surprised by his response. But the more I came to know Galbraith, both through his writings and my talks with him, the more prepared I became to expect the unexpected.

As much has been written about Galbraith as he has written. And his friends — and critics — are quoted throughout this book. A number of his contemporaries, such as William F. Buckley, Jr., Paul A. Samuelson and Arthur Schlesinger, Jr., describe various aspects of Galbraith — the man and the economist.

For example, William F. Buckley told me:

"I don't think of Ken as being primarily an economist. I think of him primarily as a social philosopher. I don't say that to disparage Ken. I just happen to think that social philosophy is far more interesting. I feel that Galbraith's place in history will be not that of an economist but that of a hugely influential and brilliant literary technician and critic. He is a great writer. Ken has great wit and is a man with some startling and highly rewarding social concepts. But, it seems inconceivable that he will be thought of in the future as having used economics other than as a sort of extended metaphor by which he has been able to ply his wares.

"Ken Galbraith is a man of great warmth. He is also someone who does not suffer fools gladly. So, he is capable of very considerable impatience. But he has tremendous capacity to enjoy any number of things, such as good company, entertainment, reminiscences, and analysis. He is hugely eclectic in his tastes. He likes the novels of Trollope, Indian art, and everything except music. Music is one of his major gaps. He enjoys all kinds of people and he doesn't mind at all enjoying people simply because they appear on the society pages."

In Buckley's opinion, Galbraith's most important contribution to the literature of economics, sociology, and political thought can be summed up in one word: "readability." "Galbraith," Buckley maintains, "succeeds by freeing himself from the shackles of his own discipline. One of the main reasons why a piece on economics by Galbraith is so enjoyable is that not much of it is really on economics."

To the suggestion that many economists are jealous of Galbraith's success, Buckley replied, "Most dull people are jealous of most bright people. But, it is also true that Ken's colleagues have never deprived him of all kinds of recognition. I would like to be able to say that they would have honored him even if he were a conservative. But, in that hypothetical respect, I am not quite sure that they would have. He has been president of the American Economic Association, and he was elected to that position by his peers. In addition, Galbraith is the best known and the highest paid economist in the world."

Paul A. Samuelson, M.I.T. professor and winner of the Nobel Prize for Economics, said of Galbraith, "I consider Ken Galbraith as an artist who looks at things in a new light and who makes us think about what we are seeing. However, like many artists who are attempting to describe a reality, Ken has his hits and misses.

"I regard Thorstein Veblen as an important figure in the history of economic thought. Veblen is not assigned in intermediate or advanced courses except to those students who have an antiquarian interest in the various schools of economics. I don't see that Galbraith's place in the history of our profession will be lower than Veblen's. But I do consider Galbraith an important figure in the history of economics. Now that doesn't mean that Ken is going to get a lot of plaudits at the annual meeting of the American Economic Association."

To some readers it may be startling to discover that Galbraith, the high lama of American liberals, counts among his friends conservatives and people who downgrade his economic and social concepts. As Galbraith explains this apparent paradox: "I always get along better with someone who agrees with me than with people who don't. But, if you confine your circle of friends to people who agree with you, it will be pitifully small."

Arthur M. Schlesinger, Jr., who holds the Albert Schweitzer Chair in the Humanities at the City University of New York, is one of Galbraith's closest friends. Schlesinger and Galbraith are two of the East Coast liberal intellectual establishment's most dominant figures. Both were Harvard professors. Both helped John F. Kennedy be elected president of the United States and served in his administration. And both continue to champion the merits of the liberal philosophy during a time when there appears to be a drift toward more conservative values in the United States.

Talking with Schlesinger, I said that Galbraith seems to derive great enjoyment from criticizing people and institutions. "I think Ken has a great skill in dishing out criticism without offending or wounding people. This is something I envy because when I tend to make a remark that wounds someone, everyone gets mad. But Ken does it in sort of an urbane, amiable way so it isn't so wounding.

"Ken Galbraith is really an artist in living. I don't know anyone who has managed to organize his life better, has more fun, gets more done, travels more, sees more interesting people, eats better, and always seems relaxed and at ease. I always feel overwhelmed by all the things on which I'm behind schedule, or agree to do or don't want to do. Ken always feels relaxed and unfussed. The other night we had dinner here in New York. He came in from Switzerland that afternoon. He was going out to the West Coast and then on to Leningrad. Whatever he does, he does with great ease. So I think he is better off than anyone I know. He has his life under control. He has been extraordinarily productive and, at the same time, he has had a life filled with enjoyment and pleasure.

"Ken likes people who have done things. He likes movie stars, writers, people in government, people who have accomplished something through their personal abilities and people who are amusing.

"He is survival-minded, ambitious, intelligent, and a fellow who is much diverted by life. And, he thoroughly enjoys the kind of life he lives. His energy, vitality, imagination and capacity for enjoyment, along with his rather caustic, ironic sense of humor which preserves his balance, enable him to distinguish illusion from reality, to know what is important in life. In addition, he has a good sense of the priorities of his own values." As Schlesinger told me, "If you can find out the secret of how he has done it all for himself, it will be well worth the effort and the search."

This "effort and the search" form the real purpose of this book. Galbraith's BBC television series, *The Age of Uncertainty*, has been seen by millions of Americans in 1977. His books — many of them best sellers, all readable, interesting, and often amusing — reach new generations of the reading public each year. My conversations with Galbraith, his friends, and his critics are an informal introduction to Galbraith, America's consummate liberal, — a search well worth the effort.

Like Galbraith, all of us want to be able to identify illusion and to discover reality. We want to know what is important and how to improve the quality of economic life — not just for the few who have the power and the money, but for everyone. Much of what Galbraith says and writes is questionable and open to debate. But his errors, as well as his correct perceptions and ideas, make us think, make us see reality in a new and more constructive way, and make our society more civilized.

Frederick J. Pratson
North Scituate, Massachusetts

1

THE MAKING
OF AN
ECONOMIST

John Kenneth Galbraith is an innovator in the social and economic sciences. He has created and presented to the world fresh perceptions of the economic, social, and political realities of the modern industrial world. In his long career he has been — often simultaneously — a novelist, politician, scholar, teacher, diplomat, reformer, journalist, and administrator. He has participated in presidential campaigns, researched Indian art, written satires, advised everyone from presidents to schoolgirls. He is also husband, father, skier, and raconteur. As he is well-known to most of the literate world, people see him in various ways — as an elegant public teacher and entertainer, as a vastly influential economist, as a wheelhorse of liberalism, as an ornament of the intellectual establishment, as a towering man of influence in a wide range of areas.

Many people believe that Galbraith is a Yankee Brahmin from Beacon Hill. This image has grown out of his long identification with Harvard and with the "Establishment."

Galbraith's roots are elsewhere; in fact, he is not a native of the United States. He was born in 1908 in Iona Station, a small farming community in Ontario, Canada, near the shores of Lake Erie.

Galbraith's father was a successful farmer whose interests and influence extended beyond the farm. The elder Galbraith had been a schoolteacher in his youth. He was active in politics as a member of Canada's Liberal party, holding offices in the county and the township. He helped to establish the local telephone company and a cooperative insurance company. Galbraith senior was a "man of standing"; his son recalls that there were "a great many people in that part of Ontario who formed their views only after they heard my father tell them what those views should be." One might reflect that in this respect the son has followed the paternal footsteps.

The horizons of the Galbraith family were never confined to the farm, although the farm work itself had broadening aspects. The family owned a herd of pure-bred short-horn cattle which they would take to county fairs, exhibitions, and auctions.

The "Scotch," as the Galbraiths and their neighbors called themselves, followed the custom of having sons succeed their fathers in the running of the family farm. Nevertheless, they maintained a commitment to education — "though never," says Galbraith, "quite as deep a one as they claimed it to be. But it existed. That commitment was very strong in my family."

While most of Galbraith's young friends became farmers, a few left the community to pursue higher education. Some went across the international border to Ann Arbor to attend the University of Michigan. Most of those who continued their educations studied medicine or dentistry or went into the ministry.

Galbraith's native community, while rural, was by no means insular and there was a considerable orientation toward the United States. Iona Station was less than a hundred miles from Detroit to the west, a little more than that from Buffalo to the east. Many Canadians worked in the United States, and it was not unusual for some to vote in the Canadian election in the summer and the American election in the autumn, since, observes Galbraith, "they wanted the best people in office in both countries."

From early on Galbraith lived in an atmosphere of a kind of dual national identity. "We thought of ourselves as Canadians, but we never dwelt on the fact. In that part of Ontario, there were very few people whose patriotism would stand more than a five-dollar-a-month wage differential between the two countries." The view toward the south was of course influenced by the strong liberal orientation of the Galbraith family. In Canadian politics, the Conservative Party had created their formerly powerful position by a strong identification with the monarchy, country, and British establishment. They talked about developing Canadian industry and Imperial trade. The Liberals wanted more trade with the United States. This principle was particularly important in the area where

Galbraith grew up, as Buffalo and Detroit were seen as natural markets for Canadian farm products.

It was customary in those days — in the alleged interest of Imperial and later Commonwealth relations — to mount a Royal Progress through Canada every four or five years. The King and Queen would land in the Maritime Provinces, and then travel across the country, to be received in each community by the mayor and a delegation of leading citizens. Flowers would be strewn in their paths; bagpipes played in their honor.

These royal proceedings were regarded with disapproval by the Galbraith family. The children were never taken to see them. Many years later Galbraith attended a party given by the late President Lyndon Johnson for Princess Margaret. The next day Galbraith received a half-amused call from his sister in Canada, who had seen his name on the guest list in the local newspaper. She told him, "You know how your father would have felt about your showing up there." Galbraith explained that he had gone out of respect for the president of the United States. "That would have been all right," his sister replied.

Galbraith's experiences of this period inculcated in him a healthy skepticism about what he sees as the "spurious class structure" growing out of monarchical institutions.

After attending local schools, Galbraith retained some interest in farming. He entered the Ontario Agricultural College and majored in agricultural economics. But his interests were increasingly devoted to another aspect of economics than that associated with working the land.

These were the years of the Great Depression, when the giant figure of Franklin D. Roosevelt was dominant in American politics and society. Roosevelt was as much of a hero to Canadians as he was to Americans. In southern Ontario, he was revered. "To my father and many of the people of southern Ontario, if they had been given the choice between voting for any Canadian politician or for Roosevelt, they would have voted for Roosevelt immediately." This was by no means because the elder Galbraith had a low esteem for Canadian politicians. He was greatly devoted to Sir Wilfred Laurier, and he admired William Lyon MacKenzie King. But Roosevelt sounded a note of national purpose that was more compelling than that heard in his native land. Galbraith's impulse toward moving into the American scene accelerated. In the autumn of 1930 Galbraith saw on the notice board of his college residence an advertisement for research assistantships at the Giannini Foundation of Agricultural Economics at the University of California, Berkeley. In the second year of the Great Depression the $60 per month stipend seemed princely. He applied, and to the dismay of his professors, who thought the people at Berkeley were crazy, and to his surprise, he was accepted.

After his graduation from Ontario Agricultural College, Galbraith made what was to become a significant trek south and west. In July of 1931 he borrowed $500 from an aunt and set off for California in company with a friend. Their trip in a 1926 Oakland took eleven days.

Berkeley was a stunning experience. He was amazed to encounter professors who not only knew their subject but who invited debate. Galbraith might have remained at Berkeley happily. But in the spring of 1933, as he was finishing his thesis, he received a telegram offering an instructorship at Harvard for $2400 a year. After a somewhat painful deliberation, he accepted.

Galbraith married his wife Kitty, the former Catherine Atwater, in 1937, around the time he became an American citizen. Catherine Galbraith is a graduate of Smith College and has a master's degree from Radcliffe. They met while she was a student there. She too has taught at Harvard (German) and has published her own book, *India Now and Through Time.*

The Galbraiths have three sons. A fourth died when he was about eight years old. Both Peter and Jamie Galbraith took up their father's interest in economics. Peter teaches economics and history at Windham College in Vermont and in autumn of 1977 became head of Vermont's Democratic Party. Jamie Galbraith was chief economist for the House Banking Committee, though he left that position to study for his PhD in economics at Yale. The oldest son, J. Alan Galbraith, is a partner in a Washington law firm.

Galbraith is a voracious reader of fiction, as well as of works on economics. His choice of reading has, inevitably, influenced his thinking and his style. He has always been fond of the nineteenth-century English novelists. "With the exception of Dickens. I have always had the feeling that Dickens told me more about the injustices of life than I needed to know. After a certain amount of time, tales of injustice cease to be entertaining and interesting. The imagery of Dickens' London or even the graphic imagery of Hogarth's London has never appealed to me."

Galbraith offers a compassionate view of Somerset Maugham. "He was a greatly underestimated novelist, in my judgment. Maugham's great mistake was one that no Harvard professor ever makes. At Harvard, we are all judged by our peers. It's recognized there that nobody will ever give a higher estimate of you than you give of yourself. A great part of the conversation at the Harvard Faculty Club is of people asserting their scholarly virtues in one form or another. This is not because they are particularly conceited, but because they know they are judged by their community, and must always seek to improve that judgment. Maugham, by contrast, once said that he was the first of the second-raters, which was a great mistake."

Galbraith admits a liking for Tolstoy, though he concedes that he has never been much taken by the other great Russian writers. In the field of philosophy, he says that he has been exposed to Rousseau, Locke and Voltaire. Of these he prefers Voltaire; "by far the most entertaining of the philosophers," Galbraith said.

Economists are not usually renowned as being fine writers. Galbraith defends the writing ability of those in his profession: "Anyone who wishes to contend that economists are bad writers is faced with the fact that no learned discipline unconnected with literature or the arts has had such distinguished ones." (*Fortune*, December 1962)

Galbraith describes John Stuart Mill, Thomas Malthus, Henry George, and Alfred Marshall as distinguished writers. About Keynes he has some reservations. He says that Thorstein Veblen's prose was "graceless, difficult and often highly contrived," but Veblen's vitality, versatility and imagery stamp him as a talented writer.

At the head of the list of economists who were gifted writers, Galbraith places Adam Smith: "In both purity of style and certainty in his command of language he is inferior to J. S. Mill. But he is effective and resourceful in exposition and far superior to Mill in imagery and humor."

It is, perhaps, that latter quality — humor — that Galbraith finds most winning. He feels that economic writing ought to contain humor; and his own writing is often quite funny — a fact which has not endeared him to some of his more sober colleagues. Note the following passage in which Galbraith supports his emphasis on humor and at the same time weaves in a bit of sly wit which is simultaneously a jab at his fellows: "I doubt that good economic writing can be devoid of humor. This is not because it is the task of the economist to entertain or amuse. Nothing could be more abhorrent to the Calvinism that underlies all scientific attitudes. But humor is an index of the ability to detach self from subject and this, indeed, is of some scientific value. In considering economic behavior humor is especially important, for, needless to say, much of that behavior is infinitely ridiculous." Galbraith's readiness to see the humorous side of his subject and unwillingness to take himself too seriously have permeated his entire career and softened the antagonisms of his enemies and critics.

In his early reading of economics, Galbraith was thrilled by neoclassical economics as it was presented by Alfred Marshall, who dominated Anglo-American pedagogy from the 1880s to the 1920s. Marshall's *Principles* is, says Galbraith, "a great and majestic book, which had the virtue of separating those who were serious about the subject of economics from those who weren't."

Marshall provided the classical groundwork. At this same time, Galbraith became familiar with the work of Karl Marx. "I have never had any doubt about the debt I owe to Marx, who is far too important to be left exclusively to the socialist countries." He considers that only Mohammed approaches Marx's ability to attract followers to a particular philosophy espoused by a single author, and that today there are far more Marxists than sons of the Prophet Mohammed.

Both in terms of Marx's influence on Galbraith's thinking and Galbraith's efforts to present Marx's ideas while stripping away the miasma of passion with which Marx's name is accompanied, it is worthwhile to consider briefly the career of Karl Marx as seen through Galbraith's *The Age of Uncertainty*.

Karl Marx is buried in London's Highgate Cemetery. His remains were interred there on March 17, 1883. Marx's grave is within a short distance of Herbert Spencer's, who once preached the gospel of a superior race. Galbraith finds a great irony in this and writes: "It would be hard to think of two men who are taking less pleasure in the company of each other."[1]

Marx was born in 1818 in Trier, a small town in the Moselle Valley. Today Trier is a part of Germany. In 1818, the town passed from French occupation into the hands of the Prussians. Galbraith says that this political change was of significant importance to Heinrich Marx and his family. The family was Jewish, and a number of Karl Marx's ancestors were rabbis. While the French were reasonably tolerant of the Jews in Trier, the Prussians were not. Although Marx's father was Trier's leading lawyer and an official of the High Court, he could not remain a Jew under Prussian rule so he had his family baptized as Protestants. Galbraith maintains that Marx made the change for practical reasons, not as a rejection of the traditions and values of Judaism. Religion, as such, was not considered important to them, and the tone of family life was secular. Karl Marx himself was an active atheist at a time when religion was far more integral to people's lives than today. Marx considered religion as "the opiate of the people" which lulled them to sleep, contented with the imbalance of wealth.

In his youth, Marx fell in love with Jenny von Westphalen, daughter of Trier's leading citizen. Baron von Westphalen liked the young Karl Marx and often described his ideas about the ideal state to Marx: It should be based on common property, not private property. At seventeen, Marx became a student at the University in Bonn, where he developed a fondness for drinking and dueling. In 1836 he moved from Bonn to Berlin and into the very mainstream of Western intellectual life. The city was the domain of the followers of Georg Wilhelm Friedrich Hegel. "The great merit of Hegel's philosophy," Marx wrote, "was that for the first time, the totality of the natural, historical, and spiritual aspects of the world were conceived and represented as a process of constant transformation and development, and an effort was made to show the organic character of this process."[2]

What was organic to Marx was the conflict between the classes, a conflict that would keep society in constant change. With the destruction of the old order, a new one would emerge, and this process of destruction and renewal would continue indefinitely. Feudalism was giving way to capitalism, and capitalism would give way to the proletariat, which would create a workers' state.

Hegel's ideas were difficult for Marx to assimilate. Intensive studying damaged Marx's health, which he never fully regained. Marx left Berlin in 1841 for Cologne where he became a journalist for the liberal *Rheinische Zeitung*, ironically financed by the leading capitalists of the Ruhr and Rhineland region. He became its editor, and the newspaper's circulation grew rapidly under his influence.

While editor, Marx took sides in a controversial Rhineland issue. Dead wood, used for fuel, had been considered free for ages. But as the population grew and became more prosperous, dead wood achieved value and became private property. The people who collected it were prosecuted for theft. Marx commented: "If every violation of property, without distinction or more precise determination, is theft, would not all private property be theft? Through my private property, do not I deprive another person of this property?"[3] Such editorials angered the Prussians. Marx moved to Paris, but before going, on June 19, 1843, he married Jenny von Westphalen.

In Paris, Marx entered a world that accommodated revolutionaries and in which revolution was a major topic of conversation. Galbraith believes that this environment had a very great impact on Marx. He resumed his occupation as editor by working on the German-French yearbook, *Deutsch-Französische Jahrbücher*. In this publication, Marx wrote: "The emancipation of Germany is the emancipation of man. The head of this emancipation is philosophy, its heart is the proletariat. Philosophy cannot realize itself without transcending the proletariat, the proletariat cannot transcend itself without realizing philosophy."[4]

The first issue of the yearbook was also the last. The Prussian police confiscated the copies at the border. Moreover, there were no French financial contributors or readers. However, at the Café de la Regence, Marx had a stroke of good luck. He met Friedrich Engels, his lifelong financial backer and friend.

Marx now began what Galbraith says was the most intensive period of reading and study of his life. During this same time he developed his ideas on how capitalism would change. But he also continued his writing, and many of his thoughts were still centered on Germany. "Germany has a vocation to social revolution that is all the more classic in that it is incapable of political revolution. For as the impotence of the German bourgeoisie is the political impotence of Germany, so the situation of the German proletariat is the social situation of Germany. The disproportion between philosophical and political development in Germany is no abnormality. It is only in socialism that a philosophical people can find a corresponding activity, thus only in the proletariat that it finds the active element of its freedom."[5] The Prussian police complained and the French minister of the interior expelled Marx from the country. He, Jenny, and their daughter left for Brussels.

In Brussels, Marx with Engels' help, wrote *The Communist Manifesto* as a pamphlet for the League of the Just, later renamed the Communist League. Galbraith says that Marx had transformed his writing in the *Communist Manifesto*. "What before had been wordy and labored was now succinct and arresting — a series of hammer blows,"[6] Galbraith writes in *The Age of Uncertainty*.

In *The Communist Manifesto*, Marx wrote: "The history of all hitherto existing society is the history of class struggles. Freeman and slave, patrician and plebeian, lord and serf, guild-master and journeyman, in a word oppressor and oppressed, stood in constant opposition to one another, carried on an uninterrupted, now hidden, now open fight, a fight that each time ended either in a revolutionary reconstitution of society at large, or in the common ruin of the contending classes.

"The Communists," Marx continued, "disdain to conceal their views and aims. They openly declare that their ends can be attained only by the forcible overthrow of all existing social conditions. Let the ruling classes tremble at a communistic revolution. The proletarians have nothing to lose but their chains. They have the world to win. Working men of all countries, unite."[7]

According to Galbraith in *The Age of Uncertainty*, successful revolution must meet three main conditions: first, determined leadership that knows exactly what it wants, and knows also that it has everything to gain and everything to lose; second, disciplined followers, people who will accept orders and carry them out without too much debate; and third, a weak opposition — "The violence of revolutions is the violence of men who charge into a vacuum."[8] Galbraith states these conditions were met in the French Revolution and in the Chinese Revolution of our more recent time.

Galbraith points out that *The Communist Manifesto* suggests a number of reforms — all of which have been adopted or continue to be seriously discussed in democratic societies, These reforms include a progressive income tax, the abolition of inheritance taxes (strongly advocated by Andrew Carnegie), public ownership of railroads and communications, the extension of public ownership in industry, the cultivation of idle lands, better soil management, full employment, free education, and the abolition of child labor.

On July 23, 1848, the workers of Paris built a barricade at the Place de la Bastille. The National Guard stormed the barricades and quickly ended the uprising. Not long after the futility of 1848 Marx was forced to leave Belgium. He returned to France and from there he went to Cologne to restart the *Rheinische Zeitung*, dedicated to revolutionary change among German workers. Again the newspaper was suppressed and failed, and Marx was once more on the move. By now only two countries were open to him — the United States and Great Britain. Because Marx didn't have enough money to go to the United States, he went to London where he lived out his days.

When Marx reached London, he was only thirty-one. Galbraith states that Marx had three key tasks to accomplish: to finalize the ideas that would emancipate the masses; to create the organization that would successfully achieve the revolution; and to earn enough money to support his family in England.

Marx got some financial assistance from Engels and his associates and he earned a partial living as a correspondent for the *New York Tribune*. But he was constantly hounded by bill collectors and landlords. He, his wife, and their six children moved several times. Prussian police spied on Marx and filed a report on him: "As a father and husband, Marx, in spite of his wild and restless character, is the gentlest and mildest of men. Marx lives in one of the worst, therefore one of the cheapest, quarters of London."[9]

Seven years after arriving in London, Marx received a small inheritance that allowed him to move his family to more pleasant surroundings in suburban Hampstead. Earlier, in 1850, the Austrian ambassador complained to the British government that Marx and his cohorts were discussing dangerous matters — even the possibility of regicide. The ambassador received a reply that said as long as regicide was only discussed and did not involve the Queen, no arrests were justified. The British home secretary offered to pay the revolutionaries' passage to the United States as a gesture to the Austrian ambassador. Later, both Austria and Prussia requested that Marx and his colleagues be deported, but the British decided against doing so.

One of the intellectual resources of London's British Museum is its library. There Marx continued his studies and wrote the book that has changed the lives of millions of people throughout the world, *Das Kapital*. "Along with the constantly diminishing number of the magnates of capital, who usurp and monopolize all advantages of this process of transformation, grows the mass of misery, oppression, slavery, degradation, exploitation," Marx wrote, "but with this too grows the revolt of the working class, a class always increasing in numbers, and disciplined, united, organized by the very mechanism of the process of capitalist production itself. The monopoly of capital becomes a fetter upon the mode of production, which has sprung up and flourished along with, and under it. Centralization of the means of production and socialization of labor at last reach a point where they become incompatible with their capitalist integument. This integument is burst asunder. The knell of capitalist private property sounds. The expropriators are expropriated."[10]

The first volume of *Das Kapital* appeared in 1867. Two more volumes were published after his death in 1883. Engels prepared the material from notes and manuscripts that Marx had left behind. Galbraith maintains that no one else but Engels could have accomplished this task.

Marx's second objective, to create the instrument for revolution, came into being on September 28, 1864. Some two thousand European workers, unionists, and intellectuals attended the First International in London. In his *Address to the Working Class*, Marx told that assembly, "No improvement of machinery, no application of science to production, no contrivance of communications, no new colonies, no emigration, no opening of markets, no free trade, nor all these things put together will do away with the miseries of the industrial masses. . . . To conquer political power has therefore become the great duty of the working classes."[11] And the famous slogan of communism was sounded: "Proletarians of all countries, unite."

The International began to grow in strength and numbers, with successful congresses in Lausanne, Brussels, and Basel. Internal dissension hurt the First International, and it was outlawed in Germany. The organization moved its headquarters to, of all places, Philadelphia, where it dissolved in 1874.

However, the death of the First International was not the end of Marx's dream of an effective instrument for social and economic change. After his death, the Second International, a coalition of workers, political parties, and unionists, was founded in 1889.

Another economist influenced Galbraith and at Berkeley, Galbraith became familiar with the man who is perhaps his favorite economist, Thorstein Veblen. Veblen was the hero of Galbraith's teachers at Berkeley, and furthermore, to Galbraith, he was a lively writer. Galbraith remarks, "Marshall has not been read for years; one can still turn to Veblen with delight."[12]

In *The Age of Uncertainty*, Galbraith describes Thorstein Veblen, who was born of Norwegian parents in Wisconsin in 1857. Life for the Veblens was at first a struggle on the American frontier; a pioneering effort to carve out of the wilderness a prosperous existence in a new and promising land. Eventually, Veblen's father had put together 290 acres of rich Minnesota farmland. Veblen worked his way through nearby Carleton College, and after attending Johns Hopkins, went to Yale in 1882. At Yale, Veblen met and impressed William Graham Sumner. After observing the rich, Veblen concluded that the American establishment was not endowed with any special gifts of intelligence, culture, or charm. Their wealth came from cunning and from adding more wealth to what they already possessed. Veblen thought the rich were particularly vulnerable to ridicule — especially their social events, such as their annual gatherings at Newport or Bar Harbor or Stockbridge.

Veblen taught at Cornell, Chicago, Stanford, Missouri, and the New School in New York City. But because university presidents then wanted professors "who affirmed the conservative truth, who treated wealth and enterprise with respect,"[13] Veblen was often requested to move on. "All were glad to see him go; today it is the pride of all that he was there,"[14] according to Galbraith. Veblen also had the reputation of being a ladies' man, which disturbed the Harvard faculty when he was being considered for a teaching position. The story goes that President Lowell of Harvard suggested that should Veblen be appointed, he was to behave himself. Veblen retorted that there was no reason for concern for he had already seen the Harvard wives!

The Theory of the Leisure Class is considered by most critics to be

Veblen's greatest book. This work, along with *The Theory of Business Enterprise*, describes the conflict between those who use their talents to produce goods and those whose only concern is making money. It was Veblen's theory that the profit-seekers increased their wealth at the expense of the producers who made the goods.

Galbraith maintains that Veblen's most important contribution was not in economics but in the field of sociology. In *The Theory of the Leisure Class*, Veblen outlined his concept of "conspicuous consumption." Conspicuous consumption applies to those who consume goods and services primarily to impress others. The cost of the product — whether a houseboat, automobile, or a diamond tiara — is the important factor. The higher the cost, the more impressive; taste becomes irrelevant.

In the United States, Newport, Rhode Island, represented the ultimate monument to conspicuous consumption to Veblen. The purpose of the Newport summer cottages — actually enormous, ornate mansions — was to indicate to the world this special American aristocracy that had fought its way to prominence in a society founded on democratic and egalitarian principles. Beyond their role as ostentatious monuments to the very rich, the Newport homes clearly delineated class differences. Obviously, many servants were required to maintain the homes and administer to the personal needs of their employers — further bolstering their sense of superiority. Galbraith maintains that most people will not remain in a servile occupation if they have other alternatives. As servants left for better jobs and more personal freedom in the industrial system, the level of ostentatious display began to decline.

Veblen also observed that ceremonial rites were vital for the very rich to display their wealth and social position. Rich men had to be, according to Veblen, "connoisseurs in creditable viands or various degrees of merit, in manly beverages and trinkets, in seemly apparel and architecture, in weapons, games, dances, and the narcotics." Veblen went on to say that "drunkenness and other pathological consequences of the free use of stimulants were valuable indications of the superior status of those who are able to afford the indulgence. . . . Infirmities induced by over-indulgence are among some peoples freely recognized as manly attributes."

Great wealth alone did not guarantee ready acceptance into society. Wealth, like good wine, improves with age.

As a point of interest, *The Age of Uncertainty* may have helped Galbraith repay some of his debt to Veblen. After taping one of his BBC broadcasts, Galbraith returned to help the Minnesota State Historical Society raise funds to preserve the Veblen house which badly needed repair.

Marx and Veblen were significant influences on Galbraith. Within a few years, Galbraith was to become familiar with the work of the economist with whom he is most closely associated: John Maynard Keynes.

CHAPTER **2**
THE
INFLUENCE
OF KEYNES

In 1937 Galbraith went to Trinity College, Cambridge, as a Social Science Research Fellow. John Maynard Keynes had been teaching at Cambridge. There Galbraith found camaraderie in a group of young economists which included Joan Robinson, Richard Kahn, and Piero Sraffa. This august group spent most of their time learning what Keynes taught and discussing his ideas.

There was another person at Cambridge, Michal Kalecki, described by Galbraith as "in some ways the most brilliant man in economics I've ever been associated with or have ever known." Kalecki, a socialist, left his native Poland during World War I for England. Later he would go to the United States. In the early 1950s Kalecki returned to Poland to become a major figure in that country's economic planning efforts. Eventually he fell out of favor, left public office, and returned to teaching.

Kalecki had considerable influence on Galbraith. "He was a brilliant conversationalist who would, in the course of an hour, throw off a half-dozen ideas, all good, which other people would pick up and use, sometimes without ever remembering they came from Michael. I was one who did. Michael died a few years ago. Several weeks before his death, I wrote to congratulate him on his seventieth birthday, and I listed a few ideas which I had stolen from him over the years, which I had never confessed. He never had a chance to answer my letter. But his widow wrote the most appreciative note I've ever received, in which she told me how delighted Michael had been in his last days to have this larceny confessed."

The paramount influence, however, was Keynes. Keynes had suffered a heart attack in 1937 and did not appear at Cambridge the year Galbraith was there. Galbraith was nevertheless immersed in Keynes' ideas by association with his now distinguished disciples. And he did meet Keynes years later.

In *The Age of Uncertainty* Galbraith dwells on Keynes' vital significance and on his own debt to this important figure in economics, and a brief familiarity with Keynes is useful for understanding the development of Galbraith's concepts.

John Maynard Keynes, according to Galbraith's *The Age Of Uncertainty*, was born in 1883, the year of Karl Marx's death. Florence Ada Keynes, his mother, had once served as mayor of Cambridge, England. His father, John Neville Keynes, was an economist and for fifteen years the chief administrative officer of the University of Cambridge.

Keynes studied at Eton and at King's College, Cambridge, which, Galbraith points out, was a stronghold of economics. Keynes had a happy youth; he had no wish to change the world. While at the university, Keynes was part of a group of intellectuals that included Lytton Strachey, Virginia and Leonard Woolf, and Vanessa and Clive Bell — known later as the "Bloomsbury Group."

Keynes graduated from Cambridge in 1905 and did badly on economics in his civil service examinations. "The examiners presumably knew less than I did,"[1] Keynes said of his poor marks. He took a job with the India Office, where, to ease his boredom, he wrote books on the theory of probability and the Indian currency. Keynes returned to Cambridge on a scholarship provided by the dean of Anglo-American economics, Alfred Marshall.

When World War I broke out, Keynes avoided the trenches by getting a job in the British Treasury. His assignment was to cover British war purchases by stretching earnings from trade, by obtaining loans in the United States, and by receiving income from securities. While at the Treasury, he received a summons to report for duty in the military which he refused to honor.

After the war, Keynes was made a member of the British delegation to the Peace Conference. In Paris he witnessed a mood that was oblivious to economic circumstances. Keynes resigned his post in disgust. Back home, according to Galbraith, Keynes "composed one of the greatest polemical documents of modern times." His *The Economic Consequences of the Peace* took severe issue with the reparations clauses of the treaty. By forcing Germany to pay more than it could, Keynes felt Europe would only be hurting itself. He urged restraint by the victors not only in the name of compassion but for fundamental self-interest. *The London Times*, however, disagreed: "In writing this book, he (Keynes) has rendered the Allies a disservice for which their enemies will, doubtless, be ever grateful."

Keynes called Woodrow Wilson "this blind and deaf Don Quixote," Galbraith notes. Clemenceau was a man who "had one illusion—France; and one disillusion, mankind . . . ." More critical of his own countryman, Lloyd George, Keynes called him a "goat-footed bard, this half-human visitor to our age from the hag-ridden magic and enchanted woods of Celtic antiquity."[2]

Galbraith feels that because Keynes remained aloof from public life, he was free and able to express the truth, in contrast to the public man who must accommodate himself to the public position. Although Keynes was kept at arm's length by the establishment, he was not totally ignored. Keynes, after all, was a Fellow of King's College, chairman of the National Mutual Insurance Company, and a director of several other companies.

In 1925, Winston Churchill was Britain's Chancellor of the Exchequer. Churchill urged a return to the gold standard at prewar values, which put British prices about 10 percent higher than those in the United States, Germany, and France. It was Churchill's attempt to create the impression that the British financial picture was as stable as ever, regardless of the recent war. Great Britain enthusiastically backed Churchill in returning to the gold standard. Keynes, however, asked Churchill in a letter why he did "such a silly thing."

Because Britain is an exporting nation, it was essential to the economy that the prices of British goods come down. A decrease in prices also meant that workers' wages had to decrease. When the world price of coal fell, the British mine owners proposed that the men work longer hours, minimum wages be abolished, and everyone work for lower wages. When the miners refused these exploitive conditions, the owners locked them out. This action, in turn, prompted a general strike in May 1926. The printing, transport, electricity and gas, iron and steel, and construction unions left their jobs in support of the miners. The men walked the picket lines for nine days before the general strike ended. Those who approved the return to gold saw the strike as anarchy.

The return to gold did not demonstrate the strength of the British pound, writes Galbraith. Instead it showed its weakness by driving potential buyers of British goods to the United States and France. In *The Age of Uncertainty,* Galbraith jokingly describes a "new law" of economics, applied particularly to the return to the gold standard: "A.J. Liebling of *The New Yorker* magazine formulated what he called Liebling's Law. It held, roughly, that if a man of adequately complex mind proceeds in a sufficiently perverse way, he can succeed in kicking himself in his own ass out the door into the street. The return to gold in 1925 was a superb manifestation of Liebling's Law."[3]

So much gold was flowing into the United States by 1927 that the heads of the banks of England, Germany, and France came to New York to get the gold back. In addition, they persuaded the US Federal Reserve to ease its monetary policy by lowering its interest rate and making more loans available. This policy, in turn, would decrease the flow of money into the United States, raise the prices on American goods, make American goods less competitive in Britain, and make it easier to sell European goods in the United States.

Though the 1920s were bad years in Great Britain, it was a boom time in the United States, particularly for those who could speculate in common stocks. Holding companies and investment trusts generated great excitement among the investing public. Individuals invested in holding companies, which themselves invested in other companies, which in turn invested in still others. Galbraith describes the layers of investment as being five to ten deep. The classic example Galbraith uses is the Goldman Sachs Trading Company. When Goldman Sachs was formed in 1928, it issued $100 million in stock — 90 percent of which was sold to the public. After a merger with the Financial and Industrial Securities Corporation in February 1929, assets stood at $235 million. This enterprise then created the Shenandoah Corporation, with an authorization to sell $102.3 million in stocks. Shenandoah, in August 1929, launched the Blue Ridge Corporation at $142 million. Then $71.4

million more in stocks was issued by the Trading Company to purchase another investment company and a bank.

When Shenandoah stock was issued, it sold for $17.50 and had risen to $36. When the bubble finally burst, it sold for fifty cents. Shares in the Trading Company itself, which once hit $222.50, were available two years later for as little as a dollar. John Foster Dulles, the best known of the post-World War II "cold warriors," was, interestingly enough, one of Shenandoah's directors.

Galbraith's *The Age of Uncertainty* describes the day of reckoning for the securities business — Thursday, October 24, 1929. Starting that morning, there was a rush to sell. Inside the Exchange there was a madhouse of confusion and eardrum-splitting noise. It seemed as if capitalism itself was coming apart at the seams. Watching the bedlam on the floor of the Exchange from the visitors' gallery was Winston Churchill. The irony of it all, according to Galbraith, was that the stock market collapse was in part caused by Great Britain's return to gold and the loosening of monetary policy by the US Federal Reserve.

The Great Crash, of course, led to the Great Depression. By 1933 nearly one-fourth of all American workers were unemployed. Nine thousand banks permanently closed their doors. The economy of the United States went from bad to worse. But in June 1930, a group of concerned citizens visited President Hoover to argue for some sort of public works program to relieve the situation. "Gentlemen," said President Hoover, "you have come sixty days too late. The depression is over."[4]

Like a plague, the depression spread from nation to nation. The more industrially advanced a nation, the more serious and devastating its slump.

Statesmen of that time, particularly Herbert Hoover and Germany's Heinrich Bruning, believed that the best cure was spartan discipline, frugality, courageous perseverance, and stoic patience. In 1931 Bruning cut wages, prices, and salaries, and raised taxes at a time when about 25 percent of Germany's workers were out of work. Hitler seemed to provide a better economic alternative.

Although Britain extricated itself from its adherence to the gold standard and free trade, the proper gentlemen in Whitehall set aside the increasing flow of advice pouring into their offices from John Maynard Keynes. Keynes wanted the government to borrow money and then spend it. This action would increase bank deposits. The money the government spent would then be respent by the workers. Galbraith writes that Keynes' philosophy "not only created money but enforced its use."[5]

In Germany, Adolf Hitler liberally borrowed and spent money to get the German economy going again. His initial projects were public works — highways, railroads, canals, and public buildings. By the end of 1935, most Germans were back at work, while grave unemployment persisted in the Western democracies. Wages in Germany also increased. To prevent inflation, wage and price controls were imposed, and they worked. By the late 1930s, Germany had both stable prices and full employment.

Although Nazi Germany achieved economic health while the rest of the industrial world suffered, the Americans and British were alarmed. Germany's economic renewal came with too high a price. Perhaps the United States held the solution.

Keynes wrote a letter to Franklin Delano Roosevelt, which was published in the *New York Times*. "I lay overwhelming emphasis on the increase of national purchasing power resulting from governmental expenditure which is financed by loans . . . ,"[6] wrote Keynes. In 1934 the English economist visited the American president. The face-to-face encounter was not successful. "A mathematician rather than a political economist,"[7] thought FDR. Keynes had assumed that "the President would be more literate, economically speaking."[8]

New York's Mayor Jimmy Walker once said that he "never heard of a girl being seduced by a book." Galbraith says in *The Age of Uncertainty* that Keynes not only tried to seduce Washington by way of a book, but the whole world as well — and "a nearly unreadable one" at that.

Keynes' book was *The General Theory of Employment Interest and Money*. In it he analyzed the business cycle — the theory of "boom-and-bust" that swings the economy from prosperity to depression, and back again. Keynes disagreed with Adam Smith and subsequent generations of economists who believed that nothing could be done about the cycle — that it would cure itself if left alone with absolutely no interference from the government.

Keynes argued that prosperity can be maintained only if there is a high level of continuing private investment or public expenditures. But private investment cannot be depended on; it fluctuates over the course of time. When private investment is low, Keynes maintained, the government must step in and spend money to keep the wheels of industry turning. It then follows that there will be more jobs, more purchasing power by jobholders, and a return to prosperity.

Although Washington ignored Keynes, he made his influence felt through American universities. Harvard was his first important entrance into America's academic world. While he was a young tutor at Harvard's Winthrop House, Galbraith first experienced Keynes' impact: "But so influential was Keynes among the young at Harvard that in later years an association of alumni was formed to combat his influence. They threatened to cease financial support to the University unless his ideas were repressed or expunged. I was singled out for attack as the Crown Prince of 'Keynesism.' I was greatly pleased and hoped that my friends would be properly resentful. That was Keynes. You came to him out of conservatism, your desire for peaceful change. And by urging his ideas you won a reputation for being a radical."9

Galbraith has acknowledged his debt to Keynes throughout all his books. It is interesting to note that Galbraith published his first influential paper in 1936 — "Monopoly Power and Price Rigidities" — the same year as Keynes' *General Theory* appeared. Keynes' ideas were first considered radical, even revolutionary — particularly using deficit spending to stabilize capitalism — but now are seen as conservative. Presidents — FDR in the thirties to Nixon in the seventies — have used Keynes' theories in their attempts to solve the nation's economic problems. For example, Roosevelt counteracted tight money policies in 1938 by instituting heavy relief and public works spending — but at half what the Keynesians recommended. And Nixon's attempt to counter inflation with Galbraithian style price and wage controls didn't cover enough of the nation's economy or last long enough to work.

Galbraith told me, "Those of us who were in Washington during the war years never had the slightest doubt that Roosevelt just hated having anything to do with economics.

"When World War II came, I am sure there were few people in Washington who were as happy as Roosevelt. In good conscience he could now wash his hands of economics and economists and delegate all economic matters, except as they had to do with war production, and concern himself with the problems of grand military strategy."

In 1939, when World War II engulfed Europe, 17 percent of American workers were without jobs; in 1940, 14.6 percent. As the war raged on, US government expenditures increased, until in 1942 American industry was begging for workers.

The war uncovered two vital aspects associated with Keynesian theory: The moral difference between spending for welfare and spending for war and the threat of inflation as unemployment diminishes. In the first instance, many people thought that government spending to help people was both immoral and economically unjustifiable. On the other hand, government spending for war was not only a safe investment, it was also patriotic. According to Galbraith, this attitude still prevails.

Keynes proposed raising taxes to finance war spending, to keep the budget deficit down, and to stabilize living costs. He hoped that wages would be frozen during the war while prices would be controlled and essential commodities rationed.

In 1941, Galbraith was put in charge of price control. It was a wartime position of great power and authority. "To say I was overjoyed would be a gross understatement," Galbraith writes in *The Age of Uncertainty*. The Office of Price Administration (OPA) grew so rapidly in staff that its offices had to be moved three times during the war.

With the wage-price spiral accelerating during the early part of World War II and taxes lagging behind government spending, Galbraith implemented comprehensive price-fixing and rationing to control the economy. He points with pride to the fact that throughout the war, as a result of these policies, price stability was maintained. Plaintiffs could appeal to higher government officials or to the courts for relief from the controls, but the OPA's position was usually upheld. Galbraith says in *The Age of Uncertainty* that his staff members felt they had failed in their jobs if any plaintiff left with a smile on his face. He maintains that price controls at that time had to be painful to be effective. "To be charged with inflicting pain, mostly on those who could handsomely afford it, was a psychologically damaging experience for a young man. I was accused of liking it, which I did,"[10] Galbraith confesses.

Galbraith did not meet Keynes until he became deputy head of the OPA. Keynes came into his outer office one day to deliver an economic paper. Galbraith's secretary brought it to him and said that the man wishing to see him was someone called "Kines." Galbraith looked at the title sheet and Keynes' name. "It was as though St. Peter had dropped in on some parish priest,"[11] Galbraith writes, still in awe of the great man's presence.

In 1944 Keynes met with delegates from forty-four nations at Bretton Woods, New Hampshire in an attempt to correct the economic errors made after World War I. "The Bretton Woods Conference was not a conference among nations. It was a conference of nations with Keynes,"[12] according to Galbraith in *The Age of Uncertainty*. Out of the Bretton Woods deliberations came the creation of the Bank for International Reconstruction and Development (The World Bank) and the International Monetary Fund.

After the Allied victory, Keynes obtained a $3.75 billion loan for Great Britain to pump new vigor into its economy and get exports again paying for imports. However, it didn't quite work out that way. In 1947, the loan was used up in a matter of a few days after speculators had converted their holdings in sterling into dollars. Keynes did not live to witness this disaster. He died of a heart attack on April 21, 1946.

If the British loan was a fiasco, the Marshall Plan worked, and because of it, Europe recovered. One of the participants in the Marshall Plan was the defeated enemy, Germany. As Keynes and the world had learned from the mistakes of the Treaty of Versailles, it made more sense in the long run to help rather than to punish a defeated enemy.

Galbraith's debt to Keynes is vast, and he acknowledges it. As Myron E. Sharpe observes in *Galbraith and the Lower Economics* (International Arts and Sciences Press, 1973), "Galbraith's anchor is Keynes. But he is neither an idolator or an uncritical recipient of Keynes' thinking. Galbraith can be critical of the British economist — sometimes in areas generally regarded to be Keynes' greatest strengths."

To Galbraith, the acid test of an economist's writing is his ability to handle difficult subjects with liveliness and lucidity. In his great work *The General Theory of Employment, Interest and Money*, Keynes does not pass the test. The book, says Galbraith, "is an acrostic of English prose and the fact that it was an important book should not cause anyone to say that it was well written or even finished." Later writers have turned Keynes' ideas into accessible English, showing that it can be done. "A better writer — patience has a certain standing as one constituent of genius — would have done the job himself."

Galbraith points out that before the publication of *The General Theory* Keynes had advocated many of its conclusions in clear, forceful language. He was able to write well; so, says Galbraith, it is all the more blameworthy that he did not do so in one of his most significant works.

It is accurate and useful to point out the great influence that Keynes had on Galbraith. At the same time, it is useful to remember that Galbraith is by no means an unquestioning worshipper at the British economist's shrine.

CHAPTER **3**

THE
SUSPECT
ECONOMIST

Ask a layman to name the first economist who comes to his mind and he is more likely to mention Galbraith than anyone else. Within the profession, however, it is a different matter. Robert L. Heilbroner (*The New York Review,* June 29, 1967) says, "John Kenneth Galbraith has not enjoyed the regard of his fellow economists to anything like the degree that he has enjoyed the acclaim of the public."

Even those who denigrate Galbraith as an economist express admiration for his style — clear, witty, incisive, cutting. Heilbroner feels that this celebrated style, far from being a great strength, is in fact Galbraith's fatal weakness.

Not everyone agrees. Bernard Nossiter (*Book World,* October 7, 1973) writes that economics itself is bankrupt; "the discipline has not yielded a fresh theoretical idea of consequence in nearly 40 years. . . ." He concludes that "if Galbraith's program for reform appears superficial and inconsistent, we are still in his debt for a clear and entertaining exposition of some of the central politico-economic problems. Galbraith's private joke, of course, is that he pretends to be a radical and is in fact deeply conservative."

Commentary on Galbraith centers on his renowned literary style. Eugene D. Genovese, reviewing *Money: Whence It Came, Where It Went* in the *New York Times,* says that Galbraith's "wit and grace have, predictably, provided an excuse for his detractors to dismiss him as superficial. In truth, however, he has admirably demonstrated that respect for the English language provides every-

25

thing necessary to demystify economics and render its complexities intelligible." The salutary effect of Galbraith's ability at demystification should, observes Genovese, make us look with some indulgence on even "so palpably poor a book" as *Money*.

Economists are not fond of the way Galbraith writes; some admit it. Scott Gordon of Indiana University wrote in the *Journal of Political Economy:* "One must begin with a candid recognition that the academic reader of Galbraith's books is under a strong temptation to react negatively to the author's style and method of discourse. He waives the scholarly conventions in favor of a rhetoric which is designed to appeal to the lay reader. But the stylistic techniques he employs to this end increase the difficulty of grasping the substance and structure of his thought and work against a fair and objective appraisal of it by an orthodox, scholarly mind."

There can be little question that Galbraith has done much to introduce clarity and zest into the gloom of the "dismal science." As a teacher and popularizer he has surely accomplished something essential. He keeps his students interested.

Joan Robinson, formerly Professor of Economics at the University of Cambridge, reviewed *Economics and the Public Purpose* for *The Spectator* of March 30, 1974. She observes that Galbraith "has cast himself for the role, among economists, of the child who remarked that the Emperor had no clothes. He proceeds by making observations that any unprejudiced reader immediately accepts as obvious while whose who are prejudiced in favor of orthodoxy are shocked and distressed. . . . Professor Galbraith has great faith in the power of reason, and since there does not seem to be anything else to have faith in, we must be thankful for that."

Has he done more? Is he — or was he — capable of doing more? Writing in the *Boston Globe* (October 19, 1975), Nina McCain quotes Paul Samuelson on Galbraith: "He could have been a top-notch agricultural economist. He could have been a top-notch industrial economist. But he went after the bigger prize of the mind of a generation and he has done that. . . . He captures their minds when they are still flexible enough to think. Everybody comes to college having read *The Affluent Society*."

In the light of these comments it is interesting to recall that two people for whom Galbraith has expressed great admiration are Franklin Roosevelt and the writer Somerset Maugham. Roosevelt, too, has been described as one who pretended to be a radical but was in fact deeply conservative. And Maugham is thought by some to be undervalued as a writer of substance because of the facility and grace of his style.

In examining the principles of Galbraith's economic thinking it is impossible to divorce the ideas from the context of style. However, one can identify some of the major elements of the message he attempts to convey to the world.

An important theme of his long discourse is the dominance of production, the affluence it engenders, the negative aspects of that affluence, and the things that society must do to restore what he calls the social balance. To establish and maintain the necessary balance, Galbraith is perceived as being willing to levy higher taxes and incur greater rates of inflation than many other economists, particularly those of the "Chicago School," among whom his name is anathema.

In his monograph *John Kenneth Galbraith* (St. Martin's Press, 1975), John S. Gambs calls attention to the subtitle of *American Capitalism — The Concept of Countervailing Power*. Gambs observes that this subtitle conveys the true meaning of the book. Galbraith describes what he sees as the rise and fall of Adam Smith's model of the competitive economy. Concentration of economic power has invalidated the proposition that the result of competing selfish interests is the ultimate social good. "Countervailing power" must be applied to restore the balance, and one form of this counter-vailing power may be government intervention through wage and price controls.

The Affluent Society, which in 1958 brought Galbraith his first great publishing success with the general public, examines the re-sults of the concentration of power. Here Galbraith advances one of his most fiercely debated arguments — that production is no longer a response to demand. Rather, he says, it is now the other way around. Production comes first; then the producer creates the demand for his goods and services.

In *The New Industrial State* Galbraith intensifies the emphasis on concentration of power which he introduced in *American Capitalism* to the extent that he says (as Scott Gordon puts it in the *Journal of Political Economy*) "that the American economy is not only no longer a competitive economy but that it is not even a market economy." Now everything — prices, production incentives, consumer preferences — is "managed" by the huge corporations.

The last book of Galbraith's tetralogy, *Economics and the Public Purpose*, restates themes found in the earlier books. Then Galbraith goes on to offer his ideas for reforms that will restore social balance and bring us back toward the ideal of a market economy.

These four books do not progress neatly in chronological fashion. Galbraith returns to previous ideas, revises, restates. A view of the works — taken in conjunction with certain retrospective observations offered by Galbraith on his thinking — may help to give a sense of his career and significance as an economist.

One trait that sets Galbraith apart from many other economists is his fascination with history. He unfailingly applies its lessons to his own work. Each of his books is replete with historical references; *The Great Crash — 1929* and *The Age of Uncertainty* are excellent examples. His style has been praised as bringing the art of poetry to history.

"But that is partly a matter of generations and partly a matter of where one has studied," Galbraith maintains. "In my generation, much more attention was given to the history of economic thought than is now. Academic subjects, such as economics, have been overtaken by a false sense of what is practical and relevant. This excludes much of the valuable feeling for the history of economic ideas. My time in England was extremely important in this regard. The British are the only people who consider the past to be as immediately and strikingly important as the present. Britain is the only country at which a dinner conversation centers around what Gladstone was really like or the nature of Lloyd George's character. Discussing Lloyd George in Britain is close to a national pastime."

In an article in *Harper's Magazine* about the 1929 stock market crash, Galbraith concludes with a paragraph that demonstrates his interest in the lessons of history, his view of the prevalence of human folly, and his casually abrasive style: "Since it was important, the question inevitably arises whether a similar cycle of speculation and collapse could again occur. The simple answer is of course! Laws have been passed to outlaw some of the more egregious behavior which contributed to the big bull market of the twenties. Nothing has been done about the seminal lunacy which possesses people who see a chance of becoming rich. On the assumption that history does not repeat itself precisely, we may never again see the particular lunacy of the late twenties. But if we survive to suffer such things, we can undoubtedly count on some variation. The time to worry will be when important people begin to explain that it cannot happen because conditions are fundamentally sound."

If Galbraith had been an active economist in the eighteenth century, there is a good chance that he might not view himself as an economic determinist. In *The Affluent Society* he refers to two important economists of that period, David Ricardo and Thomas Robert Malthus, both of whom believed that mass poverty was inevitable. There were few alternatives to poverty and almost no opportunity to improve one's lot in life in the eighteenth century — except a slight possibility of emigrating to America and taking one's chances in a frontier society.

Both Ricardo and Malthus, like Galbraith, pictured the economic reality of their time. That the masses lived close to starvation was considered normal. They also believed that access to economic factors that produce wealth was available only to those who already possessed wealth. These early English economists were not heartless, but realists in an environment that destroyed many people while it made a few wealthy. The fact that many were destroyed as a result of the capitalistic economic system was not the point. Destruction was part of life, and it was expected. The fact that a few survived and prospered was a cause for rejoicing. It is no wonder that economics is called the "dismal science." According to Galbraith, modern economic thought, which he calls the "central tradition," was founded on that system and it continues to influence modern industrial Western society.

Much economic thinking is concerned with material growth and its relation to investment in production. Since the start of the Industrial Revolution, money has been invested in plant, equipment, and labor to produce goods that are sold for a higher price than it cost to make them. Simply stated, the lower the manufacturing and selling costs, and the higher the selling price, the greater the profit. If the market demands more goods than the current factory can produce, plant, equipment, and labor supply are expanded — financed by reinvested profits and borrowed money.

Continued growth results from repeating this process. Because of the pressures of competition, the emphasis has always been on increasing productivity, on controlling — and if possible lowering — the costs of manufacturing and selling, and on increasing efficiency at all levels of the operation.

During the early stages of Western industrial development, a high level of training and education was not required to make the process work. The career of King C. Gillette, the inventor of the first safety razor, is a case in point. A bottle-top salesman in Boston, Gillette envisioned a safe, cheap, disposable blade. Unlike the straightedge razor, which lasted a lifetime, the disposable blade created repeat business. The concept of repeat sales was tied into mass production, which was developed for Gillette by William Nickerson, a graduate of the Massachusetts Institute of Technology.

As part of the early marketing strategy, Gillette gave away safety razors by the thousands. Once a man owned the razor, he would become a lifetime consumer of Gillette's blades. That merchandising technique worked with phenomenal success in the early 1900s, and it continues to work today.

Gillette not only invented a useful product, but also contributed greatly to a new concept — contriving new products in advance of consumer needs. Those products in turn require creating consumer needs to keep pace with the process of mass production and management's goals of growth and increased profits as predetermined by top management. Eventually, King C. Gillette was ousted from his company by a different breed of men with far more sophisticated visions. Nonetheless, though the Gillette Company is now a multinational conglomerate, with 1977 sales over $1.5 billion, it has yet to develop another product idea and merchandising principle to match those created by its founder. Ironically, King C. Gillette, if still alive, would probably be considered unqualified for a job today in the company he founded and led.

According to Galbraith, a large supply of well-educated people is now essential for the growth of industry. "Investment in human beings is, *prima facie*, as important an investment as material capital,"[1] he writes in *The Affluent Society*. Galbraith points out that much of the investment in educating men and women for modern private industry has come from the public sector. It is the public sector that provides and pays for schooling, from kindergarten and the elementary grades and through graduate studies in many instances.

Executives from large corporations argue that the taxes their firms pay to government help to finance a substantial portion of the cost of public services, such as education. But corporations regard taxes as part of the cost of doing business, so they pass that cost on to customers in the form of higher prices. Corporation executives also award well-publicized scholarships and grants for research and special education programs. Many such donations are restricted to research in fields that directly relate to the business of the corporation or the industry. For example, a geology department at a university might be looked on with more favor by an oil company than the humanities department. Understandable, perhaps, but a kind of self-interest often confused with public service. And contributions to higher education, even when they benefit the giver's business, are of course tax-deductible.

The private sector also benefits from public money invested in government research and development. For example, technological advances in air transportation, electronic communications, and medical science are the result of billions of dollars of public money poured into various aerospace programs. Galbraith maintains, as do many others, that the rapid rate of technological advancement in American private industry would not have been possible without the research and development achievements in the public sector.

Of course, a highly organized industrial economy cannot function and grow without well-educated people. But Galbraith also warns of a danger to the private sector — the double-edged sword of education. More than providing vocational skills, education hones critical faculties, broadens tastes, and teaches people to think for themselves. In Galbraith's view, intellectual development can offset the enticements of contrived consumer demand. If, for example, a consumer determines that a man's cologne is unnecessary to his own self-esteem and allure, eventually the profits of the company that makes the cologne will suffer. Multiply this example by millions of people and thousands of products, from chopped ham spread to hair coloring, and the problem for the entire system becomes serious indeed. Moreover, once people perceive the myth of their being masters of the marketplace with private companies battling each other to serve their wants, they will realize they are servants of what Galbraith calls the "planning system" — the mammoth corporations controlling both the supply and demand of goods and services.

Galbraith hopes this awakening will happen: "Emancipation of the mind is a no less worthy enterprise than emancipation of the body."[2] In the past, production was paramount — the cure for poverty. However, when a society becomes affluent, Galbraith maintains that production is no longer urgent; indeed, our preoccupation with production contributes to inflation and social imbalance.

Efficiency is a key element in production. The more efficient production becomes, the higher the profit. However, Galbraith holds that as production becomes less urgent, efficiency is no longer of prime importance. The people who make up the corporation are as important to it as the corporation's ability to produce goods, in Galbraith's view. Developing people into complete human beings is as worthy an objective as efficiency, even if such humanism means producing goods at a higher cost. And he asks: "Why should life be intolerable to make things of small urgency?"[3]

Galbraith reasons that as a society increases its affluence, and as the production of goods therefore becomes less urgent, fewer people need to work. A poor society, because it is poor, must exploit all available labor, both young and old. An affluent society does not require labor from either young or old. Galbraith says that if society can afford to retire the elderly because their labor is no longer required, society can also afford to provide the elderly with an income that allows them to live with dignity and independence. And since the labor of the young is also unnecessary, an affluent society should provide the young with a quality education.

Galbraith's method of allowing people to maximize every hour of their lives eliminates "toil as a required economic institution"[4] and greatly increases the investment in human potential through education (in contrast to the investment in the production of material goods). Although Galbraith uses the argot of economists, he is more in tune with the philosophers and the poets — with the exception that he believes that his vision can become reality. In fact, Galbraith states that the emancipation process is already occurring in our affluent society with the emergence of what he terms the "New Class."

All work obviously is not the same. The lathe operator, the poet, the janitor, the artist, the power company engineer, the nuclear physicist, the hospital orderly, the surgeon, the advertising copywriter, the novelist, the executive, the mailroom clerk, the assembly line worker, the racing car driver, the teacher — all perform different work roles. Toil, boredom, and drudgery are inherent in some occupations. This is true for many in the so-called "laboring class." Pleasure, prestige, a sense of individual accomplishment, and a quest for more knowledge and experience are intrinsic to others — Galbraith's New Class.

The janitor performs the same job, washing toilet bowls, emptying trash, mopping floors, day after day, night after night. The elements of toil, boredom and drudgery dominate his work. A landscape painter, who may work many more hours each day than a janitor, finds pleasure in work — and possibly even fame and fortune. The janitor toils because of a need to make money. The landscape painter "toils" for a number of reasons, one of which is that he or she likes to paint more than anything else. Money is important, but it is not the primary reason for painting.

In the same vein, although the vice president of manufacturing of an aircraft engine corporation may occasionally identify with a romantic image of hard physical work and skill of an assembly line worker, the executive would hardly trade places. The businessman knows that his job is more challenging and rewarding, even though he has to work longer hours and has less time with his family.

The lathe operator may see nothing romantic about standing behind the same machine until he retires — or is laid off — and he may be resigned to the fact that he will never become a vice president. But he also is probably determined that his sons and daughters will enjoy work that offers more challenge, prestige, satisfaction, and money. The lathe operator dreams that his children will become members of the New Class. At the same time, the business executive is determined that his children will never have to leave the New Class. As a result of those attitudes, Galbraith says, the New Class is itself self-perpetuating: no one leaves, but many join it each year.

Recently, however, young New Class members, although well-educated and relatively affluent, have rejected their parents' values and identify more closely with cab drivers, janitors, and lathe operators. However, the university-trained cab driver always has the option of rejoining the New Class. Moreover, perhaps a stint as a cab driver, for instance, will yield a new perception of the human condition.

Unfortunately, however, most workers don't have the option of switching class roles. Exclusion from the New Class is also self-perpetuating for those workers who lack education.

The New Class is growing in numbers, but Galbraith would like to see it expand even more greatly, through a more substantial public investment in education: ". . . the further and rapid expansion of this class," Galbraith writes with strong conviction in *The Affluent Society*, "should be a major, and perhaps next to peaceful survival itself, the major goal of society."[5]

To Galbraith, the affluent society's preoccupation with goods that are no longer urgent causes disorders of social balance: inflation, unemployment, poverty, toil, inequality. Galbraith, of course, is not opposed to an affluent society; indeed, he wants it to become even more affluent. At the same time he wants the quality of social balance that will equalize the provision of private goods with the provision of public services.

Through his concept of an income program, everyone will enjoy the right to a degree of financial security and a decent standard of living. This security will be protected against the ravages of inflation through his system of limited but long-term wage and price controls. Separating toil from work will be achieved through increased public investment in education. In this way more people will be given the opportunity to lead fuller, more satisfying lives, which the New Class already enjoys.

What Galbraith proposes is possible. But is it a realistic expectation? We live in a pluralistic society, in which Galbraith's view on the emancipation of the human spirit represents only one band on a wide spectrum of opinion. North American society continues to be dominated by a strong Puritan bent, which is often harshest on the weakest members of society and which fosters the concentration of great power, wealth, and privilege in the hands of a few.

Galbraith mentions that in the early days of their ascendancy, the Vanderbilts, Astors, Whitneys, Rockefellers, and Fords were considered crude by the "old wealth" — distinctions written about by Edith Wharton and Henry James. Today, of course, these families are the bastions of the American social elite. "In the last century a titled Englishman of modest means, even an impecunious and venereal Polish count, was often the equal of a Whitney or a Rockefeller. Among Americans, Lowells, Cabots and Coolidges were much better. Their wealth had aged,"[6] writes Galbraith in *The Age of Uncertainty*.

Just as Newport was the watering hole for the very rich in America, the Riviera was the special enclave for the aristocracy of Europe. Appropriate marriages were arranged between the titled nobility of Europe and the daughters of American millionaires. Of course, along with the daughters flowed money to improve the health of the bank accounts of European aristocrats. In *The Age of Uncertainty*, Galbraith offers an impressive statistic: "By 1909, by one estimate, 500 American heiresses had been exported for the improvement of the family name, along with $220 million."[7] The Duke of Marlborough struck a deal to marry Consuelo Vanderbilt for a first payment of $2.5 million; this convenient familial arrangement later reached $10 million. But it was worth the price to purge the robber baron image from the Vanderbilt name, as Galbraith points out.

Another function of the Riviera, particularly at its casinos, was to provide the rich with an elegant way to lose their money — through gambling. Galbraith makes the point that most people believe gambling is a way to make money. But for the already rich, gambling, in the company of other wealthy and influential people, provided an opportunity to lose money with style. In fact, losing even several thousands of dollars was unimportant. The real game was to demonstrate to everyone that money was inconsequential. The loser's prestige was enhanced by nonchalant indifference to a poor turn of the dice, cards, or roulette wheel. Conversely, winning was accepted coolly and with proper grace.

Speaking of the situation today, Galbraith maintains that the wealthy hostess in New York or Washington derives more prestige from entertaining a well-known politician at dinner than she would an industrial millionaire. Even entertainers, journalists, high-ranking members of foreign diplomatic corps, and intellectuals seem to command more interest in social circles than the contemporary millionaire-entrepreneur. Indeed, minority leaders are often found mingling with society in exclusive parlors — Thomas Wolfe's "radical chic." Galbraith points out that conspicuous consumption is frowned on in New England, however. "More wealth does nothing for a family except as it makes them an object of attention for those collecting money for charitable or political causes."[8] In New England, esteem is achieved by cultural and conservation pursuits — museums, symphonies, etc. — and by associating with an infinite variety of intellectual groups.

Galbraith considers the handling of New York wealth to be similar to that in New England. New England women may be more "horsey-tweedy," whereas New York women spend far more time and money on making themselves elegant and attractive. Wealthy New Yorkers pride themselves on their expertise in such contemporary matters as foreign policy, the arts, and often, liberal and radical causes.

Texas wealth personifies contemporary conspicuous consumption. Big cars and bigger ranches, jewelry, furs, luxurious homes, sumptuous furnishings, and private jet planes are to be praised and admired. According to Galbraith, Dallas is the "world's most notable market for costly consumer artifacts."[9]

In Los Angeles, ostentatious homes, automobiles, swimming pools, and other luxuries are still necessary to the life style of the wealthy, but they are no longer considered the pinnacle of achievement. Today, one's self and public esteem are enhanced by associating with important names in television, motion pictures, politics, and even crime. Before the presidential resignation, associating with Richard Nixon and leading members of his administration was the ultimate ego inflater.

But have the manners and morals of America's rich improved since the days of the robber barons? Galbraith believes that the manners have. No one would dare shout "the public be damned," for example. Indeed, today's wealthy person speaks of concern for the public good and defends the free enterprise system. But Galbraith is less sure about any improvement in morality. He cites several examples of modern scoundrels who have separated people from their money in *The Age of Uncertainty*. "My own thought is that if men are sufficiently concerned to acquire money," writes Galbraith, "their behavior will reflect that preoccupation and be much the same, whatever the time or place. . . . The manners of capitalism improve. The morals do not. But, equally, they do not get worse."[10]

During the recession of the mid-1970s, the downturn in all forms of manufacturing and service businesses resulted in a corresponding decrease in production. This, in turn, necessitated massive layoffs of workers. When people lack jobs, their security and ultimately their economic survival are at stake. At that point production becomes very important: as it rises, the work force increases. And once people are working again, their sense of security returns and they view the future with less anxiety.

Galbraith's concept is that in an affluent society the traditional relationship between worker security and production must be divorced. His attitude is that the individual should not be the victim of an ethos based on production, which one day offers security and the next discards the worker to the uncertainties of unemployment.

Galbraith places great emphasis on strengthening the system of unemployment compensation. Most employers, in contrast, prefer that the unemployment compensation system be weakened for several reasons: Their firms pay the taxes that fund it and they maintain that the system encourages indolence and malingering. But Galbraith states that income and employment have become far more important economic problems for our time than production. Most employable people would rather work than stay at home. He noticed wryly that indolence is also found among the rich — who have raised it to a fashionable art form. With the poor and unemployed, on the other hand, indolence is most often attributed to them as being some kind of socioeconomic or even theological evil.

Galbraith dismisses malingering as an aspect of unemployment compensation not serious enough to sway us from strengthening the system. Unemployment compensation, he believes, should benefit the large majority who are innocent victims of a capricious ideology that places the production of "silly" goods above maintaining the dignity of human beings.

Galbraith offers three steps of action to divorce security from production. First, unemployment compensation should be brought up to the level of real wages and the number of weeks for benefits extended. Galbraith proposes that this function be nationalized and administered by the federal government. An increasing number of governors would also prefer that the federal government relieve the states' burden of unemployment compensation.

Galbraith's second step would provide income to those who cannot find work or who cannot work. Each individual should receive a guaranteed income. Several years ago, President Nixon proposed a family allowance plan developed by Daniel Patrick Moynihan. The conservative economist Milton Friedman has developed a similar concept — the negative income tax.

Galbraith counters fears that a guaranteed income will entice more people to remain unemployed by pointing out that working people will have a larger income. Current wages at or below welfare level do not provide incentives to work.

Galbraith's third step is the imposition of a system of wage and price controls on large corporations and powerful unions to slow inflation. Obviously, a guaranteed income cannot be effective if inflation is allowed to erode its value.

People and, indeed, entire societies — no less affluent ones — resist change, especially that which would redistribute wealth. But Galbraith maintains that an affluent society has the luxury to make substantial changes. For example, it can choose to correct social imbalance. He contrasts the plenitude of private goods produced in the United States with the far fewer public services provided. Galbraith calls this condition bizarre. His solution is increased corporate and personal taxation to raise more money for the government to provide new and improved public services.

He also favors making private goods more costly through a more intensive use of the sales tax. Increased revenues from higher sales taxes, he believes, could be used by government to provide more public services which would improve the quality of life in our communities. Then health care facilities, mass transportation, education, community safety, and recreation will have equal priority with such private goods as automobiles, cigarettes, perfume, and whiskey. Instead of an economy subject to the production of private goods based on and susceptible to the vagaries of contrived wants, a socially balanced economy will be stronger and healthier because a broader range of needs, both private and public, will be satisfied.

"One of the worst mistakes that economists have made in the last ten years has been the recurring advocacy of federal tax reduction instead of keeping taxes up," Galbraith told me. "Tax cuts, in the main, benefit the affluent. They are a slow and inefficient way to expand employment because people can't be relied on to spend this extra money. However, if these same revenues, instead of going back to the taxpayer, were spent on the urban unemployed, the employment effect and the social effect would be much greater. Through this application of revenue, we would have done something to prevent the kind of agony we see New York City passing through at the present time. Oddly enough, Walter Heller was the first to get hold of the idea that the fiscal structure of the United States requires the turnback of money to the states and the cities.

"Unfortunately, Heller has never been willing to embrace fully the strategies necessary to control inflation. However, these were essential to his success when he was head of the Council of Economic Advisers. He instituted the policy of guideposts and voluntary price and wage restraints, which held prices stable through the early 1960s against rising employment. But then — one really doesn't know why — he never became an active proponent of controls or restraints after that. Sadly, Heller did become an active proponent of tax reduction to expand employment while he was a member of the council. He has come up with that idea repeatedly ever since. It is one of the most conservative and damaging ideas of modern times."

One of the strongest arguments against high personal and corporate taxation is that it kills incentive. In Britain, for example, high social costs — such as pensions, health insurance, unemployment benefits, and welfare payments — have pushed income taxes up as high as 98 percent. Britain's well-publicized recent economic problems are almost as familiar to us as those of New York City. It is difficult to say whether expenditures for the public good are the source of all its economic problems — but the high tax rate and inflation certainly have curbed individual incentives to work harder for more money. But Galbraith does not believe that high taxation would have any effect on incentive in the United States.

Galbraith does not think there is the slightest reason for anyone to believe that the American tax system as it is now structured has any counterincentive effect. For example, no corporation would promote a man who was slackening his effort because he was taxed too heavily. "The corporate ethic requires that one should always be putting one's best foot forward and making maximum effort. The diminishing of incentive as a result of taxation is a fear that can only be attributed to the special pleading of the rich," he says.

When Galbraith was a *Fortune* magazine editor many years ago, one of his fellow editors came into the office with a proposal for a study on the counterincentive effect of progressive taxation. This was just after World War II, when tax rates were very much higher. Eric Hodgins, who was then also an editor, kicked Galbraith under the table and said, "I think we should do that story. I know a lot of businessmen who, because of those rates, are constantly struggling to increase their income in order to protect what they have left. They smoke too much. They drink too much. They have high blood pressure. We are losing a lot of good talent because high income tax rates are forcing people to work too hard."

Galbraith agreed that there wasn't any doubt that people were concerned with their after-tax income. The higher the taxes, the more they had to struggle to maintain their after-tax income at the level they wanted. But, he said, we shouldn't worry about the health-effects part, because there was an enormous benefit to society to have this extra effort. In the end, the editor said, "Well, maybe we better drop the whole idea."

Galbraith thinks it is possible that there is a counterincentive effect on certain types of entrepreneurs when they reach a high income level — as in Great Britain. He says, "I have never seen the slightest evidence that the United States is suffering from a shortage of entrepreneurial or executive talent because of a lack of incentive due to taxation."

Paul Samuelson, among others, takes issue with Galbraith's ideas on taxation. "Galbraith was once here in a debate at MIT, and we were amazed that he insisted that it was not a value judgment that the public sector should be expanded. He insisted that it was an objective fact. I regard it as a value judgment. But it is not something you can prove to people such as Milton Friedman, who holds the opposite value judgment from Galbraith."

What does Samuelson believe increased taxation will do to incentive in the United States? "It is very difficult to devise a progressive, graduated tax system which achieves a greater measure of redistributional equity according to value judgments which Galbraith and I share without having some effects on incentive, of course," Samuelson told me. "When you get a marginal tax rate, tax avoidance becomes colossal. It has different effects upon risk-taking. The sophisticated economist has to go over the redistribution of the social pie, but he also has to have some interest in what size the whole pie is."

Sweden has, over the years, made a great effort to achieve social balance. In recent years economists have come to regard the Swedish system with marked skepticism. Typically, Paul Samuelson told me, "In Sweden you also see a 20 percent absenteeism on Friday and a 10 percent absenteeism on Monday. And an elaborate system of working outside the tax system. But Sweden in many ways is admirable from my point of view. However, one should not believe that it is a country without problems."

Samuelson believes that the exceptionally high taxes needed to maintain the immense cost of a cradle-to-grave welfare state cause great problems.

"It certainly is a problem, but reactionaries exaggerate the problem. Some abuse — for example, tax avoidance — could be cured by lowering taxes, which is Milton Friedman's proposal. Or high taxes could be cured by getting rid of the loopholes. When George McGovern proposed to really get rid of tax loopholes, he helped create an electoral victory for Nixon, a landslide. You only have one electorate to work with. The electorate is, of course, torn. A man making over $15,000 a year, even if he is a man of good will, is concerned that he does not go below that income level. That is what scared people about McGovern.

"Galbraith completely misjudged the temper of intellectuals and the American electorate when he announced that the Democratic Party should become a socialistic party, and that it would win elections on that basis. You should look at this idea in his book, *Who Needs the Democrats?* That book is an absolute prescription for disaster."

Swedish socialism is also of interest to William F. Buckley, Jr., who does not see any appropriate parallels between Sweden and the United States. He told me: "Sweden has a terribly high concentration of people living in a very small area. Sweden has a kind of transnational mobility on the basis of which it has fought unemployment and gradually converted itself from an agricultural to an industrial society. And it is a country which sat out rather peacefully a world war in which other countries made considerable sacrifices. However, there is more government money available for private enterprise in Sweden than in any other country in the world. If you want to set up and finance a private company, go to Sweden, because that's where your chances are the best.

"Sweden is an example of a society that has experimented with socialism but has not gone totalitarian. However, this experience with socialism is not of a very long duration.

"And the tone of Swedish culture has a sense of procrastination to it. They make one good car. They have beautiful blondes. And they have one good movie director; that is, they did have one good movie director. But that's about all," Buckley said.

Buckley, of course, disagrees with Galbraith's social and economic philosophy, which includes taxing corporations more heavily to raise money to serve the public purpose and improve the quality of life. "I think this is a considerable act of autohypnosis," Buckley said. "As far as I am concerned, there is no question that we would be much better off without any corporation taxes whatsoever. What I resent are the billions of dollars of wasted energy by corporations attempting to seek tax shelters. That's a misallocation of energy.

"Ken Galbraith is worried about somebody pissing in the Hudson River. I would just as soon they wouldn't either, because that's a form of ecological profanation. But there are also economic profanations, and one of them is the company which is spending $15 million a year on lawyers and tax authorities simply to run around and survive a heavy, heavy overhead of taxation."

Buckley also attacks Galbraith's notion that incentive would not be impeded by increased taxation. "He is incorrect . His colleague, Professor Martin Feldstein at Harvard, has documented that a worker in Massachusetts who earns $6,000 a year, married to a woman who earns $4,000 a year, loses only 18 percent of his net income by not working at all. Now 18 percent is not an awful lot to lose in return for being relieved of 160 hours of work each month. So even at the lower level, the incentive is not high enough. And at the upper level it is very hard to quantify the extent to which things don't get done as a result of a 70 percent tax on earned income."

I turned to Arthur M. Schlesinger, Jr., to get a liberal's view on increasing taxation to improve the quality of life and to maximize human potential. Will Americans tolerate increased taxation for the provision of more public services? "I think it all depends on how far it goes," he told me. "People can be taxed more than they are being taxed in the United States without coming anywhere near the English tax levels."

But would Schlesinger be willing to be taxed another 20 to 40 percent of his income? "Not another 40 percent," he answered. "I would not necessarily be cheerful about paying extra taxes. But if this money could be effectively used to produce a number of positive changes in our society, I could reconcile myself to the increased taxes on my income."

In the end, Galbraith's enduring contribution is likely to be seen as his ability to write and teach about economics rather than in some original contribution to the discipline.

"Ken is by all odds the best writer — that doesn't even do him justice — in American economics," according to Walter Heller. "Ken has really been a wholesome influence on the profession — even when he's wrong. There are many economists, especially those of a more modern bent, who think that a person like Galbraith is not scientific and mathematical enough to suit them. Ken has performed an enormously useful service in putting economists on their mettle, in looking at the broader aspects of problems, and deflating some of the jargon, rhetoric, and excessively abstract reasoning. Sometimes he's jogging us. Sometimes irritating us. Sometimes stimulating us into rethinking our positions. He has always been a force to be reckoned with."

Wassily Leontief, Nobel Prize winner and New York University economist said this about Galbraith's contribution: "I think his work has certainly brought to public attention some of the most important problems society will have to solve one day or another. His greatest contribution has been to be a public educator and questioner in the widest global sense. Businessmen, labor leaders, blacks, whites, people on different sides of a fight listen to Galbraith."

"If economics were written in algebra, if it eschewed all ideas not yet adumbrated by Adam Smith, if it claimed austere separation from the politics which engulf it and simply served the conventional wisdom of collective or private establishments, would we read economics?" Barbara Ward (Lady Jackson), the noted historian, commented. "So, let us be grateful to Professor Galbraith who keeps the subject witty, lively, relevant, and eminently readable."

This emphasis on style rather than substance may not be altogether unrelated to Galbraith's wry, mocking view of his own discipline and his fellow economists. This is demonstrated by an exchange I had with him, touched off by my question about the inability of economics to forecast events with any degree of accuracy.

"Economic forecasting is largely witchcraft," Galbraith said. He appreciates computers and mathematical models as new tools of his profession but is not beguiled by them. "Even the econometric models," Galbraith maintained, "have the great defect that they can only take into account past events. It is the old problem of the computer. Garbage in, garbage out. The computer models which economists use, with the exception of one at MIT, never took into account the deflationary effects of those large slumps in the stock market and in the real estate market. And these, after all, were precipitating factors in the slump of the mid-1970s. The computer models were not programmed to deal with an oil embargo. There were many other disturbing factors which the computers could not handle.

"The personal strategy of an economist should be to avoid prediction. At the end of every December and the beginning of every January, I can count on a dozen telephone calls from various publications. The editors say to me, 'We have this special weekend edition coming out on the economy. What are your predictions for the New Year?' I never give mine because people only remember the predictions you make which are wrong. The people who do make predictions are mostly people who either don't know, or don't know that they don't know. And why run the risk of making a prediction unless one is being paid for it?"

Because American presidents are usually not experts in economic matters, they need economic advisers. On a formal basis, the president has access to his Council of Economic Advisers, his secretary of the treasury, the chief of the Bureau of the Budget, and the chairman of the Federal Reserve System, who can, by law, maintain a position independent from that of the President. In addition, the president can call on economists teaching at universities or working in consulting firms. Galbraith, Paul Samuelson, Milton Friedman, and Walter Heller are only four of many economists who have advised presidents. During the administrations of Presidents Nixon and Ford, Alan Greenspan, chairman of the Council of Economic Advisers, was one of the most dominant figures in the shaping and implementing of public policy to deal with a high rate of inflation coupled with a recession.

I asked Galbraith about the role of the Council of Economic Advisers — and particularly its chairman — in federal economic policy.

"You have to keep this in perspective," Galbraith told me. "The economic advisers, and this has been true under the Democrats as well as under the Republicans, do not function as economists. They function as a priesthood. They use incantation to explain that what the president needs to have happen will in fact happen. Alan Greenspan's predictions were based on what Gerald Ford needed to have happen. When Alan Greenspan said that inflation would taper off, that it was really the result of mistakes made back in the Johnson administration, and that employment would rise steadily with no danger of another recession, he wasn't making any economic judgment. He was trying to justify what the president needed to believe.

"But this was also true under the Democrats. Back in the Johnson administration an economist could not base his public economic judgment on the fact that the Vietnam war was going to get worse, that it was going to get more expensive, and that it was going to last longer than the administration expected. Even though he expected this, he had to adjust his forecasts to the political needs of the administration.

"There is a growing feeling in my mind, and one I share with a lot of other people, that the Council of Economic Advisers is becoming a major disaster area for economists," Galbraith said. "The corruption of the forecasting and policy planning process in the federal government is professionally bad. There is a superficial impression that the three members of the council bring a quasi-judicial view into the proceedings. This seems to suggest, in some spurious way, that they may be honest about it all, which they are not. The Council has served its purpose and should probably be abolished.

"The president should have an economic adviser. However, no economist should suppose that he or she is anything but the full-time servant of the president's needs. In addition, this adviser should not be identified with the integrity of the economics profession but with the politics of the president.

"However, one shouldn't exaggerate the role of the Council of Economic Advisers. It is a more influential body today than one might have expected it would become when it was created thirty years ago. It has power over economic matters once assumed by the Bureau of the Budget and even more by the secretary of the treasury.

"The rise to power of the Council of Economic Advisers (and the Bureau of the Budget) is a reflection of the diminution of the powers of the secretary of the treasury. The secretary of the treasury now has one of the most banal jobs in Washington. The Internal Revenue Service functions autonomously and with very little control from the secretary. He still has some involvement with taxes, but that power is still very strongly with the Congress. In addition, the secretary has a little to do with international finance. But this is all. Customs, currency and bond rules largely run themselves. The secretary of the treasury, who at the time of Alexander Hamilton and even in the time of Andrew Mellon was a man of decisive importance in Washington, has now become a figurehead in the federal government."

Do economists have what might be called a compassion deficiency? They are often on television with their charts and statistics speaking in somber tones about percentage points rather than people. I asked Galbraith whether economists are removed from reality — the reality of the young mother or the elderly pensioner or the unemployed man trying to survive.

"That isn't peculiar to economists," Galbraith responded. "It's a very common and a very central tendency to enunciate a dry principle and never associate it with the consequences. This is something with which I dealt in the first of my television programs (*The Age Of Uncertainty*). At the time of the Great Famine in Ireland,

Trevelyan, the Britian Treasury official, said that the famine was a kind of preordained solution to the Irish problem — the best remedy for Ireland's overpopulation. That was a solution which he completely separated from the starvation and death of human beings. In more recent times, it's the kind of solution you heard enunciated during the Vietnam war when the Pentagon talked about a preemptive strike. This was a solution that didn't consider the consequences of bombs falling on populated farming villages in the Vietnamese countryside."

In a 1968 *(Playboy)* interview, Galbraith expressed an unusual degree of optimism about the evolution of economic opinion in the United States when he observed that, under John F. Kennedy, "we finally got away from the cliches of the balanced budget and came to see the Federal Government as an affirmative instrument for maintaining the level of employment. This has become an accepted fact." Observers of President Carter's priorities during his first year in office would wonder about whether that "fact" were as "accepted" as Galbraith thought it was then.

Galbraith has always rejected the notion of a "classical" economics that can be neatly compartmentalized and kept apart from such vulgar realities as poverty and bombs. His wide-ranging mind, his unwillingness to conform to stereotype, and his facility with pointed words do not endear him to traditional economists.

Nevertheless, there are those within the discipline who value his contributions. Myron E. Sharpe, editor and publisher of *Challenge: The Magazine of Economic Affairs*, wrote in *The Journal of Economic Issues* (June 1977): "I wish to assert that Galbraith has met a pressing need in economics. . . . Political economics must be restored to its place of respectability alongside more esoteric undertakings. No man has done more to accomplish this than Galbraith. . . . The quiet man in search of truth would never have been heard. Economics required the audacious man, the ingenious man, the abrasive man with an instinct for attack on the weak flanks of the enemy. Thus Galbraith."

Perhaps we may permit Galbraith the last word. An interviewer *(Playboy* 1968) asked if writing about economics in clear English had lessened his stature. "Not with anyone whose opinion I would respect," he replied. "Economics, like all sciences, has its crotchets, its petty jealousies and its minor feuds. I have no doubt that a certain number of people have said from time to time, 'Galbraith is unfair; by not making use of the normal tendencies to obscurity, he's as guilty as a doctor who writes prescriptions in clear English instead of illegible Latin.' But these are the attitudes of inconsequential people, and I've always successfully ignored them."

4
THE
PERILS OF
AFFLUENCE

John Kenneth Galbraith's career as an influential and popular author began with *American Capitalism,* published in 1952. Since then he has written a score of books while pursuing parallel vocations as educator, diplomat and politician.

Along with *American Capitalism,* four of his books may be grouped in an economic tetralogy: *The Affluent Society* (1958); *The New Industrial State* (1967); and *Economics and the Public Purpose* (1973). Through these works run his major themes: the concentration of economic power; the nature of the economics of abundance; the dynamics of the corporate "technostructure" which deeply influences our lives; and the need for social balance. These themes, woven together, form the spine on which Galbraith has fleshed out his philosophy of modern economics.

Each of the latter three books offers a social and economic model of our contemporary society. *The Affluent Society* argued for new economic structures based on an economy of wealth. *The New Industrial State,* the next step in the evolution of Galbraith's theories, is an analysis of the great "mature" corporations that dominate our economy and culture. *Economics and the Public Purpose* sums up many of Galbraith's key economic points. It offers a fairly complete model of the social and economic order, by rounding out "the theme of unequal development and the associated inequality in income,"[1] as Galbraith says in its foreword.

The Affluent Society was not Galbraith's first book, but it was his first *big* book. It helped make him an international celebrity, a

49

position which he has held and reinforced ever since. Today, *The Affluent Society* is considered a classic, in the same distinguished category of social thought as C. Wright Mills' *The Power Elite* and William H. Whyte's *The Organization Man*. Even William F. Buckley, Jr., includes *The Affluent Society* in his special *National Review* reading list of important books about America.

In this book Galbraith focuses on the other side of the coin of success. We have succeeded, he says, in solving the problem of production; but that success has brought with it new problems.

A key factor in economics is the production of goods and services. Production is vital for the survival of private enterprise. Producing and selling goods brings back income that pays the expenses — labor, overhead, taxes. If all goes well, production results in profits, some of which are reinvested in future growth and some of which are proportioned out to investors. According to Galbraith, the question is not one of production as such, but rather the *kinds* of goods and services that a society produces.

An affluent society typically produces a superabundance of private goods, far in excess of the real needs and wants of individuals. And because production levels must be increased, or at least maintained, the consumer must be convinced, through advertising and other marketing techniques, to buy the goods and services, whether needed or not. Galbraith not only includes the production of consumer goods but also the excessive and unnecessary production of goods and services for government use; for example, weapons systems, developed and produced at extraordinary costs, quickly becoming obsolete as even more sophisticated systems are developed.

The problem then becomes one of production for the sake of production, or production for the sake of those few who have the most to gain from a constant flow of superfluous goods and services. If all this production is heaped on one side of a scale, the platter drops, sending the empty platter on the other side upward. At this point in Galbraith's theory are goods and services produced for the public benefit: education, police and fire protection, housing, recreation, child care centers, mass transit — and most important — the elimination of poverty. Place these public-sector goods and services on the scale, and the consumption of private and public goods and services should come more nearly into balance.

Our society is affluent for some people and not for others. One of the ironies of any affluent society, including that of the United States, is that it tolerates the existence of poverty in a land of plenty. According to the U.S. Census Bureau in November 1977, 11.4 percent of all households in this country are classified as poor. Perhaps it is part of human nature for someone who is comfortably affluent to ignore the economic plight of others. "The worst sin towards our fellow creatures is not to hate them, but to be indifferent to them: that's the essence of inhumanity," George Bernard Shaw once stated.

In *The Affluent Society*, Galbraith separates poverty into two categories: case poverty and insular poverty. Case poverty occurs when individuals or families do not or cannot adapt to their environment, for example, alcoholics or drug addicts, the mentally retarded or illiterate, the chronically ill or physically unemployable, and families with too many children and too little income. Those conditions, not necessarily caused by the community, nevertheless prevent individuals and families from benefiting from whatever economic prosperity exists in the community.

Insular poverty occurs when everyone in an urban ghetto or a rural slum "island" lacks enough money for shelter, food, and other necessities. Insular poverty suggests a defect in the community that keeps people poor. Galbraith feels that most poverty in an affluent society is insular. He cites the movement of poor people from impoverished rural areas into urban slums. The number of poor farm families declined from 1.8 million in 1959 to 295,000 in 1973, according to 1975 Department of Commerce figures. The rural poor feel that more opportunity lies in a large industrial city, even though they often lack the skills and training to get and keep an industrial job.

Almost all people living in insular poverty are subject to restraints that prevent or frustrate their sharing in the economic well-being of the larger, more affluent community surrounding them. Such restraints, according to Galbraith, include race discrimination, poor educational facilities, and the disintegration of the family structure. Moreover, he feels that insular poverty cannot be cured by increased income alone. A few who can qualify for jobs outside the ghetto escape their environment; most are trapped, he stresses.

As one solution to eliminating insular poverty, Galbraith strongly recommends a guaranteed annual income that would provide a decent standard of living for individuals and families at the bottom of the social structure. Such a basic income would prevent poverty from perpetuating itself and would free the children of the poor from the sufferings of their parents. According to Galbraith, poverty is a vicious cycle "because the poorest communities are poorest in the services which would eliminate it."[2]

He proposes that communities invest "more than proportionately in the children of the poor"[3] — in the form of quality health services, quality schools, and quality recreational programs. Case poverty, in Galbraith's theory, can be solved by attending to the physical, psychological, and educational deficiencies of human beings. Galbraith says that knowledge to solve the problems of poverty is available; it is the financial commitment that has yet to be made.

Galbraith calls the presence of poverty in the United States a disgrace. In the 1960s the plight of the poor was a fashionable cause — witness the War on Poverty. But it, like other wars, has passed into history, and the poor are still among us. Today, among liberal causes, women's rights, nuclear plant safety, food processing, and the environment are fashionable. These issues are vital, but they are of primary concern to the affluent. A poor person — of whatever race or color — is far more concerned about food and shelter. The fact that bologna contains ground bones and sodium nitrate is of minor concern.

Galbraith states that "there is a persistent and never-ending competition between what is right and what is merely acceptable."[4] Most of us would rather believe in what conforms to our self-interest than face a reality that may make us uncomfortable. His view is that economic, social, and political ideas emerge not necessarily because they will solve a problem or bring enlightenment, but because the particular community or audience for which they were designed will find them acceptable. Galbraith goes on to say, "To a very large extent, of course, we associate truth with convenience — with what most closely accords with self-interest and personal well-being, or promises best to avoid awkward effort or unwelcome dislocation of life."[5]

He believes that self-interest is one of the most important forces motivating the actions of individuals, groups, and institutions. Those ideas or truths which mesh well with self-interest are both convenient and acceptable. We are all susceptible to self-interest, even Galbraith. To a selfish society, those truths — no matter whether they accurately reflect reality — which detract from self-esteem, or profits, or comfort, or the realization of some opportunity are to be discarded.

Exxon, General Motors, and many of the other 498 leading corporations on *Fortune*'s listing of leading industrials grind out press releases and place expensive advertisements on the glories of the free enterprise system. Such self-congratulation is both convenient and acceptable for corporations because they create their own reality and thereby benefit from it. The general public also benefits from corporate jobs, products, and eventual enrichment of the local economy — but hardly from their self-serving ideologies.

The ingredients of convenience, acceptability, and stability in ideas form one of Galbraith's many neologisms — "conventional wisdom."[6] Conventional wisdom is his surgical tool for severing illusion and obsolescence from the prevailing reality as he perceives it. He feels that liberals are no less guilty of conventional wisdom than conservatives. Liberals, like conservatives, bring an intense moral righteousness to those ideas with which they are most familiar; not that the ideas are original but only that they are familiar.

For example, liberals in both the United States and Great Britain say that they are constantly searching for new ideas to improve society; however, the search, at least to some degree, is a substitute for actually finding those ideas, according to Galbraith. In this way, the process becomes more important than the result. Galbraith loves chiding his fellow liberals for their failings as much as he enjoys jousting with conservatives.

But conventional wisdom is an artificial condition. It is an idea, or a series of ideas, and ideas are subject to the movement of time and therefore to change. Adherents of conventional wisdom, according to Galbraith, fail to recognize when their ideas have become obsolete because the idea is acceptable and convenient.

When the very rich complain about the American system of personal taxation, their complaints are in fact strategic ploys for diverting the public's attention from the tax advantages they enjoy,

Galbraith says. Indeed, the complaints of the rich about the injustices of progressive income taxation get louder when the rest of society talks about reforming the system.

But an entire society can be the victim of conventional wisdom as well. The long public credulity about Vietnam is one example. The belief that America should democratize every corner of the world in its own image is another. The continued expenditure of billions of dollars on unneeded weapons systems while our cities decay and our environment stagnates is yet another. "Only posterity is unkind to the man of Conventional Wisdom, and all posterity does is bury him in a blanket of neglect,"[7] Galbraith writes in *The Affluent Society*.

Because the term conventional wisdom has been fully accepted in the English language, it is now frequently used — or misused. Despite television anchormen and newspaper reporters, conventional wisdom does not mean any prevailing truth or real opinion from such places as the White House or corporate boardrooms. Rather it represents that which the politicians and the captains of industry want people to believe, in Galbraith's view.

There is an inherent danger, of course, that both time and change would make Galbraith's own perceptions of reality the conventional wisdom of the present. He readily acknowledges that problem: "Oh, absolutely! Galbraith on the environment, for example, has become the conventional wisdom of the present," he told me.

The Affluent Society made great waves because it indicated a harsher and a more complex reality in the so-called happy days of the late 1950s. It was not Galbraith's purpose in *The Affluent Society* to deny people their hard-earned comforts but to show them that affluence has a higher purpose than conspicuous consumption. Affluence should be used to improve the quality of life for everyone.

William Manchester, in *The Glory and the Dream*, tells about a rare bit of good luck which the Russians inadvertently gave to Galbraith. Manchester wrote that "Galbraith had been awaiting publication of *The Affluent Society*. Neither he nor his publishers had expected much of a sale. 'Then, in the autumn of 1957,' he wrote in an introduction to the second edition, 'the Soviets sent up the first Sputnik. No action was ever so admirably timed. Had I been younger and less formed in my political views, I would have been carried away by my gratitude and found a final resting place beneath the Kremlin Wall. I knew my book was home.' "

Nobel Laureate Paul Samuelson sees *The Affluent Society* as Galbraith's most important book. It had, he said, impact in several directions "and one of the most important of them emphasized how wealthy America had become.

"This has nothing to do with regard to the desirability of an equitable sharing of whatever social pie there is. Ken's impact on readers is that there is a tremendous amount of social pie. However, this is not the way the voters perceive the problem. The gap between the poor and the rich is not a point which has been made more eloquently by Galbraith than by a whole army of mandarin writers in economics whom he always criticizes. Ken thinks that we ought to be concerned with redistribution of wealth and with equality.

"A few economists disagree with this. Some economists feel that he doesn't go far enough. I once devised a test to determine what is affluence and most of the people who took it went against Galbraith's concept of it. The American people are now, of course, *not* feeling very affluent."

I asked if it was true that Galbraith's concept for improving the quality of life, for example, by diverting money from some consumer production to a public service like ecology, was only something out of the rhetoric of the 1960s? -

"I think there are cycles," Samuelson said, "and we are in a retrenching cycle. This is certainly true of the field of ecology. In Plymouth, Massachusetts, for example, the people voted to put in a second nuclear power plant by a four to one margin. And in Eastport, Maine, 40 percent of the townspeople voted against having any oil refinery built in their area. However, the majority who wanted jobs and associated economic benefits voted for the refinery.

"Certainly, almost everyone is for ecology, that is, until the bill for it is brought home for them to pay. Then people look at the price tag on an ecology project and decide on it the same way they do when they wonder about paying for a pound of chocolates or peanut butter. They try to decide if its value is worth the price. When people find what the price will be to make the Hudson River clean enough in which to swim, they'll discover that it would be astronomically expensive. Very few rational people would opt for that.

"It is certainly desirable to have a cost-benefit analysis to find out what it would cost for the last bit of cleanliness. And when I say what it costs, I mean what it would cost to clean up the Hudson River at a sacrifice to building new hospitals, to providing more kidney machines, and to making money available for other important projects which would benefit people, and not just the money that would be made available from producing and consuming less bubble gum," Samuelson concluded.

The ideas presented by Galbraith in *The Affluent Society* can still engender lively debate. There is no doubt that the book — through its title — brought a new term into the language; and there can be little doubt that it gave many Americans a new viewpoint on American life — whether that viewpoint was welcome or not.

CHAPTER **5**

THE
NEED FOR
SOCIAL BALANCE

The achievement of the affluent society and the rise of the corporate techno-structure or professional managers have, in Galbraith's view, created vast inequities. His response lies in the concept of *social balance*, considered by observers of Galbraith to be most important in understanding his "socialistic" stance on economic affairs.

The essence of social balance is that the provision of public services must keep pace with the production of goods. When this does not happen, the imbalance between affluence and poverty grows until it reaches explosive proportions.

Detroit is a good example to demonstrate his theory. Although there are many industrial centers in the United States, Detroit conveys the strongest image of production and marketing. Greater Detroit is home for the big three of the automobile industry, General Motors, Ford, and Chrysler. Other major industries there, such as steel, rubber, plastics, glass, and textiles, contribute to the manufacture of automobiles.

When people are buying cars, millions of new units are sold each year. Employment in the automobile and allied industries rises. Workers are able to purchase goods, including the cars they helped assemble. When the auto industry is healthy, economists consider, so is the United States.

But Detroit is also a place of violence; it has had one of the highest murder rates in the United States. It has a high unemployment rate, especially among the young and the poor and the black. Despite the vast sums of private money spent on the

Cobo Hall convention center and the Renaissance Center, both designed to attract people to the core city, Detroit also has huge slum areas that are cesspools of prostitution, narcotics use, disease, and illiteracy.

Thus, on the one side of the scale are the glamour and the profits associated with the automobile industry. And on the other are the waste of individual human potential and the decline of a great city.

During the recession of the early 1970s, people suddenly stopped buying cars. Our national monetary policy tried to check inflation by cooling demand through higher interest rates and a tightened money supply. In addition, the petroleum exporting countries decided both to limit the supply of oil and to raise prices. Driving one's own car became an expensive luxury. These were important reasons for the sharp decline in sales of American-made automobiles. Of course, that decline led to massive lay-offs of auto workers.

Then, in 1975, came the turnaround. And a year later, General Motors announced the best profit year in its history. So it was natural in 1976, the Bicentennial year, for the people of Detroit to feel optimistic about the future.

Thousands of suburbanites and city residents turned out to celebrate the renaissance of the new urban spirit of Detroit. The party was festive and colorful, filled with song and dance — and togetherness. But gaiety faded into the summer night when marauding bands of young men, many of them teenagers, attacked at random, robbing, beating, and raping brutally.

Newspaper headlines the next day shocked the nation. Mayor Coleman Young acted quickly to prevent his city from passing out of responsible control into the hands of the young terrorists. He called back to active duty two hundred police officers whom he had recently laid off because Detroit, like cities all over the United States, was in a financial bind.

Detroit was and still is a city out of balance. It is one example of massive expenditures on private goods and services on the one hand and a minimal provision of public services on the other. The gangs had their brief time of dismal glory when they took advantage of that imbalance.

Social imbalance in Detroit and other American cities is not only the result of poor police protection, but other socioeconomic factors as well: substandard housing, minimal job opportunities for the poor — particularly for young blacks — an impoverished school system, and a general street philosophy that promotes the rip-off as the means of survival.

William Serrin, a Detroit journalist, wrote angrily in an article reprinted in the *Boston Globe* about his city's decline. "Taking the money and running is an old game in this country. It was not invented by the black gangs on the Detroit East Side. Old Henry Ford took his money and ran to Dearborn a long time ago and the big merchants in downtown Detroit have been doing it for years. This is a country of selfish people seeking money and comfort. This is what is wrong in Detroit and that is what is wrong in this country."

American suburbanites are not immune to the problems of their city neighbors. Travel from the town to the city office is expensive, whether by private car or public transportation. Property taxes in the suburbs rise each year as well as in the cities, and usually as sharply. Those looking for homes face the same high interest rates, along with grossly inflated property values. Suburbanites also discover that crime is not just a phenomenon of the city.

The suburbanite knows that narcotics are being used in the town's schools and that the town itself is becoming more congested as more people flee the city. Suburbanites feel that they are already contributing their share of taxes directly to their towns and indirectly to the city.

While people complain about the decline of the quality of life in cities and towns and the tax burdens they share, they rarely complain about the private goods and services they consume — unless, of course, a particular product or service fails to live up to its claims.

Galbraith, however, is not against privately produced and marketed goods and services. He himself makes good use of those which please him and satisfy his needs. He flies first class. He usually stays at the Ritz Hotel in London. He skis in Vermont and Gstaad. If Galbraith is a socialist, he is hardly one of the stoic variety; rather he has epicurean tastes and inclinations.

Nonetheless, Galbraith the economist has often pointed out the distinction between the high rate of production of automobiles, for example — which provide pleasure and mobility — and the accidents and foul air they cause and the subsequent need for safer highways, better hospitals for accident victims, and more effective antipollution devices.

Galbraith began articulating his theory of social balance in *The Affluent Society:* "Just as there must be balance in what a community produces, so there must also be balance in what a community consumes. An increase in the use of one product creates ineluctably a requirement for others."[1]

Similarly, every increase in the consumption of private goods will normally mean some facilitating or protective step by the state. In all cases, if these services are not forthcoming, the consequences will in some degree be ill.

To continue the automobile analogy, the more cars a community uses, the more gasoline will be consumed. In addition, because much of our culture is centered on the automobile, the automobile will be subjected to more uses: commuting to work, shopping, vacations, and transporting children. When the number of automobiles increases, the community must build more roads — with public funds.

Galbraith has shown the interrelationship that exists not only between the privately produced automobile and privately produced gasoline, but also between the automobile and the need for new or improved public services that it generates.

Yet another element in the consumption of privately produced goods and possible explanation of America's powerful youth fixation is that youth is a huge consumer market. The tragic irony is that youth, whether rich or poor, is courted to consume the goods that the private sector produces. Indeed, for many young people, consumption is the core of life itself. If that is what they believe, some way for the young to get their fair share needs to be found. The problem is that the methods of the rootless — the street mentality, in a way — are invariably opposite to those of the community.

"The case for social balance has, so far, been put negatively," Galbraith writes in *The Affluent Society.* "Failure to keep public services in minimal relation to private production and use of goods is a cause of social disorder or impairs economic performance. The matter may now be put affirmatively. By failing to exploit the opportunity to expand public production, we are missing opportunities for enjoyment which otherwise we might have had."[2]

Most of what is learned about our social and economic ills is depressing, even when it emanates from Galbraith, who is ordinarily an entertaining writer even on economic theory. But Galbraith also states that the effort to create social balance can also produce pleasure and opportunity for a community. There are few, if any, economists who use the term "pleasure" with the ease and conviction of Galbraith. The "pleasure" and "opportunity" of which he speaks could be translated into a day care center in which the high spirits of the young are meshed with the warmth and tenderness of the elderly. It could mean continuing education programs for adults to improve their skills or learn more about the art of living. It could mean a well-trained police force working intelligently to prevent crime.

What Galbraith implies strongly is that social balance can provide both pleasure and opportunity for every community, a society in harmony with itself. "An austere community is free from temptation. It can be austere in its public services. Not so a rich one,"[3] Galbraith writes.

Why hasn't social balance been achieved? According to Galbraith, there are two reasons: "the truce on inequality and the tendency to inflation."[4]

One difference between private goods and public services is the way in which they are purchased. For example, a family sees a need for a new station wagon. They go to an automobile dealer, find the car they like at a price they can afford, and buy it. The new station wagon is theirs alone.

At a city council hearing, on the other hand, a group of concerned citizens may present their case for a youth recreational center and a new library, which could also be used for various cultural activities. The elderly propose a shuttle bus to transport people who have no other way of getting around town or city. The fire chief complains that the existing fire department is antiquated. What is needed is another fire station, signaling equipment, and five more firefighters. Everyone present agrees that each proposal has merit. At that point, a general mumbling of those looking on culminates in one angry voice shouting, "Who in hell is going to pay for all this?"

That, to Galbraith, is the key question: "Who in hell is going to pay for all this?" That question represents the breaking of the truce on inequality. He maintains that liberals want improved and new services paid for by progressive taxation. On the other hand, conservatives oppose that kind of taxation because, if they are rich, it will affect them the most. Galbraith feels that the debate itself is responsible for holding money aside while the community goes without the services it needs.

In the area of public money and its effect on social balance, Galbraith makes a distinction between the federal government and state and local governments. Because the federal government relies on money coming in from personal and corporate income taxes (the Internal Revenue Service is one of the government's most efficient agencies), its revenues increase faster than economic growth in the private sector. Local governments, on the other hand, rely on property and sales taxes, license fees, and lotteries, for example. Such revenues rise at a slower rate than private sector revenues. An appropriation of funds for a particular public program on the federal level influences the social balance of communities, such as providing mass transportation aid to cities, without regard to the question of inequality.

On the federal level, as Galbraith writes in *The Affluent Society*, "Public services are considered and voted on in accordance with their seeming urgency. Initiation or improvement of a particular service is rarely, except for purposes of oratory, set against the specific effect on taxes."[5]

In contrast, state and local governments must reconcile each service — whether a youth center, a senior shuttle, or another fire station — against the amount of money it can collect, most typically by property taxes. Moreover, that community will have to face, unlike the federal government, the problem of inequality: who will pay the bill?

Because local communities cannot achieve social balance alone, Galbraith states that the federal government should take an increasing role. But he feels that the impact of the federal government on social balance has been weakened because it has diverted so much money from domestic needs into expensive and perhaps unnecessary defense programs. Moreover, federal agencies appear to have a prior claim on public money. The Central Intelligence Agency, for example, seems to be able to get whatever resources it wants. In contrast, the city of Detroit, a major production and distribution center, cannot afford a decent police force.

Just as Galbraith sees the eradication of poverty as one of the fruits of social balance, he also envisions a different way of life for those who are not poor. One of the most significant changes would be in the way people work.

Economists and businessmen like to point out that today people work fewer hours per week, while at the same time production has increased. It is estimated that the average work week has shrunk by some thirty hours over the last hundred years. Galbraith uses that statistic to illustrate further his thesis that private goods have become less urgent: even more goods could be produced if more hours were devoted to production.

To Galbraith, the proper balance is for the individual to have access to both more goods and more leisure. And instead of being constricted by the same wage week after week, each person would be able to earn additional income from overtime work to satisfy individual tastes and needs. The current weekly wage system operates for the convenience of business and assumes that all individuals are the same. Galbraith's thesis is that people should have more control over how long they work and how much money they earn. He considers this an important expansion of individual liberty.

While the number of hours worked per week has been reduced, a significant portion of a person's time is still spent at work. Galbraith feels that work itself can be made less fatiguing and safer, and that the work environment can be made more pleasant.

Many businesses have tried to eliminate or reduce boring jobs through more extensive use of automation and computers. Offices and plants have become more colorful and comfortable; work schedules in some businesses are arranged for the mutual convenience of the worker and the employer. Federal safety and health legislation, considered by business an expensive burden, nonetheless sets up strict regulations to make factories and other places of work cleaner, safer, and less depressing.

It is difficult to determine what influence Galbraith has had on the recent trend to improve working conditions. Since the late 1950s a number of architects and interior designers have sought to create a more humane and inspirational industrial and commercial environment for workers. Even with these changes, Galbraith holds fast to his contention that "fewer working hours are not always preferred to working more pleasant ones."[6]

The means to accomplish social balance, spending money to

educate the illiterate, to feed the hungry, to provide decent housing and health care — the public programs that would tend to
improve the quality of life in our society — is suspect. Such expenses are considered causes of inflation by the corporate technostructure and deemed harmful to the moral fiber of the nation.
Defense spending, in this view, is supported because it contributes
to the security of the technostructure and provides income to
people who are persuaded to buy the products the technostructure
sells. But public programs are condemned. They do not necessarily
serve the goals of big business.

Galbraith considers Sweden to have come closest to the ideal
economic society, one which makes a great effort to achieve social
balance. (After forty-four years in power, the Swedish Socialist
Party was defeated in 1976 elections. The Socialists, of course,
created the modern welfare state in Sweden. The upset is not seen
as a rejection of socialism's goals, but as a move toward making the
system more responsive to the needs of individuals.) To finance a
wide range of public services, which take up over 50 percent of its
GNP, Sweden has an exceptionally high income tax rate on corporations and individuals. Carl G. Holm, a Swedish writer, reported
in the *National Review* that in 1975, "Parliament legislated a special
tax for private entrepreneurs (authors, artists, lawyers, shopkeep-
ers, etc.) earning more than 150,000 Kr. [$33,000], a tax rate of 102
percent. The well-known Swedish author, Astrid Lindgren, wrote
a widely publicized fairy tale on the absurdity of the 102 percent tax
rate, which eventually forced the government to change the tax
law." Taxes remain exceptionally high, however, as film director
Ingmar Bergman's recent self-imposed exile from Sweden shows.

Almost every community faces an increasing need for more and
better public services. Perhaps the theory of social balance is
somewhat responsible for the trend. In the late fifties and sixties
people began to take a closer look at the quality of life in the nation
and in their communities. They discovered needs for public services that assumed a priority at least equal to that of goods and
services attracting their attention from the private sector. Many
states, Massachusetts, for one, with the help of the federal government, spent vast sums on health care, education, mass transportation, urban development, the environment, and other public
services. But as those services expanded, so did the cost of maintaining them.

Inflation has pushed the cost of providing public services to such heights that the current trend is to cut services, or personnel, or both. And, while public services are deteriorating, local governments are forced to raise more money from their citizens. As a result, people find themselves in the uncomfortable position of paying more and more for less and less. And that, according to Galbraith, is a situation that can bring about serious disruptions in our society.

Throughout Galbraith's books, he reiterates time and again that education provides democracy with the power and the wisdom to make it work for all the people. I asked Galbraith how society will be able to absorb so many educated people in times of high unemployment.

"I do not think this is really a very serious problem in the advanced industrial countries," he replied. "It is, however, a serious problem in India, Pakistan, and Indonesia, where you have a small number of prestigious, quite well-paid people who hold commanding positions in their societies, and where the gap between them and the working proletariat in agriculture and in industry is enormous.

"In the advanced industrial countries, the trend has been to upgrade progressively both the pay and the prestige of the blue-collar and the white-collar worker. In that way we make it increasingly easy for college graduates to take those jobs.

"For example, in the past, nothing was considered more routine and required less qualification than the policeman on the beat. But even forty years ago, when I was at the University of California at Berkeley, nearly every member of the Berkeley police force was a graduate of the university," Galbraith recalled. "A person would go into this police job to get some experience after receiving his degree in criminology. He would then move on and become police chief in some other community. Donald Graham, for example, the son of Katherine Graham, owner of the *Washington Post*, got a job with the Washington, D.C. police force after he graduated from Harvard. He felt this would be the best way of gaining experience in his community," Galbraith continued. "He served with the police for a while and then went to work at the newspaper.

"There are many indications of just how blurred these vocational lines have become in our society. But they are very sharp in the developing nations, and the problem of the educated unemployed in those countries is a serious one. From a different perspective, I have seen a certain number of Harvard graduates who were admirably qualified for unskilled labor," Galbraith added with a twinkle in his eye.

When there is a high level of demand for labor, there are numerous job openings for those who have college degrees and many of these jobs are not filled because the educational system has failed to keep up with the requirements of our industrial society. Moreover, even when companies are hiring, some people will still not find work because they lack the necessary education, or they do not have work experience, or they have no seniority.

Galbraith equates quality of education with quantity of education; the less schooling a person has, the poorer in quality that schooling will be.

Galbraith sees the universities as critical to the emancipation of belief, as freeing the public from the "conventional wisdom," his term for the outdated myths and truisms of the past clung to by both liberals and conservatives alike. But they are placed in a dilemma in the Galbraithian system. There is the symbiotic relationship between business and the academic community: business needs the graduates and the colleges need the support that business provides. To the extent that the universities are constrained by this dilemma — as liberal arts loses to job related training — they cannot play the role Galbraith envisions for them.

During the 1960s, when the student movement was at its radical peak, the question of business involvement in academia was intensively debated and often dramatically protested. But American campuses have since quieted down. Inflation has increased the cost of advanced education, and made operating a university more expensive. In addition, the recession of the first half of the 1970s made it difficult for many university graduates to find jobs. As a result, the industrial system and the academic community have become congenial once again.

Because the industrial system benefits from education in terms of qualified workers and research, Galbraith recommends that it support educational enlightenment for people and in other fields — not just those which relate to the goals of corporate management.

Galbraith sees in the increasing growth of the academic-scientific estate the emergence of a new political power. But like most new sources of power, he feels that it lacks confidence. The intellectual community expressed its strength during the Vietnam war, in the social explosions of the late 1960s and early 1970s, in the presidential campaigns of Eugene McCarthy and George McGovern, and in the environmental movement.

Though the Vietnam war and the draft eventually ended and important steps have been taken to preserve the environment, McCarthy and McGovern failed in their bids. Many of America's serious social problems persist and grow, and the faculties and students at our schools and colleges become more preoccupied with their personal career goals than with the emancipation of the human spirit. Even Harvard's department of economics is becoming more conservative in its point of view. Indeed, one wonders if Galbraith would be hired by Harvard today, considering his liberal — even socialistic — stance.

In 1941 Walter Lippmann wrote pessimistically about the condition of modern Western society: "The social problem of the modern world arises not out of the objective difficulty of providing an adequate material existence but out of men's subjective expectations, which because they are unlimited and insatiable, cause violence, inequality, hatred, and frustration."

Galbraith does not disagree with Lippmann's assessment. However, he might add that individuals have very few alternatives other than satisfying their "unlimited and insatiable expectations." Modern mass production creates such expectations for its own continued growth; and the public sector has not provided adequate services to prevent "violence, inequality, hatred, and frustration."

William F. Buckley, Jr. feels that the capitalistic system breeds a tendency to want even more. "One should want more and more," Buckley told me. "That is what keeps the consumer satisfied. The more profit I desire as a businessman, the more people I satisfy. That satisfaction is the only way I can accumulate profit, assuming there is competition.

"Now, that which motivates you can be considered greed to the extent that the motivation dislodges other concerns. If you want to accumulate a lot of money in order to do praiseworthy things — that isn't technically greed. If you want to accumulate money only because you have an obsession with the accumulation of money, then that is greed. And it is a theological sin. It is not, in my opinion, an economic sin. It is only an economic sin if you exert yourself in the accumulation of wealth to upset the rules of the economic system; such as, for example, exercising monopolistic rights, getting government intervention, or asking for protective tariff legislation.

"But so far as I am concerned, if the local hot dog vendor elects because of greed to keep his store operating twenty-four hours a day instead of closing at midnight and getting a good night's sleep, I might sympathize with this obsession of his. But the fact that I can go around the corner at 2 a.m. to get a hot dog — even though I am making him richer by only a nickel in the virtue of doing it — does not upset me socially at all."

Galbraith has continually repeated the theory that the provision of public services suffers in relation to the production of private goods. In *The New Industrial State* he continues with this theme by saying that the selling of toothpaste is in competition with the establishment and operation of public dental clinics; the provision of recreational facilities is in competition with the production of color television sets; and the provision of day care centers is in conflict with the production of pantyhose.

In the last section of *Economics and the Public Purpose,* Galbraith proposes a detailed theory for reforming the social and economic inequities of the current imbalanced system. His solutions are radical and unorthodox, but he believes that reform is inevitable. Public management — through government planning and controls–is organic to his system of putting the citizen consumer back in control. As he wrote in the foreword; "For on no conclusion is this book more clear: Left to themselves, economic forces do not work out for the best except perhaps for the powerful."[7]

The opposition to this kind of thinking is epitomized by some comments from William F. Buckley, Jr.

"I think that is probably the most fundamental superstition of the whole socialist creed," Buckley stated vigorously. "What you are really talking about is not the money held by the rich that you need for other purposes; you are simply finding an acceptable way to say that you don't want these people to have that money.

"Now, some people — I suspect that Ken Galbraith is one of them — have insomnia because some cultural barbarian like the late H.L. Hunt and Howard Hughes had companies worth one or two billion dollars. It doesn't bother me in the least," Buckley said. "I don't know what they have done with their fortunes. All I know is that the possibility that capital formation and risky investments in behalf of large or small enterprises will go forward is much more closely allied to the question of whether there are residual fortunes which are permitted to accumulate, than to whether some bright young planner in Washington using the public money is going to come up with bright ideas. Mostly you don't come up with bright ideas for the very simple reason that the planners are not familiar with the discipline of the market.

"Also, I like much better the notion of losing private money on silly ventures than losing public money on silly ventures. As far as I know, I haven't lost a penny of my money as a result of the excesses of a Howard Hughes or an H.L. Hunt. But I have lost fortunes as a result of the excesses of government."

Galbraith's theory of social balance appears to be new. However, though his words and ideas relate to our contemporary industrial, urban, technological society, they are rooted in a universal tradition thousands of years old.

According to Plato, beyond the simple need for food, "the desire for a whole variety of luxuries is unnecessary. Most people can get rid of it by early discipline and education; and it is as prejudicial to intelligence and self-control as it is to bodily health. Further, these unnecessary appetites might be called expensive, whereas the necessary ones are rather profitable." Like Plato, writers in every century and culture have sought the possibility of balance and harmony in their particular social order. They tried to design a peaceful, productive order in a congenial and enlightened civilization out of the human confusion around them.

The theme of social balance and social order runs through Galbraith's major economic works. His suggestions for achieving these goals have brought him into conflict with many of his contemporaries. Some of his most iconoclastic and controversial ideas are devoted to the corporation — its power and what should be done about it.

CHAPTER **6**

INDIVIDUALS
VS.
THE SYSTEM

Galbraith invariably emphasizes that the planning system, his term for the mammoth corporations, and extremely wealthy individuals possess most of the economic power in the United States. Most medium-sized and small companies have very little power. The individual has even less power. And there are large numbers of individuals who have been deprived of their due. He returns again and again to this question of the struggle of the small against the large, the weak against the powerful, the individual against the organization.

He begins with the concept of work.

According to the conventional wisdom, people work to get paid. And, most economists assume higher pay generally motivates individuals to work harder and increase their commitment to the organization. However, as might be expected, Galbraith has some different ideas. Just as profit maximization is no longer the single goal of the technostructure, other forces as well as monetary compensation bind the individual to the organization.

The new managerial structure, or technostructure, of the corporation requires coordinated, collective decision-making. In *The New Industrial State*, Galbraith maintains that such coordination requires people to set aside their individual goals to pursue those of the organization. "He's a good team player" is high praise in the industrial system as well as on the basketball court.

According to Galbraith, the problem is to motivate individuals to exchange personal goals to work for the collective aims of the organization. He lists several major inducements.

Compulsion, either by force or punishment, is associated in varying degrees with compensation. This method invariably means a loss of free choice, but for the modern industrial employee compulsion has lost much of its sting because of unemployment compensation and other welfare benefits.

Galbraith has a name for the process of compelling people to perform menial or unpleasant services. He defines the pervasive force that binds servants to masters, orderlies to hospitals, and janitors to schools as "the convenient social virtue."[1] "Inconvenient behavior," he says in *Economics and the Public Purpose*, "becomes deviant behavior and is subject to the righteous disapproval or sanction of the community."[2] As industrial employment increasingly lured away much of the servant class, Galbraith notes, the convenient social virtue reached its ultimate success "converting women to menial personal service" as surrogates.

In identification, individuals become associated with an organization because they believe its goals are better than their own. People seek a special identity from a group that they do not possess themselves. For example, introducing oneself as "Tom Smith from General Motors" provides more prestige than the simple "Tom Smith." The name Tom Smith may mean very little to most people, but General Motors suggests money, power, and dominance. Moreover, "Tom Smith of General Motors" is more a reflection of a corporate image than of an individual. In this process of identification, some individuality is lost as the organization man emerges.

Another inducement, adaptation, allows employees to retain a measure of their individuality. Galbraith theorizes that adaptation allows the individual to work for an organization not because he believes that its goals are better than his own but because he anticipates that he can make them conform more to his own. In practice that person is pursuing two sets of goals: his own and those of his organization. His hope is that the two goals are compatible. Politicians, for example, are visibly adept at adaptation.

Galbraith refers to pecuniary motivation as a paradox because the higher the salary a person makes, the less important it becomes in relation to other personal goals. Once a person rises above a certain salary level, according to Galbraith in *The New Industrial*

State, the motivations of identification and adaptation overshadow the motivation of compensation. The executive who admits that the effort he is expending is in direct relation to what he is earning will probably not advance very far. "A decent respect for reality requires that we recognize that men serve organizations in response to a complex system of motivations,"[3] Galbraith writes in *The New Industrial State.*

Galbraith pictures the mature corporation as a series of concentric circles. The outermost circle is made up of stockholders, whose interest in the corporation is money. Most stockholders are more concerned with dividends and the rising value of the investment than with identification with the corporation or its goals. The next ring contains production workers, who are motivated by a combination of money and identification with the company. Moving inward from circle to circle — from supervisors to white-collar workers to engineers and technicians, and finally to management at the center — identification and adaptation, according to Galbraith, become more important motivators.

Because the technostructure has power of its own, it can adapt its goals, within reason, to those of the corporation. "Adaptation, as a motive, will be stronger as one approaches the inner circles of the technostructure. Here both the illusion and the fact of power are the greatest,"[4] according to his *The New Industrial State.* Galbraith adds that the process of adaptation permits the goals of the corporation to coincide with those of the technostructure, and to arrange the many goals into a kind of "hierarchy of goals"[5] or priorities.

Galbraith states that two other important labor changes have occurred in the industrial system: blue-collar workers are decreasing both in numbers and in influence, and the traditional notion of unemployment has less meaning today. Because the large industrial corporation is a product of ever advancing technology, it has an increasing need for educated workers. Although highly skilled craftsmen, such as tool-and-die makers, are still in demand, Galbraith maintains that industry's overall requirements for both skilled and unskilled labor are progressively being reduced in direct proportion to the need for more highly educated technicians.

Increasing automation is not only changing the shape of the labor force but also the shape of the work week. One of the main collective bargaining issues between the United Auto Workers and Ford in 1976 contract negotiations was the reduction in the number of working days per year. This issue has been interpreted as a major step toward the four-day week, as a variety of sophisticated machines improve production. The benefits won by the United Auto Workers in past bargaining sessions have set the pattern for workers in other industries.

Machines, of course, do not strike and equipment costs can be predicted with more certainty than labor costs. As a result, the technostructure is assured of continuing production. Any interruptions in production create demands on the technostructure and conflict with its goals. One possible solution may be to emulate recent labor-management experiments in Europe.

A new West German law requires that all companies establish a supervisory board divided equally among shareholders and representatives of the rank-and-file workers. As an article in *US News and World Report* explained: "The idea of letting the rank and file into the boardroom is widely accepted in most countries of Europe, although no other nation has embraced it as wholeheartedly as West Germany. Austria, Sweden, Luxembourg, the Netherlands, Norway, and Denmark also have introduced codetermination systems."

Management prerogatives are fiercely defended in the United States, however. It may be some years before an assembly line worker shares management power with the technostructure of, say, General Motors or United Technologies.

As machines continue to replace blue-collar workers, industry will require more white-collar workers and more members of the technostructure, educated people who use their intellectual energies rather than physical strength. White-collar workers tend not to organize into labor unions (with the exception of teachers and government workers). They are more likely to identify with the goals of the corporation. Despite that, the white-collar worker can be fired more easily than can a union member. Moreover, the white-collar worker ordinarily has no route of appeal, whether or not the firing was capricious. White-collar workers lead a paradoxical existence: They identify with corporate goals and hope to advance into the upper levels of the technostructure, while at the same time they have comparatively little job security.

Everyone is familiar with the wage-price spiral. To the working man or woman, the concept is made evident when shopping for the week's groceries. Prices on meat, canned goods, soap powder, and other essential household items have risen. When workers complain they cannot make ends meet, thanks to rising costs for insurance, fuel, rent, property taxes, clothing, repairs, medical care — as well as food — the union enters into collective bargaining with the corporation. The result: a wage increase which is passed along by the corporation to consumers in the form of higher prices. The wage increase is thus negated; the worker needs more money to pay for higher prices of goods. And so it goes, in an ever-upward spiral. Galbraith, of course, believes that a system of wage and price controls is the solution to restraining corporate price increases and union demands.

Although large trade unions share some responsibility for the wage-price spiral, Galbraith believes that unions today are less militant and powerful than they once were, because of the decreasing number of blue-collar workers. Nevertheless, the large corporations prefer to accede to most union demands rather than suffer a strike that could affect earnings seriously and, therefore, threaten the technostructure's power. Indeed, when the United Auto Workers led a brief strike against Ford in 1976, representatives from both Ford and the UAW stated that neither side really wanted the strike, especially because business was picking up following a prolonged recession. The strike seemed to be more a fluke than any serious arm-twisting by the union.

Galbraith thus argues that collective bargaining for unions dealing with the technostructure of large corporations has become easier. No more are the sessions punctuated by anger, by shouting and fist-shaking, as in the days of John L. Lewis, for example. Rather, corporation executives and labor leaders conduct themselves in fairly much the same manner. George Meany may represent the last of a unique breed of men. So, if the process of collective bargaining has become easier, the union becomes less important to the worker. At this point, the technostructure, by giving its workers union benefits, in a way virtually replaces the union. And when that happens, obviously, the union is no longer necessary.

But Galbraith believes that unions do offer some advantages to their membership. Unions have succumbed to technological advances — many of which have resulted in the loss of jobs — but in exchange for smaller employment the unions have won significant pay increases, a shorter work week, and better working conditions for their members. On the whole the technostructure rewards the unions' attempts to accommodate by avoiding strikes when possible. The cost of any benefits won is passed on to consumers, of course, in the form of higher prices.

Unions also help stabilize the demand for products bought by government. When industry pleads for larger defense contracts, it is considered self-interest. But if the cry comes from the unions, it is merely accentuating the need for jobs and for a strong local economy. The public generally accepts the latter approach. For example, closing a Strategic Air Command base in Maine may make good economic sense overall, but removing Air Force operations from that location would cause severe economic hardship to the workers and businesses that depend on it. Therefore, the announced removal is vigorously protested by trade unions and businesses alike — not necessarily out of patriotic motives or out of an understanding of the overall defense plans, but out of self-interest: the desire to maintain the standard of living that the air base has brought.

Large manufacturers of defense hardware, such as United Technologies, act out of similar motives. The International Association of Machinists is just as interested in receiving lucrative contracts for jet engines as is United Technologies' management. The union, therefore, becomes one of the technostructure's most effective lobbyists.

Unions benefit the technostructure by contributing to that organization's most important function, planning. Unions help standardize wage increases with an industry and ensure that wage increases will take effect at approximately the same time. When the United Auto Workers pick Ford for negotiating a new contract, the technostructures at General Motors, Chrysler, and American Motors know that, in effect, the union is also dealing with them. The agreement between Ford and the union ordinarily sets the pattern for contracts with the other oligopolistic automobile manufacturers.

Unions provide yet another important service for the technostructure. Each contract is in force long enough to determine its effect on productivity. From that determination, the technostructure can calculate what further wage increases would not upset price stability. Once again, the unions help the technostructure plan for earnings and growth. Because unions provide these services to the corporation, they are no longer antagonists but are referred to — by Galbraith, for one — as handmaidens of the industrial system.

Today, many people are unable to find work in which they can use their particular skills and experiences — perhaps because the industries for which they have been trained have moved away and the workers, for whatever reasons, are reluctant to follow. Shortly after World War II, for example, the New England textile industry packed up its machinery and moved to the South where workers were unorganized and wages were lower. A great many skilled workers, many of them middle-aged, suddenly were without jobs and had no fresh prospects. After Nixon was elected to his first term in 1968, New England suffered major cutbacks in the electronics industry, which was a major employer during the "anything goes" years of the sixties when massive amounts of federal dollars were spent on sophisticated weapons systems and space exploration. Suddenly not only production workers were let go but thousands of scientists and engineers as well. The price for a new job was relocation. But many qualified professionals were reluctant to leave what they felt was a pleasant and stimulating environment — New England — for something less. The result was, of course, that the nation, as well as the individual, suffered the loss of trained and experienced professionals.

Galbraith says that, in addition to inadequate demand and the difficulty in matching human skills with the needs of the industrial system, a third characteristic of modern unemployment is a lag in cultural accommodation. Society's inability to provide the educated manpower that the industrial system needs creates a shortage of qualified workers in many technical and managerial specialties. Just as flowers attract bees, those areas of the country that place a high priority on education, Galbraith maintains, will entice corporations that require this cultural accommodation for their continued economic security and growth.

One of the most persistent problems in economics deals with the wants of individuals. In eighteenth-century Great Britain, the wants of the common individual coincided with immediate physical survival. Food, clothing, and shelter were the imperatives. Getting drunk on gin, as depicted by Hogarth, was perhaps another imperative, for it dulled the very real possibility that there might be no tomorrow. However, the Industrial Revolution — which increased productivity dramatically, introduced competitive markets, and transformed the economic structure to capitalism — raised individual wants beyond the survival level. It then became self-sustaining; it had to hire workers for wages to produce the goods workers wanted to buy.

This process of working to make money to meet wants has today evolved into one of the most sophisticated and well-organized economic activities of all industrialized societies. Galbraith makes a very positive point of that in *The Affluent Society*: "It is the increase in output in recent decades, not the redistribution of income, which has brought the great material increase in the well-being of the average man."[6]

Once an individual's concerns move beyond mere survival, in addition to wanting better food, smarter fashions, and a finer home, there arises a desire for better health care and education, more recreation and travel, and cultural pleasures. The traditional economists maintain that the consumer is the sovereign of the marketplace. They reason that companies search out the wants of consumers and attempt to satisfy those wants with new and better products and services; the words of Thomas Alva Edison, "Find a need and fill it," are the marketing manager's credo. And, further, those companies which best serve the consumers' wants not only survive, but have earned the right to the rewards of profits and increased corporate growth.

Galbraith disagrees with this traditional view. He maintains instead that demand arises out of production. The "planning system"[7] creates needs because it can't afford to be at the whim of the consumer market. Galbraith's concept of the planning system is fully detailed in *Economics and the Public Purpose*. The planning system represents those few large corporations that produce approximately half of the annual sales in the United States. The remaining half is produced by the thousands of small firms that make up the "market system." All the firms on *Fortune*'s annual listing of America's 500 leading industrials are components in Galbraith's planning system. The corner delicatessen, the women's boutique, or the small manufacturing firm with $2 million sales are representative of his "market system,"[8] which he says does respond to consumer needs. (The implications of these two systems will be explored more fully in later chapters.)

As Galbraith outlines it in his *Economics and the Public Purpose*, the planning system is sovereign over the consumer, because it creates products before consumers are aware that they have a need for them. Such advance planning of new product strategy helps ensure the future growth of corporations. Through the heavy use of advertising ($28.3 billion in the United States and $52.5 billion spent in the world in 1975, according to McCann-Erickson), consumers are then convinced that they have all along had a real need for these products.

Effective advertising and psychological motivating techniques that convince consumers of the need for a corporation's products, the way consumers perceive their wants, and why they shift from one product to another are far more complex phenomena than even Galbraith has been able to articulate. However, something deep inside each one of us makes us want to upgrade our wants. Old Irish priests might call it temptations of the devil. But it is entirely reasonable that once a basic need for personal transportation has been satisfied with a Volkswagen that one should then desire a Mercedes sedan with a sunroof. Another might buy an inexpensive bottle of Scotch but thirsts for a bottle of Chivas Regal. It is not only Chivas' elite image projected through a form of whimsical advertising — Chivas does indeed taste better than the cheap stuff.

Galbraith told me, "There are hierarchies of wants and it is a matter of common sense to recognize this. It also follows that as you increase income and as you supply more and more goods, you have also created a choice between spending on more private goods, such as cars, washing machines, hair dryers, or surf boards, or spending on public goods, such as cleaning up polluted rivers and lakes, providing better health care and housing for more people, or making our cities more aesthetically pleasing and safe. Now if people don't have enough to wear, there is a case for getting a higher production of textiles at whatever the damage to the countryside. But, if society is producing textiles for relatively unimportant purposes, you then have a stronger case for spending money on preserving the integrity of the landscape, rather than on unnecessary clothing," says Galbraith.

William F. Buckley, Jr., as one might expect, disagrees with Galbraith's concept that the companies use advertising to contrive consumer needs:

"That fails to take into account not only the tremendous failure rate of a number of corporations," Buckley told me, "but also the extent to which these companies devote their advertising dollars in persuading people to go from one particular product to a competitive product. Most of the money that is spent on cereal food, for instance, is not spent to promote cereal food in general. It is spent to promote corn flakes or grapenuts as opposed to raisin bran, or whatever.

"The fastest way to make somebody dissatisfied with his hi-fi set is to have gaudy advertisements about how awful the hi-fi sets of yesterday are. I don't find it particularly venal because somebody goes and listens to a hi-fi set which is manifestly better than his own, and then spends his savings on it. I don't see why the consumer should resent the fact that this better alternative was brought to his attention."

Although advertising is an enormous industry that employs many highly creative and intelligent specialists, the profession itself has long suffered from an image of hucksterism. Galbraith's books have given advertising a degree of respectability by describing its immense power to influence people in economic decisions.

Galbraith points out that a starving person does not have to be told he needs to eat. He says that production stimulates more wants and that these increased wants, in turn, create more production. Galbraith calls this process the "dependence effect,"[9] the contrivance of wants to increase production. Advertising and its allied specialities, such as market research, sales promotion, motivational research, and salesmanship, are some of the tools that make the "dependence effect" work. It is the centering of our industrial society on increasing production and the contrivance of wants that are at the heart of *The Affluent Society*. He is not against replacing an old hi-fi set with a new one or even changing a car every year. Rather, he believes that the planning system creates superfluous consumer needs in its own self-interest, while urgent social needs — housing, health care, and community services of every kind — go unmet.

The market system uses production to meet the specific needs of individual customers. Compare, for example, a deli sandwich with a frozen dinner by Swanson; the labor of a backyard garage mechanic with repairs by a General Motors dealership; a hand-made suit from an old tailor in a corner shop with the mass-produced synthetics from Burlington Industries — the list seems endless.

In the planning system, the consumer is the faceless servant of the large corporation. In the market system, the consumer is served, and his and her business is valued on an individual basis. In the planning system, the consumer is confronted with a product and the seductive persuasion of the abstract image of the corporation behind it. In the market system, the consumer is confronted with another human being, who, most of the time, seeks to please because repeat business is vital to survival and success.

The need to control prices, by which supplies and services are bought and products sold, is essential to the planning process. Galbraith says that the control of prices, though imperfect, is *organic* to the industrial system and that it serves the system's primary goals. Price control provides security to the technostructure and allows it to go after its other goals, not so much profit maximization as security, earnings, and growth, according to Galbraith. Control is further extended over individuals; that is, by contriving consumer demand. The technostructure needs to control both how income is spent and how much the individual has to spend. Therefore consumer behavior must be controlled. All large consumer product companies use motivational research to determine which psychological wants can be exploited to the advantage of selling a particular product.

The consumer doesn't need many of the products that promise greater sex appeal, social acceptability, or a sense of good feeling, but he or she wants to participate in what's been presented as a necessary American experience. Demand management is used to make people go out and purchase what companies produce, regardless of whether or not a real personal need exists for these products. And it is essential to the goals of the technostructure that these products be sold at prices which are controlled. Constant advertising creates brand recognition and then brand loyalty. According to Galbraith, this recruiting process builds an "automatic corps of customers."[10] In addition, because corporate growth results from increasing sales, the objective of modern marketing is to recruit more and more consumers into an ever-growing and loyal army.

Television has become the indispensable tool in this selling and recruiting process. Television advertising can reach more people at a lower cost per person than any other sales medium. The price of being bored or entertained by commercial television is to suffer through a barrage of messages from a variety of sponsors. Television exists for managing consumer demand through the persuasive power of repetitive advertising to the greatest number of potential buyers; it is not for the enlightenment or entertainment of the public. The planning system has become so dependent on television that it could not exist without it. Currently, large sponsors are seriously discussing the need for a fourth commercial TV network in the United States. ABC, NBC, and CBS find it difficult to meet the demand for prime time, and the companies have excess money to spend; though recently some financial analysts predict a flattening out of the demand for more prime time advertising.

The management of demand is not based on influencing the individual, but on the mass. When "All in the Family" pauses for a "few friendly messages from our sponsors," the individual can say "the hell with it!" and go to the refrigerator for a ham sandwich and a beer. No doubt, many individuals do just that. But each week "All in the Family" reaches many millions throughout North America, and the network and the program's advertisers are reasonably certain that the vast majority remain in their chairs watching the commercials.

Galbraith respects the power of advertising: "Advertising and its related arts . . . help develop the kind of man the goals of the industrial system require — one who reliably spends his income and works reliably because he is always in need for more. . . . Advertising by making goods important makes the industrial system important. And therewith it helps to sustain the social importance and prestige that attach to the technostructure."[11]

The *accepted sequence,*[12] according to Galbraith, is the general belief that the consumer is the master of the market place, with private enterprise identifying and serving, through competition, his every need. Galbraith turns this belief around into what he calls the *revised sequence*,[13] in which the corporation is the master because it controls the market. In the revised sequence the consumers serve the corporation. Because the accepted sequence is the prevailing belief or conventional wisdom in our industrial society, Galbraith says the government is prevented from acting in behalf of the individual in terms of consumer reforms and remedies. To meddle with the accepted sequence is considered the same as tampering with individual liberty. Thus, Galbraith maintains, the individual's right to buy is not protected. What *is* protected is the right of the corporation to manage the individual.

To serve its fundamental self-interests, the corporation must regulate aggregate demand. Consumers must not only buy products in predetermined quantities, they must also have enough reliable purchasing power to buy what the corporation produces at the prices the corporation charges. Unless industry manages aggregate demand, large firms would be subject to economic vagaries, such as wide fluctuations in the amount of goods they make and sell. These vagaries would undermine the planning process, which is the soul of the technostructure. The absence of aggregate demand management would endanger the technostructure because there would be a failure in earnings because of decreases in sales and production. Earnings protect the interests of the technostructure; without earnings, the technostructure is vulnerable to outside interference, and it cannot achieve its most basic goals, the first of which is survival. According to Galbraith, only government can regulate aggregate demand, and industry is dependent on government for this function.

Both corporate and personal taxes serve the function of regulating demand. The more money people make, the more they pay in taxes. This damper of progressive taxation on income controls the amount of money people have to spend. According to Galbraith, corporate income increases at a far greater rate than any other form of income. This increase in the rise of earnings also produces an increase in the amount of revenue the government takes in from corporate taxes. When there is a decline in business, government revenues from corporate taxes are proportionally less.

Galbraith maintains that large government, with its power to affect changes in expenditure, is the instrument for regulating aggregate demand. While increasing government spending is a source of anguish to businessmen, those who complain the most are the entrepreneurs representing small and medium enterprises in the market system, who are directly affected by taxes on their businesses. The executive of a large corporation may complain about the level of government expenditures on domestic programs, waste in government, and the size of the bureaucracy, but there is almost no criticism of the money spent on defense, which is one of the "big-ticket" items in the federal budget.

The revised sequence comes into play once again, but in a different manner. The huge amounts of money spent on defense serve the needs of the technostructure. Large corporations benefit from the defense contracts they receive. This type of government spending is encouraged by the technostructure, often in the guise of serving the national interest or the appearance of patriotic duty.

Galbraith returns again and again to the inequities which the structure of society imposes on large classes of people. One of his abiding concerns is with the role of women. He calls women the crypto-servants of the planning system. William Manchester wrote in *The Glory and the Dream*, "Men's rooms in genteel establishments had long displayed a sign over urinals: PLEASE ARRANGE CLOTHING BEFORE LEAVING WASHROOM. Well-brought-up boys didn't need to be reminded; they had been taught never to fasten the flies of their trousers in public. They were therefore startled when Francoise Dorleac, in the 1966 film *Where the Spies Are*, emerged from a dressing room, reached for her crotch, and casually zipped up her slacks in the presence of her costar, David Niven. It was one of those moments which served as reminders that the delicate balance between the sexes had been altered, probably forever."

The fact that women are in the process of emancipating themselves did not prevent Galbraith from basing his concept of convenient social virtue on them. He made it clear that the convenient social virtue was what had put women in the role from which they were now being liberated.

Before the Industrial Revolution, in addition to their common household chores, women — as part of the cottage manufacturing system — also produced such goods as textiles. And in rural areas, most families lived off the land, except for exchanging agricultural goods in the nearby town or city for ready-made clothing, tools, or whatever.

As more people began to participate in the industrial system, the traditional servant class diminished. This left the management of consumption to the woman of the house, and intelligent home management and shopping became social virtues. The good wife was perceived, by others and by herself, in terms of good homemaking. Even today's emancipated women still praise other women for their excellence in culinary, sewing, and cleaning skills. Or, as Thorstein Veblen once remarked, "According to the ideal scheme of the pecuniary culture, the lady of the house is the chief menial of the household."

The modern housewife's day is both complex and demanding. She is usually the first in the family to arise each morning. Breakfast has to be made, and the husband and children organized and sent their separate ways. The dishes have to be cleaned, beds made, and the house put in order. If a sink is plugged, she gets the plumber. If the family auto needs repair, she takes it to the garage. Time is spent at the supermarket playing the game of trying to make the budget stretch to fit ever-increasing food prices. Then she has to be ready for the children's return from school. Then the evening meal and the return of her husband, who himself may well need ego-stroking. And of course, hers is a seven-day-a-week job, with few fringe benefits and little recognition.

The emerging modern feminist movement has resulted in many women shedding their crypto-servant role. In *Economics and the Public Purpose*, Galbraith strongly advocates that one sex should not be subordinate to another. Of course, that is what women have been arguing for years. But Galbraith, a male economist, makes a major issue of it. As the chief administrator of the household and of the family's consumption, the woman, Galbraith feels, should have the decisive voice about the life style for herself and for her family. But if family decisions are made jointly, the husband should also share in the cooking, cleaning, and the tasks involving the management of the household.

He also questions the traditional concept of the family, in which the man goes outside to work and the woman stays home to take care of the children and manage the affairs of the home. With increasing affluence, Galbraith argues, a person can do both. Galbraith also encourages women to consider life styles other than marriage — life styles that may be more suited to the development of their individuality. The traditional concept of marriage requires that the woman subsume her individuality for the sake of the family.

Whether a woman seeks a life style outside of marriage or more independence within a family of her own, emancipation requires that she have her own income. Income gives the woman more power over decisions regarding consumption. The married woman then can dispense with the humiliation of her husband's questioning how she is spending "his" money. Moreover, a woman with an income of her own need not tolerate an unsatisfactory marriage.

Of course, Galbraith is not advocating that wives leave their husbands, or that families have become unimportant. Indeed, he himself has been married since 1937. What he does advocate is more power and freedom for women within the home and equal opportunity outside of it.

Today the law ensures that American women have equal access to jobs, and affirmative action programs in corporations are creating job opportunities for women. Galbraith recommends four reforms to strengthen the position of women in industrial society.

First, he recommends that women be provided with professional care for their children. The key word here is *professional*. In *Economics and the Public Purpose* he says, "In a child care center one person can care professionally for numerous children; in the family one person cares unprofessionally for one or a very few."[14] The child care center frees the women to pursue self-development or employment without neglecting her children. As Galbraith implies, the professional care her children receive may, in fact, be more effective than the care she herself could administer.

Galbraith's second recommendation is that women be given special treatment regarding working hours. Rather than the traditional 9-to-5 five-day work week, Galbraith proposes a more flexible schedule that reflects the needs and the preferences of individuals, whether man or woman. His concept assumes that some people would give up some income for more leisure. A more flexible work schedule would allow women to apportion their time among several important activities; those which tend to promote their independence and those which they assume on behalf of their families.

Third, Galbraith recommends that male domination of the better jobs in the technostructures should cease. As Galbraith suggests in *Economics and the Public Purpose:* "In 1969, in excess of 95 percent of all jobs in industry paying more than $15,000 a year were held by males. This reflects, in some degree, the sound instinct of the technostructure. If the latter is successfully to pursue the affirmative goal of growth, there must be women to administer the resulting increase in private consumption. Sensing this, the technostructure sets a sound example by excluding women from its membership, reserving them for the required household administration."[15]

Galbraith thereby maintains that the technostructure of the planning system is in constant need of educationally qualified members who will contribute to its goals. And, because women are no less intelligent than men, the corporate technostructures should look to women as one of their most abundant sources of the supply of available intelligence.

Galbraith's fourth recommendation concerning women stresses the importance of increasing educational opportunities and the ending of discrimination against women at universities and in professional training.

Two observations about Galbraith's analysis of women in our industrial society are necessary. First, a great many women derive great satisfaction from their combined roles as wives, lovers, mothers, and homemakers. Second, what emancipation women now enjoy has been achieved by women. Indeed, women have been far more perceptive of their own condition than men — including Galbraith. But Galbraith's influence cannot be dismissed by feminists.

Gloria Steinem, the feminist editor, described Galbraith in this manner: "His thinking has pointed out the economic inequities with regard to women in very logical and readable terms. I cannot think of another major male economist who has included the economic role of women in any way. His chapter on the economic uses of the housewife is unique. It is very important. In addition to what he writes is the fact that he acts on his beliefs. One example of this is his administrative assistant, Andrea Williams. He thought enough of Andrea to dedicate his book, *The New Industrial State*, to her.

"He has dared to be readable. Apparently it's a great sin to be referred to as being a *literary* man. Education seems to be valued to the degree to which it's impractical. Galbraith has changed that. And I think in many ways he has been punished for it by his colleagues."

Andrea Williams has been Galbraith's administrative assistant and alter ego for more than eighteen years. If people wonder how Galbraith is able to write all the books, articles, and reviews that he does, and still constantly travel the world and speak to countless groups, Andrea Williams is the answer.

I asked her if Galbraith practices what he preaches about women. "He certainly does," she replied. "He has been wise enough to realize that there is a third role for women in the era of liberation — a woman need not be either a housewife or a bank president. She can find outlets for her talents, her administrative ability, her business acumen by managing the life of a talented (and self-confident) man who allows her to take over 'those things he doesn't want to do himself' (in his oft-repeated phrase). In his stead I can deal with publishers, accountants, lawyers; edit his manuscripts, organize his travel; learn and grow exactly as if these projects were my own, while leaving him free to think and write and lecture, all of which he does so well."

The role that Mrs. Williams has chosen is of inestimable value to Galbraith. Overall he wants a wider range of options opened to women, and at the same time he recommends practical measures to restore the imbalances that have built up over the years. This, in general, is the approach he takes to enhancing the status and function of all individuals who have been shortchanged by the industrial society.

CHAPTER **7**
THE SYSTEM
VS. ARTISTS
AND ENTREPRENEURS

Galbraith feels that industrial society is endangering our aesthetic experiences because increased production, not individual well-being, has primacy. Simply stated, the goals of the technostructure are not those of the artist. What Galbraith condemns is the assault on the human spirit by the ugliness of our communities. For example, New York City subways are dirty, foul, and hostile. The trains are covered inside and out with graffiti (which, incidentally, some critics think is an important new urban art form). The riders, physically close, are nevertheless alienated from each other, partly by fear and partly because indifference is one defense against an urban environment nearly unfit for human beings.

Paolo Soleri, the great Italian architect who lives in the Arizona desert, once wrote in the book *Architects on Architecture* that "there are *instrumentalities* and *finalities.* Technology is an instrumentality; science, in its purest form, may have some kind of finality. The tools we are producing are instrumental — shown by the way in which they become obsolete. Aesthetic expression does not become obsolete because it has a finality to itself — which we tend to ignore or forget in our attempts to define the true nature of things."

Unfortunately, in most of our industrial urban centers, such as New York or Detroit, there has been very little attempt even to define "the true nature of things."

The Montreal subway is far more pleasant than the one in New

89

York is. Each station is clean, safe, and decorated with paintings, murals, or stained glass. The trains, too, are clean and comfortable. The whole system creates a feeling of well-being in passengers. But subways are only one part of our urban aesthetic experience.

The late architect Frank Lloyd Wright also expounded on the aesthetic experience. In *A Testament,* Wright delineated the nature of the confusion afflicting industrial humanity: "Modern machine masters were ruling man's fate in his manufacture as in his architecture and arts. His way of life was being sterilized by marvelous power tools and even more powerful machine systems, all replacing hand labor by multiplying — senselessly — his activity and infecting his spirit.

"Everywhere these inventions of science by ignorant misuse of a new technique were wiping out the artist. He was himself now becoming a slave. The new chattel. I saw in these new 'masters' no great motive above the excess of necessity-for-profit, all likely themselves by way of their own assembly lines to become machines. The kind of slavery that now loomed was even more monstrous and more devastating to our culture now dedicated to senseless excess, so it seemed to me, than ever before."

Some cities — notably Boston, Montreal, Toronto, Atlanta, Minneapolis, and San Francisco — have apparently begun to save themselves from physical decay. However, most urban centers of North America continue to spread out in a confusion of poorly built homes, parking lots, and plastic neon shopping centers with their gasoline stations and garish fast-food emporiums. Absolutely tasteless, and hardly functional. Even in the central cities, impersonal monuments to business continue to be built with little regard for the surrounding environment and the aesthetic feelings of the people who are confronted by them or who must work in them.

Nor does Galbraith see any real hope that improving aesthetic experience will come from the private sector. Modern urban renewal projects that protect the value of corporate-owned real estate in the core of the city by bulldozing ethnic communities out of existence are a case in point. But they have failed as a place for people to congregate, except to work. The rich and diverse human activity one finds both day and night in the centers of many European cities is missing in most North American cities. Why? Because such activity is considered not compatible with the goals of the technostructure.

Galbraith's remedy rests with the public sector. The intellectuals and an educated public will have to demand a better quality of life and insist that the elected officials see that it is accomplished. Galbraith foresees the day when elected officials, from mayors to presidents, when retiring from office will be judged partly by whether they are leaving behind a more livable community than they found when they entered office. Moreover, just as the technostructure relies on planning to attain its goals, Galbraith stresses, informed government planning that serves the individual instead of the technostructure can achieve a community's requirements for better housing, public transportation, education, health services, employment, recreation, culture, and an aesthetic, human environment.

The artist resides within the context of the market system according to Galbraith. Like the small business owner, the artist, too, is an entrepreneur — whether a sculptor, a potter, a weaver, a jewelry designer, or a musician. After all, artists create and sell goods. As entrepreneurs, they are as valid members of the market system as the home appliance repair firm, the local cobbler, the drug store, or the fisherman who sells his day's catch on the town pier. But, however artists sell their wares — alone, through cooperatives, on consignment, or outright to galleries — they are by nature the most resistant to organizing and, therefore, most vulnerable to the vagaries of the marketplace.

A potter or weaver, for example, can plan production. But the potter has no control over the price of clay, chemicals, and the fuel to fire the kiln. Because the potter's resources are usually meager, it is difficult to advertise the product. Because the potter has no control over demand, he or she is dependent on people wandering into the shop. The potter can control prices — but they may be too high for prospective customers, or too low to permit a profit. In addition, the potter may have to compete with others whose work and economic problems are similar.

However, Galbraith does not necessarily view the potter's situation as dismal. Because the potter's work requires the talent to produce goods of exceptional aesthetic merit, he or she can compete effectively with the large firm. In a very real sense, the potter's work is unique; it is produced to meet the individual consumer's demands. A large corporation, such as Corning Glass Works, manufactures its cooking and dinner ware for the masses. An exceptional artist would more than likely find it difficult to work for Corning. A designer with lesser aesthetic sensibilities — one trained to adapt his or her talent to the requirements of mass production and mass selling — may find Corning more congenial.

A similar case can be made for the graphic designer. Working on new packaging or advertising for soap, jewelry, candies, or toilet bowl cleanser, the graphic designer's talents are concentrated on the pragmatic requirements of creating a more effective selling image. The consumer products graphic designer is well rewarded for services to the planning system, but may never know the freedom of expression of an artist as long as he or she is dependent on the large corporation.

Down the street may work another kind of graphic designer, one who creates shapes and forms for no other reason than that they must be expressed. This graphic designer participates in the market system by selling to galleries, museums, or private collectors, or by acting as an independent consultant for small firms within the market system.

Obviously, the demand for individually produced art is small in comparison to that for commercially designed products. But one incentive to individual art, according to Galbraith, is that there are a sufficient number of people who seek out excellence in crafts, furniture, foods, books, clothing, jewelry, or whatever. As Galbraith points out, "A small market, in which cost is secondary to the quality of artistic achievement, also lends itself well to the individual or the small firm."[1]

In a sense, Galbraith is overly optimistic about the "carriage trade" environment for the individual entrepreneur and the small firm. The failure rate of small firms in the United States is astronomically high; some 12,000 go out of business each year. In addition, it is impossible to calculate how many artisans and artists have been forced by such basic and essential needs as food, shelter, and clothing to lower their high standards. Even Galbraith is puzzled by the fact that so many individuals and firms in the market system are able to survive.

Increasing numbers of people are leaving the cities to set up small enterprises so that they can be their own masters.

"I have lived in Vermont for about thirty years," Galbraith told me when I interviewed him for *Yankee* magazine, "and during this entire period we have been subsidized by people moving into this part of the state, all of whom have planned to make a living for themselves. They've started inns. They've started small handicraft enterprises of one sort or another. They've sold vegetables. They've sold art and antiques. I remember one person, twenty years ago, who came here. He was going to have the world's largest business in African violets.

"These ventures generally last for about two or three years until two things develop. First, their capital is gone, being used up benefiting other people who live off these enterprises by buying the products below cost. And second, particularly when there is a young couple involved, they find, not surprisingly, that they can stand each other's company in the summer but not through an entire Vermont winter. So at the end of two years the natural and inevitable antipathies that developed from December to the end of the mud season flourish. The family breaks up, and their enterprise comes to an end.

"My impression is that there is a romantic view of this rural countryside and a romantic view of the possibilities of making a living here. I feel that most of it is done by people who are not escaping the city but by those who have never really experienced this life. Most of them tend to be young romantics who have seen how their parents live, and they have assumed that they could find some other more agreeable design for living. However, every once in a while, somebody does make it. But the cases of success are very few.

"I was always asked what I thought about the economic prospects of such an enterprise. I would always be honestly pessimistic. For example, people would come to me and ask about raising sheep. I always pointed out that there was a long feeding time in the winter, that fencing was expensive, that there was an inordinate population of dogs which bothered the sheep, that sheep shearers were not available, and that the price of wool was often not that high. But I found in the end — I never discouraged anybody — that I was getting a reputation for being a pessimist. So whenever anyone came and asked me for my advice, I said go ahead, because you're only going to do it anyway."

Galbraith has pointed out that in the past, people and societies expressed their affluence by spending money on the arts. Renaissance Europe, particularly Italy, provides a sumptuous panorama of private, public, and church architecture. And in the Western Hemisphere, the colonial architecture of France, Spain, and England continues to survive as reminders that good aesthetic taste can be congenial with industry, politics, finance, trade, and religious devotion. The redevelopment of Quincy Market on Boston's waterfront may be a step in the right direction. Its small shops and restaurants retain a human scale and charm unique to an urban American city.

The abandoned mills and factories from New England's Industrial Revolution era also have a rather solid beauty and represent an important part of America's heritage. Galbraith also sees their beauty and their continued usefulness, but in more humane ways:

"The older New England cities and mills are rather beautiful. I would like to see them subject to the same kind of rehabilitation and development that has been done so brilliantly along Boston's waterfront. I would like to see some kind of comprehensive design that would convert some of these old mill buildings into retirement centers and pleasant residential communities. This is where the future lies."

Galbraith perceives that our society, because of its preoccupation with the Soviet arms race, is far more impressed with its scientific and engineering accomplishments in developing new, quickly obsolescent and often unnecessary weapons systems and moon landings than with improving the quality of life in our cities and towns. "Engineering and science are socially necessary; art is a luxury,"[2] he has written. Despite that, he feels that the arts will become increasingly more important to economic development as more people have more and better education, as they develop better taste, and as they have more money to spend on those goods and services that are best supplied by the market system.

But first, Galbraith argues, people's present attitudes regarding art and science must be changed. Galbraith believes that people have been conditioned to believe in the dominance of science over art — even to the extent that artists themselves are victims of this conditioned belief.

Although the market system plays an important role in our economic society, according to Galbraith, self-exploitation is essential to the survival of the small firm. There are two vital ingredients for the success of an individual or a small-business owner in the market system: hard work and long hours. This self-exploitation is necessary for the restaurant owner and the farmer, for example.

The executives, scientists, or engineers, who are members of the technostructure of a large corporation, can leave work each day confident that the business and their jobs are relatively secure. They can play tennis or golf or sail or camp over weekends and forget the company. They have, if they want, the luxury of disassociating themselves from their work and relaxing.

The business of farming, in contrast, is always with the farmer. Feeding his patrons is the constant preoccupation of restauranteurs. They, for example, must prepare menus, purchase commodities, supervise chefs, busboys, bartenders, waiters and waitresses, greet the guests, listen to their complaints, oversee the advertising, maintain quality standards, pay the bills, and make sure that the house is clean and ready for the next day's customers. The gruelling work and the number of hours that are involved day after day indicate self-exploitation. But that is the choice of the entrepreneur in the market system.

As the entrepreneur exploits himself, he, in turn, exploits the people whom he employs, Galbraith maintains. The entrepreneur resists unions, maximum wage laws, and any other worker's benefits because it is difficult to pass on these costs to his customers. According to Galbraith, the entrepreneur survives by paying lower wages — including his own — than the number of hours worked justify. Unlike the large corporation, the small business entrepreneur is almost powerless against the unpredictabilities of the market.

CHAPTER **8**
WHAT
TO DO
ABOUT INFLATION

Inflation is one of the economic realities of our time. Is it a side effect that must be lived with so that we may enjoy a greater measure of social balance? Or is it the archenemy against which every respectable economic policy must be aimed?

Critics accuse Galbraith of being too casual about inflation. Some say his policies carry an unpayable inflationary price tag. Galbraith is not hesitant to respond.

Like the weather, the effects of inflation are felt by everyone. Everyone — the ten-year-old who remembers the good old days when ice cream cones cost half as much, the wife who has gone back to work to make two incomes stretch to cover what one afforded in 1967, the small businessman, the large corporate executive, politicians, and presidents. And, like the weather, almost no one seems to know what to do about it.

Such economic troubles have far wider implications than pinching just the consumer's pocketbook, of course. Even the largest corporations and conglomerates suffered from the combination of existing tight money policies and ever-declining demand for their products. Some of the largest and most over-extended went under — Penn Central into receivership, Grant's into bankruptcy.

In *The Affluent Society*, Galbraith writes, "Through most of man's history, the counterpart of war, civil disorder, famine, or other cosmic disaster has been inflation."[1] And, recalling post-World War I Germany in *Money: Whence It Came, Where It Went*, he writes,

97

"By November 27, 1923, domestic prices stood at 1,422,900,000,000 times the pre-war level. . . . Men and women rushed to spend their wages, if possible within minutes of receiving them. . . . Notes were trundled to the stores in wheelbarrows or baby carriages. . . . All of the countries of Central Europe that suffered a collapse of their currencies following World War I were eventually to experience Fascism, Communism, or — as with Poland, Hungary, East Germany — both."[2]

Although Americans are not yet wheeling their pay envelopes to the stores, recent figures show that the purchasing power of the dollar has declined drastically in the past decade. It now takes more than $1.75 to buy what a dollar bought in 1967.

To Galbraith, the recession of the first half of the 1970s and the double-digit inflation of 1974 were predictable and will happen again and again. Unless, that is, his policies are applied — an indefinite system of wage and price controls and the power to use them. But why was the recession/inflation predictable? What events set off the period of economic instability?

Galbraith states in *The Affluent Society* that "the wage, price, and profit spiral originates in the part of the economy where firms with a strong (or oligopolistic) market position bargain with strong unions. These price movements work themselves through the economy with a highly diverse effect on different groups. Where firms are strong in their market and unions are effective, no one is much hurt, if at all, by inflation. . . . Those individuals and groups will suffer most which have least control over their prices or wages and hence the least capacity to protect themselves by increasing their own return."[3]

In 1968, a year of exceptional prosperity in the United States, a handful of money managers were warning of impending economic disaster. At the same time they issued their warnings, the managers were converting common stocks into other, more stable, investments for their clients. Those money managers were reacting to President Lyndon Johnson's policy of providing both guns and butter without increasing taxes. During his term in office, Johnson spent vast sums of money on space exploration and research, on new domestic programs of every conceivable sort — and at the same time he was fighting a war in Vietnam.

Hindsight has proven the wisdom of the money managers who

issued the warnings, of course. By 1974, the absurd had happened. The country experienced simultaneous inflation and recession, a double-edged calamity that most economists once believed was not possible. At the same time, planning his response to the Watergate disclosures, President Nixon was forced to relegate all other domestic matters including the economy to second-level importance.

When Nixon resigned office and Gerald Ford became president in August 1974, the economy continued to worsen. Ford's solution was the WIN button — "Whip Inflation Now." More people were unemployed or dropped out of the job market completely. OPEC, the Organization of Petroleum Exporting Countries, raised the price of oil. Detroit raised the prices on new model cars at the very time the market was glutted with unsold models from the previous year. As prices on the stock market declined, many investors felt the effects of the most serious economic crisis since the Great Depression of the 1930s and remember it with the same bitterness.

Although increases in consumer prices and inflation have recently begun to level off — though still at high rates — it is necessary to ask why the crisis continued so long. Economists, with their statistics, computer models, and game plans, should have been able to come up with solutions, tentative or otherwise, for checking the slump. Galbraith believes that his system would have worked and faults administration economists for relying too heavily on monetary policy as a means for controlling the business cycle.

Orthodox monetary policy directly or indirectly controls the amount of money available for lending, which in turn inhibits investments and cuts back on consumer spending.

As Galbraith told me, "I have long since come around to believing that we cannot tackle a boom through monetary policy without running unacceptable risks of a recession. When you tighten up on monetary policy, two things are certain to happen. First, you are going to do a lot of damage in those specific industries which depend heavily on borrowed money. The housing industry is one good example. In 1975, there was a devastating depression in the housing industry, the lowest level of activity since 1961. Second, if you depend extensively on monetary policy, the results are uncertain. That is why the use of monetary policy has sustained such a priestly discussion among economists. If some outcome is uncertain, you debate it. That is the case against using monetary policy: It is uncertain — risky."

In an article in *The New Statesman* (February 1976) Galbraith writes, "The democratic Left, in all Western industrialized countries, has two major failures — or dilemmas. The first involves, not surprisingly, inflation and unemployment — what economists have come to call macroeconomic policy. The Left, like the Right, has no generally accepted policy for reconciling substantially stable prices with substantially full employment. Present measures in all countries involve either substantial inflation, which is socially damaging, or substantial unemployment, which is socially intolerable, or most likely both.

"Inflation in the modern industrial economy is ultimately the result of the claims of various groups on the always limited capacity to supply them," Galbraith continues. "These claims are enhanced by the progressively more classless character of consumption. The rich still feel, on the whole, that they should have more than others. But, there is now no large group — not blue-collar workers, not unskilled workers, not blacks, not women — who accept that they are meant to have little."

In his 1976 book, *Economists at Bay*, economics professor Robert Lekachman writes: "As a group, economists are slightly more entertaining than bankers and a trifle duller than lawyers. The excuse for perpetrating an entire volume about their shortcomings is only this: when respectable economists are wrong en masse, other people usually suffer the consequences. The economists who encouraged Richard Nixon in early 1973 to dismantle a comparatively effective set of wage and price controls neither expected nor desired the price explosion that immediately followed this dash for freedom. That explosion, however, was the pretext for the Nixon-Ford actions which deliberately deepened and prolonged the 1974–75 mini-depression. Various people, most of them black, poor, female, or young or sufficiently unfortunate to combine in themselves several of these attributes, lost employment and income because reputable economic advisers urged a pair of conservative presidents first to restore free markets and then to counter the inflation with this action stimulated with high unemployment."

Galbraith has not only written about inflation, and with great deliberation, but he also played a key role in controlling inflation during World War II. He remembers his days as deputy head of the Office of Price Administration (OPA) with genuine satisfaction.

"One of the most powerful of the domestic economic jobs in Washington was to be in charge of price control. We had all prices under control. By the summer of 1943, when I left the job, there were no prices left uncontrolled."

In the early days of the OPA, one of Galbraith's employees was Richard Nixon, who had come to Washington for his first job in government. Writer William Manchester maintains that Richard Nixon went to Washington as a liberal but became a conservative after his OPA experiences. Years later as president (and before adopting controls himself), Nixon publicly condemned the use of wage and price controls as a throwback to the OPA days, emphasizing their abuses of freedom and their enormous bureaucracy.

In *The Glory and the Dream,* Manchester speaks of the OPA's size and problems. "By the war's end the Office of Price Administration had become a government-within-a-government, with 73,000 full-time employees, 200,000 volunteers, and an office in every community down to the town level. It was an intolerable tyranny, a mockery of freedom, and all that could be said for it was that there was no alternative. Somehow it had managed to hold price rises to 30 percent over their 1939 levels. . . . In 1946, the economy was virtually glued together on the back of red and green stamps."

Galbraith, of course, does not feel that the OPA was an "intolerable tyranny, a mockery of freedom," but does agree that, at the time, "there was no other alternative." Apparently Richard Nixon changed his mind about wage and price controls in the early 1970s — at least for a time.

"I suppose the first real disciple for wage and price controls I've ever had was Richard Nixon," Galbraith said with a broad smile. "In early August 1971, when prices were going up and unemployment was also rising, somebody asked Nixon, at a press conference, what he proposed to do. Nixon replied by saying, 'I know that some extremists on Capitol Hill are following Galbraith's ideas.' And then he said — very nicely — 'I'm not criticizing them. I'm just describing them.' That was about two weeks before he put in wage and price controls. He applied them to the big corporations and the unions, which was essentially the arrangement I've always urged."

But Nixon's commitment to the Galbraithian cure was too short-lived. As Galbraith notes in *Money: Whence It Came, Where It Went*, "On January 8, 1973, Secretary of the Treasury George P. Shultz . . . met with newspapermen to affirm his continued opposition to the policy. He noted controls had worked well in a slack economy but expressed the conviction that they would work less well now that full employment was being approached and they were not needed. The election had been won. Steps were taken to dismantle the controls."[4]

Although the Republican administrations of Nixon and Ford may not have given Galbraith's theories an adequate test, other leaders are adapting his cure to government policies.

On January 19, 1976, Prime Minister Pierre Elliott Trudeau of Canada made an important speech to his countrymen. The speech unveiled Trudeau's new attack on Canada's high rate of inflation (above 11 percent in 1976): selective wage and price controls were imposed on business, labor unions, and the government itself.

Trudeau stated, "The free market system, in the true sense of that phrase, does not exist in Canada. I have said that we haven't been able to make even a modified free market system work in Canada to prevent the kinds of problems we are now experiencing, and that it will do no good to try to create a pure free market economy to solve our future problems, because that won't work either.

"Every reasonable person," the prime minister continued, "now recognizes the duty of the federal government to manage the country's economy in the interests of all its people and all its regions. That duty carries with it the consequent responsibility to intervene when necessary to stimulate employment, to redistribute income, to control inflation and pollution, to protect the consumer and to promote conservation, productivity, and an adequate supply of the things we need."

Galbraith could not have said it better himself. Indeed, much of the substance of Trudeau's speech can be found in *The Affluent Society* and *The New Industrial State*. It is said that once government bureaucrats realized the impact of Galbraith's philosophy on the prime minister's new economic policy, the bookshops of Ottawa were rapidly emptied of his books.

Robert Lewis of *MacLean's*, Canada's leading news magazine, in an interview asked Galbraith, "The anti-inflation program in Canada is virtually a perfect mirror of some cf the suggestions you have made, except for one point. You advocate permanence to controls, which the Canadian government has not."

"I have only advocated or urged what circumstances require," Galbraith began in his reply. "If the market still works as it does in most small retail trade, the individual retailer (or the service trades, agriculture, small manufacturing) has no power and no unions. I would never dream of urging controls there.

"You can have inflation in those areas, but that is the result of a general excessive demand in the economy. The proper control for that is through fiscal and monetary policy. A massive bureaucracy would be required if you were regulating every price down to those in Iona Station, Ontario, where I was born. As to the question of permanence, I expect that as long as we have competitive trade unions, they are going to be reaching out for higher wages than the other unions. This process is going to lead to wage hikes well in excess of what can be paid for out of improved productivity. This is going to start the inflationary spiral, and strong corporations will protect themselves by passing it on to the public. As long as we have strong unions and strong corporations, which I accept, being a conservative on these matters, we are going to have the controls. The hope that somehow or other there will be a blessed day when they become unnecessary is romantic."

Controls seemed to have worked in practice and in theory for Canada, although not without widespread social and political repercussions. After almost a year of wage and price controls, Canada's inflation rate dropped from 10.7 percent in Autumn 1975 to 4.4 percent in August 1976 — two full points lower than the August 1976 figures for the United States. Instead of a nation grateful to Trudeau — and Galbraith — for devising a formula to combat double-digit inflation, the response to controls in the land of the red maple leaf was quite different. Organized labor struck back at the federal government's system of wage and price controls with a fury unmatched in any other sector of the Canadian economy.

On October 14, 1976, thousands of workers representing organized labor and led by the large Canadian Labor Congress (the equivalent of the AFL-CIO) quit work and held a "day of protest" against the controls. Labor's protest was that the Anti-Inflation Board had rolled back pay settlements that had been won through collective bargaining. For example, auto mechanics in Newfoundland settled on $6.45 an hour. This rate was cut back to $6.30 by the board. The workers appealed this decision, and as a result the board cut the rate back even more to $5.50.

Controls also mean keeping prices down and they have affected the profits of Canadian businesses. Wage and price controls have not only dampened US investment and expansion in that country, but brought on a reverse phenomenon. Instead of increasing their investment and expansion in their own country, Canadian business is seeing greener, more profitable pastures across the border in the United States. Economic growth in most of Canada is moving at a snail's pace because of the lack of the American investment in the country and the diversion of Canadian investment into the United States.

On November 15, 1976, the Parti Quebecois took political control away from the Liberal Party in the Province of Quebec. This election was not only a setback for Prime Minister Trudeau, the head of the Liberal Party, but it also put into power a party pledged to separate from Canada and form an independent republic. About two months after it assumed control of the French-speaking province, the Parti Quebecois unilaterally, without asking the federal government's permission, took approximately 200,000 civil service and public-sector related workers out of the nationwide scheme of wage and price controls.

As of this writing, there is a strong feeling in Canada that Trudeau will lift his wage and price controls on the country's economy in 1978. Although the inflation rate is down from its previous high, its current rate is still adversely affecting economic growth in Canada. It will be interesting to observe if labor and business restrain themselves after controls are lifted. Or perhaps there will be a mad rush to the well to make up for what is perceived to have been lost during the years when controls were attempting to regulate the economy.

In discussing the Canadian inflationary situation and the impact of wage and price controls, Galbraith indicated that "the British have in one way or another been working out the same policy over the years. In the smaller countries of Europe — for example, Switzerland, Sweden, the Low Countries — and for slightly different reasons in Germany, you come by indirection to the same policy. Prices and foreign sales set an implicit ceiling on collective bargaining. This is particularly effective in a country like Sweden, which has one wage bargain for the whole country. You have the classic example in Switzerland where wage bargaining has been very cautious in recent years. Over-time and over-contract payments have been eliminated, and substantial wage reductions have been accepted in order to keep Swiss industries competitive. Here, too, prices have been set in relation to what can be sold abroad. You have an implicit wage and price regulatory mechanism which grows out of a recognition of the competitive position of the country in international trade. The Canadians, therefore, are hardly unique in wage and price controls.

"You either have an income policy or more unemployment than you want or more inflation than the country can stand. This policy sets aside the whole textbook argument as to how wages are determined in relation to the marginal productivity of workers. It suspends the whole operation of the market as it is taught by economists. It's a policy that affronts neoclassical economic instruction and it would be, therefore, hard to imagine a step that more radically departs from the conventional structure of beliefs. It would be hard to imagine a policy which more radically affronts the vested interests of economists in their textbooks, in what they teach, and what they were taught. It's a far more radical step than the Keynesian revolution, which propped up the economy but left the market and wage determination processes intact.

"But our situation isn't going to be any different from that of the other industrial countries. We are going to control inflation by having a lot of unemployment, or we're going to have — which we also don't want — a little less unemployment but a lot of inflation. Or, we are going to try some form of controls. Once you try controls, you commit yourself, among other things, to a substantial amount of economic planning, Controls are an idea that people come to only after they discover that inflation, or unemployment, or both, are worse."

William F. Buckley, Jr., comments that "Trudeau was forced to adopt wage and price controls in the same sense that Nixon was forced to adopt them in 1971." Buckley maintains that "prices were slipping out of control. Some people were shouting for wage and price controls. So you try them for a time, then you give them up because they don't prove anything. They haven't proved anything in England. And of course wage and price controls didn't prove anything in America."

The debate over how to control inflation continues, and it directly affects the economic security of every individual. Late in the summer of 1976 a group of prominent American executives representing both profit and non-profit interests organized the Committee for Economic Development. It subsequently issued a report titled *Fighting Inflation and Promoting Growth*. Countless such committees, organized by well-meaning people trying to do something about inflation, have been formed before. They hold a few meetings, debate, issue reports, and fade into obscurity — still overshadowed by inflation.

However, the Committee for Economic Development seemed to be different. Its report criticized a monetary policy that restrained demand, thereby causing idle industrial capacity and unemployment. The report went on to say that "federal policies should seek to increase supplies and stimulate investment instead of curbing demand. . . .

"The role of monetary policy should be diminished and that of fiscal policy, (i.e., spending and taxation) increased."

Although the committee came within shouting distance of Galbraith's approach to solving the problem of inflation, it appeared to damage its cause in the same breath. Its report stated that "there is no single policy that will solve the inflation problem. Instead, an appropriate policy will require a mixture of many different measures to supplement market forces." In so waffling, the committee strengthened Galbraith's premise that everybody — liberals, moderates, and conservatives — desperately wants to do something about inflation, but nobody knows what to do. Except, of course, Galbraith.

"So long as we depend on the instruments that we are now using, such as monetary policy, we are going to keep on having inflations or recessions or, more likely, both at the same time,"

Galbraith told me. "Until we go on to develop a comprehensive incomes and price policy, which directly grips inflationary forces — particularly the competitive pressures to increase income and drive up prices on the part of large corporations and wages on the part of unions — we are continually going to be faced with either recession or inflation. At the present time we have no way of controlling inflation except by creating a lot of unemployment."

Galbraith's plan for stabilizing inflation is inextricable from his plan for reforming the economic world. His thesis, set out clearly in *Economics and the Public Purpose*, proposes that the state should serve the public purpose rather than the "planning system" — the mammoth corporations that control selling and buying prices as well as demand, the amount of goods they produce or sell.

Progressive taxation tied to public expenditures, wage and price controls, and an astringent fiscal policy are the keystones of Galbraith's solutions to our economic problems — a visionary system of logic and planning to provide economic opportunity to every person.

CHAPTER **9**

HOW
THE CORPORATION
SHOULD BE
REFORMED

The United States is an affluent society because it is a highly industrial society. Most of its private economic power is concentrated within a relatively few large corporations. That concentration of power is an *oligopoly*, as distinct from *monopoly*, in which one firm has complete control over an industry.

As Galbraith has written in *The New Industrial State*, the two thousand largest industrial corporations in the United States account for about half of the private sector's total output of goods and services. Although Galbraith was trained as an agricultural economist and spent his early years in that field, his most important — and most controversial — contributions to social and economic thought have been his ideas about the nature of the corporation in society.

After World War II, Galbraith traveled through Poland and Yugoslavia, studying their postwar economic recovery and lecturing at universities. Characteristically, he recorded and later published his observations of that trip. One day, as he was strolling through the gates of the American Embassy in Warsaw, he noticed a Marine Corps guard reading *American Capitalism*. As Galbraith passed, he gave the Marine a kindly nod and thought to himself, "That fellow will go far in life."

What degree of success the Marine enjoyed is unknown, but *American Capitalism* was a decided hit. In it the expression "countervailing power" first appeared. Countervailing power is somewhat akin to a move on a chess board which seeks to bring to bear a power equal to or greater than that of the opponent.

For example, a strong labor union exerts countervailing power against a strong corporation. In the early days of the auto industry, before labor was organized, each worker sold his labor individually to the company. Obviously, power was concentrated in the hands of the company, which could hire its employees at terms favorable to itself. However, once the individual workers organized themselves into a union — with the power to shut down production through strikes — countervailing power became a potent factor in negotiations for better pay and working conditions. Today the United Auto Workers Union has such power that the results of its bargaining with one company can be expected to set the standard for the entire automotive industry.

Auto companies themselves exert countervailing power — in dealing with suppliers of steel, for example. Steel is the primary material in the manufacture of an automobile, and sales to auto companies represent a major portion of the steel industry's business. Thus countervailing power works both for and against large corporations. Galbraith maintains that other economists failed to recognize that when power is concentrated in fewer and fewer corporations countervailing power would emerge as a new restraint.

Countervailing power is also energetically exercised by large-volume buyers representing discount stores and supermarket chains. Moreover, jobbers and wholesalers who distribute manufacturers' products to a variety of independent retail outlets, from neighborhood Mom-and-Pop grocery stores to small pharmacies, employ countervailing power. A manufacturer can obviously sell more goods more easily and with less expense in a single transaction with a chain store buyer than in the expensive and comparatively inefficient process of having his salesmen go from one store to another. Because the chain store buyer purchases large quantities of goods, the buyer is able to exert countervailing power on the seller.

Gillette, for example, is a major producer and marketer of shaving and personal care products. It spends over $100 million dollars annually on advertising and special promotions in the United States. That effort is directed primarily at large volume buyers, the retail chain stores. Those buyers can substantially affect the profitability and market dominance of particular Gillette products. In other words, by exerting countervailing power, the buyer can extract terms and concessions favorable to his organization.

Countervailing power is less effective in times of increased demand, however, at least for the buyer. Given a strong consumer demand for a new Gillette shaving system or for Gillette products in general, the buyer's leverage is virtually nonexistent: he needs the products on his shelves to satisfy his customer's wants.

Since the publication of *American Capitalism* in 1952, another type of countervailing power has emerged. Consumer advocacy groups, such as Common Cause and Ralph Nader's movement, attempt to exercise countervailing power on the buyer's behalf. Other similar ad hoc and permanent groups have led boycotts against the rising cost of food and lobbied against high energy costs.

It is Galbraith's opinion that "countervailing power performs a valuable — indeed, an indispensable — regulatory function in the modern economy. Accordingly, it is incumbent upon government to give it freedom to develop and to determine how best it may do so."

Is John Kenneth Galbraith the relentless enemy of the large, highly organized corporation? Quite the contrary, he is intellectually fascinated by both the internal workings and the external influences of the corporation. Moreover, he believes that the large corporation is a necessary and important entity in an advanced industrial society. Galbraith, however, objects to the present nature of the large corporation because he believes that consumers have become slaves to the modern system when they should be its masters.

As Galbraith was writing *The Affluent Society*, in which he explored the phenomenon of industry's creating consumer wants to increase production, he began to question the more comprehensive anatomy of the large corporation. In the foreword to the first edition of *The New Industrial State*, perhaps his most important book on economic and social thought, he writes: "This was a world of great corporations — a world in which people increasingly served the convenience of these organizations which were meant to serve them."[1]

The New Industrial State lays the foundation for Galbraith's conceptual structure of an industrial economy composed of two main parts: the *planning system* and the *market system*. The planning system is made up of a comparatively small number of large corporations that control the production of more than half of America's private goods and services. Those corporations are managed by a highly educated and organized professional elite. The market system is made up of the thousands of small and medium companies and of individual entrepreneurs who provide the remaining portion of goods and services to our society.

Obviously, the industrial system itself has changed over the years. As machines — the key factor in the Industrial Revolution — replaced unskilled labor, industry began to rely more and more on skilled labor and on more highly trained human intelligence. Concurrently, corporations themselves changed. Diversification — several enterprises under a single corporate umbrella — provided insurance against the risk of marketing a single product. Gillette, for example, which started by making only razors and blades, now sells pens, cameras, and home appliances, and owns the Welcome Wagon service.

Today, multinational conglomerates such as ITT and AVCO are involved in all kinds of businesses — food, entertainment, finance, electronics, among others — which require offices, plants, machines, and workers scattered all over the world. Moreover, although many corporations were once owned and operated by their entrepreneur-founders, virtually all large corporations today are managed by a different breed: the sophisticated, trained executive theoretically responsible to a board of directors and to outside stockholders. The modern manager is both a slave to and a master of the corporation.

In Galbraith's view, the other key factors that changed our industrial system were the expanding role of government in the purchase of goods and services, the ability of advertising to contrive and exploit consumer wants, the current decline in union membership as a percentage of a growing labor force, and the increasing number of people seeking higher education.

According to Galbraith, one important characteristic of the modern large corporation is its technology — the systematic application of organized knowledge to a specific task. The manufacturer of an automobile, for instance, requires a large, resource-rich corporation. The product involves the distillation of talent from many disciplines: scientific skills in the development of metals and other materials for construction; engineering skills for performance and safety; design skills for consumer appeal; manufacturing skills for setting up an efficient assembly line; and, of course, marketing skills to get the product into the hands of the consumers.

Obviously, no small firm has the resources and skills to perform such a comprehensive series of tasks, except in a very expensive and inefficient manner such as those firms that specialize in manufacturing custom-made automobiles.

Galbraith considers six consequences of the nature of technology, each having a distinct influence on the way in which the modern corporation performs: first, the more complex the task, the greater the amount of time separating its conception from its completion; second, the more time that a task needs to be completed, the more financing it will require; third, with an increasing commitment of time, technology, and money, the parameters of the task become more constricted (a prolonged effort to develop a quieter and more efficient jet engine for an executive jet aircraft, for example, could not suddenly be diverted to the design of a combat aircraft without repeating the engineering, tooling, and materials processes); fourth, the task to be completed requires a high level of scientific, engineering, and managerial talent; fifth, because the total task is made up of many complex subtasks, coordinating all its elements is essential to ensure successful completion of the task; and sixth, because time, money, and talent have been invested, and to ensure that the anticipated needs of the corporation and the problems of the market have been met, planning is necessary. Underlying all six consequences is the belief that risks must be reduced to ensure some certainty of success.

Galbraith is emphatic that technology leads inexorably to planning. Despite the fears of some conservatives who equate planning with socialism and the loss of personal freedoms, planning is simply a process that implies "a sensible concern for what might happen in the future and a disposition, by forehanded action, to forestall avoidable dysfunction or misfortune,"[2] Galbraith says in *The New Industrial State*. Planning is a process by which goals are established, problems in attaining the goals are anticipated, and courses of action to prevent failure or minimize its effects are determined. It is an intelligent attempt to capitalize on future opportunities while minimizing risks.

Galbraith insists that planning is essential in our industrial society because the market economy, based on the vagaries of prices and demand, has ceased to be reliable. He believes that much corporate planning has to do with minimizing or eliminating the influences on the market. Any large corporation needs to know in advance what price it can charge for a product, what volume of sales it can expect, and what labor, materials, and services it will need to ensure that its goals are realized. Planning is based on past and present data plus a projection of the future. And therein lies the inherent weakness of planning: constant and unpredictable change always introduces an element of uncertainty. For example, the recent tightening of foreign oil supplies plus a substantial rise in prices provided an incentive for Americans to buy more economical automobiles. It made sense for the nation's automobile manufacturers to replace opulent, gas-guzzling monsters with a more practical machine.

As *The New York Times* reported: "October 1976 brings the beginning of the end of the iron monster, at least in its grossest forms: the long, low, wide, bulge-sided road ship; the zoomy, rubber-peeling, power-packed 450-to-500 cubic-inch V-8, 4,500 pound-plus gasoline waster. In Detroit, fat is out and thin is in."

Large corporations have three weapons at their disposal to avoid the uncertainties of the market, according to Galbraith. The first is vertical integration, in which a corporation controls the entire process from the source of supply to the selling of the product to the consumer. The large oil companies, such as EXXON, practice vertical integration. EXXON finds the oil, pumps it out of the ground, refines it, ships it to its distribution points, delivers it to retail outlets, and pumps it into the consumer's cars.

The second weapon is control of the market. General Motors flexes its muscles both as a buyer and as a seller. Because GM purchases so many products and services in such huge quantities, some suppliers depend on GM for their own existence. They must then bend to the planning requirements of GM.

In the role of seller, General Motors controls the prices at which its products are sold. Ordinarily, demand is down and inventories are high during a recession. Companies then lower their prices to stimulate buying by consumers. But in the recession of the early 1970s, when automobile sales were at their lowest in years, GM actually increased the price of its new models. Ford, Chrysler, and American Motors followed suit. As Galbraith maintains, the only possible winner in a price-cutting war would be General Motors.

In addition to controlling the price of its products, General Motors controls the number of units that it sells. By determining how many vehicles — and at what prices — it will sell in a given year, GM can estimate how much money it will have for future planning.

The third weapon that large corporations have at their disposal to avoid uncertainties of the market, according to Galbraith, is their ability to establish prices and the amounts of raw materials they will buy over an extended time. For example, a company that employs a dozen or so craftsmen making custom-built cars is a less influential customer for the steel industry than, say, General Motors. The demand for custom cars is subject to fashion trends. The chief designer of a small company may suddenly leave. General Motors, on the other hand, will go right on making Chevrolets. It really doesn't matter if its chief executive officer is fired or if a natural catastrophe like a blizzard closes down one of its plants. General Motors will prevail.

"In a world of large firms," Galbraith says in *The New Industrial State*, "it follows that there can be a matrix by which each firm eliminates market uncertainty for other firms and gives them some of its own."[3] Because General Motors is a large company dealing with large suppliers, it creates a favorable degree of economic certainty for its suppliers and they for GM. This, in turn, promotes a mutually favorable business environment.

Who runs these mammoth enterprises? Galbraith's phrase for this new breed of managers is the *technostructure* — a network of professional scientists, administrators, and managers that increasingly is taking control of the economy.

The repository of organized knowledge within a corporation is its technostructure, according to Galbraith. It is the aggregate corporate brain, with each individual a kind of brain cell, contributing his or her specialized knowledge in concert with others. Galbraith states that the industrial decision-making process — collecting and analyzing data from a number of individuals — has three main sources.

The first is industry's own technological requirements. Ordinary men and women acquire knowledge in their specialized fields and then combine their knowledge with people from other fields. Galbraith stresses the word "ordinary," in contrast, say, to genius. For example, moon landings succeeded because ordinary men and women were organized around a common purpose. The Apollo missions were accomplished by a bureaucracy. The astronauts were the well-publicized heroes, the glamorous members of a vast organization of human beings who made those missions possible.

In *The European Discovery of America: The Northern Voyages*, the late Samuel Eliot Morison wrote, "The three young heroes of the moon landing did not supply the idea; they bravely and intelligently executed a vast enterprise employing some 400,000 men and costing billions of dollars; while Columbus' first voyage cost his sovereigns less than a court ball; and Cabot's, which gave half of the New World to England, cost Henry VII just fifty pounds. The astronauts' special voyage into space, a triumph of the human spirit, was long prepared, rehearsed, and conducted with precision to an accurately plotted heavenly body. Their feat might be slightly comparable to Cabot's if the moon were always dark and they knew not exactly where to find it and if they had hit the wrong planet."

The second source of industrial decision-making in Galbraith's scheme "derives from advanced technology, the associated use of capital and the resulting need for planning with its accompanying control of environment,"[4] he writes in *The New Industrial State*. The vegetable grower who sells his produce from a roadside stand has a relatively simple planning process to follow. He plants, nurtures, and harvests vegetables which the people in his area like and which he can grow. His prices are the same or lower than those of neighboring vegetable stands and the nearby supermarket, possibly even higher if his produce is something special.

The large industrial firm, on the other hand, is engaged in a far more complex planning process. The Boeing Company, for example, must obtain and organize enormous amounts of information about people, plants, equipment, and materials to produce a new generation of commercial aircraft. Boeing also requires information about the anticipated needs of the airline industry, its ability to pay for new equipment, and the projected growth in the air travel and freight markets. New technologies in exterior metals, fuel utilization, and sound and sonic-boom abatement must be developed. Both the cost of manufacturing and selling of a selected number of the new aircraft must be planned. Of course, if the aircraft is meant for military rather than commercial use, a whole new set of information will be required.

The third source of industrial decision-making is applying human talent to a common purpose. Although each individual of the technostructure obtains, analyzes, and exchanges knowledge and information within the corporation, Galbraith maintains that only the committee produces action and makes decisions. He views corporations as being a "hierarchy of committees."⁵ This committee approach is the only efficient way for a large corporation to operate, according to Galbraith's argument. He acknowledges the popular notion that individual effort is supposed to be of a higher quality than collective effort, but he argues that highly paid persons working together are not necessarily inefficient.

Nevertheless — and a reality that Galbraith fails to consider — the corporation holds specific individuals, such as division managers or presidents of subsidiaries, directly responsible for setting and attaining, performance goals such as sales and profits. If these goals are not met, then individuals — not necessarily the committees that made the decisions — may suffer the retribution of higher management.

Galbraith firmly believes that the collective intelligence — the corporate brain — of the technostructure is essential to its growth. However, at the first sign of a recession, management apparently is wont to slice off a portion of that brain. Why do companies lay off intelligent, experienced people? Why don't they save money in other ways? Indeed, aren't the companies destroying the very brain cells of the technostructure with such lay-offs?

"Human overhead may be the only item that can be easily cut," Galbraith said.

The chief executive officer of the corporation is often perceived as wielding the power and making cosmic decisions that affect worldwide markets and the lives of thousands of people. Harold Geneen, the architect of today's ITT edifice, seems to be the archetypal corporate man at the top: hard-driving, powerful, ruthless.

But Galbraith takes another view: The function of leadership is to assign tasks to committees, which themselves produce substantive decisions. For example, in many corporations the executive committee represents the governing body. This does not imply that a chief executive officer does not wield power. Indeed, each corporation is different in its nature and the style in which it is managed. But to Galbraith, it makes no sense for the top-level executive to second-guess or ignore the substantive decisions of his committees — which represent organized intelligence.

Galbraith believes that small and medium corporations are more subject to the market's vagaries of price, demand and supply than larger conglomerates. On the other hand, large corporations overcome such vagaries through planning and by their sheer size.

As an illustration of the magnitude of large corporations, each year *Fortune* lists the top thousand industrial corporations in the United States. In *Fortune*, 1975, the combined sales of the first five hundred — the largest — were $865 billion; their profits were $38 billion. EXXON, ranked first, recorded 1975 sales of $45 billion. General Motors was second with sales of $36 billion. The next group of 500 industrials had combined sales of $82.6 billion and profits of $3 billion. From the corporation's point of view, bigger is better, because bigness as such allows it more control over supply, capital, demand, and risk.

The technostructure of a large corporation requires autonomy to function effectively, according to Galbraith. It must protect itself from meddling by outside forces — consumers, government, labor unions, and stockholders. The intrusion of government and labor unions can be resisted on ideological grounds. Even though the stockholders' right to become involved is guaranteed through legal ownership, they can be "excluded by giving them the impression but not the substance of power," Galbraith says in *The New Industrial State*.

In seeking autonomy, the corporation at once resists government interference. Yet paradoxically, it looks to government for subsidies, protective tariffs, research and development support, and education of people to fill the ranks of the technostructure. For example, Frank Borman, former astronaut and now chief executive officer of Eastern Airlines, needs government subsidies to ensure his firm's profitability. Yet Borman wants no government interference in the internal affairs of Eastern — even though the alphabet soup of government agencies (the FAA, CAB, ICC, and the like) establish Eastern's routes, flying levels, fares, and myriad other airline procedures. Borman's situation is even more paradoxical because his education and his ensuing military career as a pilot and astronaut were financed by American taxpayers.

Corporations depending on yet desiring independence from government may appear paradoxical, but not to William F. Buckley: "It is preposterous to say that a guy is not going to take a welfare check if he can get it, because he is going to. And, by extension, I think it is ridiculous to say that capitalists are not going to try to use whatever government leverage they can for their own benefit. They do it all the time. This is one of the reasons why one has to affirm capitalism not only against the socialists but against capitalists, because capitalists have a dismal record in making use of whatever instruments are available for their own benefit.

"If Frank Borman were sitting here with us, he would undoubtedly say that his education was paid for by the public. But, by the same token, in signing up for West Point, he had to sign up for a four-year hitch in the military service," Buckley told me. "And very probably his salary during those four years was half what the salary was for somebody who had gone to Harvard or to Yale. Regarding government subsidies, there are any number of answers he might make. One is that Eastern is required by the government to provide service to certain cities which is unprofitable for his airline.

"If you decide, as a matter of public policy, that we require flights to Hanover, New Hampshire, then you should first see whether or not some private enterprise carrier will do the job. In fact, Hanover has air service — a lousy, little, uncomfortable airplane that charges first class rates. But it gets people to Hanover. Government regulations ought not be made a matter of public policy such that they will dominate the economic policies of the private airline."

The right of a stockholder, seen as another meddling outside force, to become involved directly in the affairs of a corporation is guaranteed by right of legal ownership. Yet stockholder interference in substantive decisions is rejected by the technostructure because it might interfere with the self-interests of the corporation, especially in planning. The large number of outstanding common shares easily minimizes the influence of stockholders. Very few people control enough shares to affect votes in an important way. Those few who do on occasion make banner headlines on the financial pages.

Another way in which the technostructure ensures its autonomy is by maintaining its own source of new capital through retained earnings. This lessens the corporation's need to borrow money and minimizes the banker's intrusion into the affairs of the business. When it is not the lender, the bank obviously cannot control the way in which the technostructure uses its own capital. And most stockholders know little or nothing about how wisely retained earnings have been invested.

However, banks are now heavily involved in the trust management business — thereby owning and controlling large blocks of stock — and many corporations have been forced to borrow money because of skimpy retained earnings during economic downturns. I asked Galbraith whether these changes suggest that bankers have power with the technostructure?

"You could make the same case for the mutual funds and for insurance companies," observed Galbraith. "The knowledge that the technostructure possesses does not filter back to the insurance company, the mutual fund, or to the bank. Therefore, even though these institutions may have representatives on boards of directors, they do not have any great impact on corporate policy. EXXON, for example, once had a board of directors made up entirely of its own executives. Then it added some outsiders who represented financial interests. But, this changed little or nothing. When the board does meet, once every two or three months for half a day, most of the key decisions have already been made."

One of the most important developments in capitalism to Galbraith is that large corporations have been able to amass significant sums in retained earnings. They have used such money at their discretion — thus bypassing more traditional sources of capital. "It is hard to overestimate the importance of the shift in power that is associated with the availability of such a source of capital," he writes in *The New Industrial State*. "Few other developments have more fundamentally altered the character of capitalism. It is hardly surprising that retained earnings of corporations have become such an overwhelmingly important source of capital."[6]

In *Money: Whence It Came, Where It Went*, Galbraith writes that "the study of money, above all other fields in economics, is the one in which complexity is used to disguise truth or to evade truth, not to reveal it."[7] To Galbraith, bankers are chief among those who perpetuate an aura of mystery around money, making it their exclusive domain. James Howell, senior economist at the First National Bank of Boston, the largest bank in the New England area and one of the oldest in the nation, is a Texan widely known for blunt language. His notions about any change in relationship between large corporations and banks because of retained earnings differ from Galbraith's.

Are large corporations in fact financing their expanding programs from radically different sources, as opposed to those of one or two decades ago? The answer is no, Howell told me. "They are not. There has been a revolution in corporate cash management practices, but I don't believe this is a source of new strength to the corporations at the expense of the banking system. Indeed, I would argue that most of my banking colleagues consider this to be a constructive step forward in rationalizing business financial practices along lines that bankers have long advocated.

"Galbraith seems to have had a political flair in describing economic theories that he believes accurately reflect the realities of the economy," Howell continued. "But, finally, I suspect that the Galbraithian world in which he lives in his country-day school [Harvard] across the Charles River is a world of his own rather than indicative of the true realities of the American market economy."

A corporation's failure to produce earnings is another source of danger to the technostructure. If a corporation records losses rather than profits, stockholders and financial analysts will want to know why. In addition, losses mean that little or no internal capital is available from retained earnings. In this respect, when the autonomy of the technostructure is most vulnerable, Galbraith maintains the "power of the capitalist is revived." However, if earnings are maintained at an acceptable level, stockholders are kept quiet, bankers are more subservient, and the autonomy of the technostructure is preserved.

But in reality do large corporations ever register losses? According to Galbraith, on the whole they do not, because both the corporation and the industrial system have adapted themselves to the requirements of the technostructure. However, each year some losers appear among the giants in *Fortune*'s annual list. In 1975, for example, Singer lost $42 million, Chrysler $250 million, and Anaconda $40 million. There were twenty-five other large corporation losers in that particular assembly. Then, in 1976, one of the leaders of American retailing, WT Grant, folded. But those losers represent only a small portion of a select group of large corporations that over the years have maintained an adequate level of earnings for future investments and stockholder appeasement.

In his analysis of the modern large corporation, Galbraith stresses that owner involvement in management decisions has become the exception rather than the rule. Aside from those exceptions — the Houghton family of Corning Glass and Edward Land of Polaroid come immediately to mind — the days of the Morgans or Carnegies are gone forever. Owners can no longer make the important corporate decisions; these decisions are now the responsibility of the technostructure.

Where then in the process of decision-making does the board of directors fit? According to Galbraith, directors no longer have a place of corporate importance or influence. They are nothing more than a collection of older men and women — some outsiders, some executives within the corporation itself — who routinely pass on previously made decisions submitted by the technostructure.

"The typical board of directors has strong geriatric tendencies," Galbraith said. "Some of the members have trouble keeping awake during the meetings. Substantive corporate policy is formulated in and resides in the management structure. This is why putting trade union leaders, consumers, or blacks on the board is largely window dressing. If I were a member of the senior management of General Motors, I would put a black, an American Indian, a priest, a Chicano, and a woman on the board, knowing full well that this would not alter in the slightest degree the present power structure of the corporation."

Galbraith also considers the annual meeting of stockholders

merely an illusion of participatory ownership. The annual meeting is most often an orchestrated public relations event, at which the past year's financial results are reviewed, top-level personnel changes announced, new product commercials viewed, incantations for continued progress aired, and slick annual reports distributed. Any stockholders brash enough to ask an embarrassing question of the board are stoically tolerated or rudely ignored. Indeed, Galbraith feels that the two most significant aspects of an annual meeting are that no important decisions will be made and that only a handful of eligible people will attend.

Like any organization, the technostructure has goals. Survival, a favorable growth rate, and a secure level of earnings, according to Galbraith, are its three principal aims. Survival requires that the technostructure protect its autonomy. Freedom from interference by government, labor unions, stockholders, and capitalists gives the technostructure the power to make whatever decisions it chooses. As long as the company earns enough to allow for both reinvested earnings and reasonable dividends, it is safe from aroused stockholders and the cold analysis of bankers — or takeover.

The second goal of the technostructure that Galbraith identifies is to attain the greatest rate of growth based on annual sales. A favorable growth rate in sales means that the technostructure itself can grow. Growth creates jobs for the technostructure — more promotions and more decision-making power in the hands of more people. Growth also means higher salaries and more perquisites. When the technostructure accepts economic growth as a social goal, Galbraith believes its members can identify with a purpose that is larger than their own, even though their own self-interests may lie behind that purpose. The well-educated technicians and managers who make up the technostructure are by nature ambitious — hardly people who would be satisfied with dead-end jobs. If they are employed by a firm with a strong growth rate, and they see people around them being promoted, their hopes have to be positive.

The third goal is, in Galbraith's words, "a rate of earnings that allows, over and above investment needs, for a progressive rise in the dividend rate."[8] However, that earnings rate must not be achieved through a price structure that might well dampen growth — implying that maximizing profits is not the primary goal of a large, mature corporation.

Indeed, as Galbraith argues, when a corporation reaches a certain "bigness" and maturity, it is able to control the market. Therefore maximizing profits becomes less important. And because profit maximization is no longer a primary goal, the technostructure can divert some of its attention to pursuing other goals, such as educating the public on the virtues of the free enterprise system, participating in local Chamber of Commerce activities, providing vocational training programs to inner-city youth and executive talent to minority business, or sponsoring public television broadcasts. Pursuing such secondary goals serves the interests of the technostructure. Its prestige and self-esteem are enhanced by contributing to the social good, but only so long as such convenient social virtues do not interfere with its primary aims of survival, growth, and earnings.

The large corporation, because it is large and powerful, is a convenient target for critics of our industrial system. The public generally admires the rugged individualism of the entrepreneur. He is perceived as a latter-day extension of North America's pioneering spirit. Executives of large corporations, however, like to think of themselves as rugged individuals. This role they can assume, of course, without having to undergo the risks and disappointments of the entrepreneur. The mechanic working alone in his garage has far more in common with the Henry Ford of the early twentieth century than the current president of The Ford Motor Company. The popular conception of the entrepreneur is that he is master of his own fate, one who can talk with any person, regardless of stature, on an equal basis.

The other side of the coin, according to Galbraith's theory, is that the entrepreneur is at the mercy of suppliers and customers. He has no planning system, no industrial-government matrix working in his behalf. He cannot survive, let alone prosper, on the image of rugged individuality. His creditors may admire him because of his entrepreneurial qualities, but he must still make his payments on time, suffer high interest rates, and constantly worry about cash flow or go out of business. In *Economics and the Public Purpose*, Galbraith sums up the predicament of the small business entrepreneur in these words, "His is often the freedom of a man who is pecked to death by ducks."[9]

Considering that the market system is really at the mercy of the planning system, some reform, Galbraith feels, is necessary. He puts forth six steps. Galbraith would like to see small businesses receive a general exemption from antitrust laws so that their firms can join together to stabilize their prices and output. Independent gas station operators, for example, could benefit from such an exemption; small businesses could not only exert power in the marketplace, but could also compete more equally with the large corporations.

Second, Galbraith feels that strict regulation of prices and production is important in the market system to benefit all small businesses. Galbraith feels that government should regulate prices and production. As an objective force, government would tend to ensure that prices remain stable and that production be more efficient. Left alone, the firms would most likely go their own way, thus breaking down the cooperative system they need to prosper in the marketplace.

Third, Galbraith encourages trade unions to develop a strong and effective organization of the market system. The bargaining position of a worker in a small firm is weak and, according to Galbraith, his employer survives because of this weakness. Galbraith cites the National Labor Relations Act as discriminating against the casual laborer, the domestic worker, an employee of a small service company, or a farm worker. He calls such discrimination "illogical" and "barbarous." But he also points to recent progress in organizing, particularly by such advocates as Cesar Chavez with farm workers, and the growth of membership in the service employees' and retail clerks' unions.

Fourth, Galbraith feels that minimum wage laws should be extended to include every business in the market system. The minimum wage protects employees of small businesses from outright exploitation by the entrepreneur. The minimum wage tends to eliminate the differential between wages received by workers in the market system and those in the planning system. People who buy products and goods from the market system should have to pay prices that reflect a decent living wage for workers in small businesses. The era of sweatshops may virtually have disappeared in the United States, but vestiges of it remain in the garment and domestic servant industries, as well as agriculture — particularly among illegal immigrants and migrant agricultural workers.

One negative effect of minimum wage laws is that they have encouraged US firms to shift some of their manufacturing operations to nations which have a large supply of cheap labor, such as Mexico, Taiwan, and South Korea. The American shoe industry has been particularly affected by the shift of manufacture to foreign countries.

During the golden days of Puerto Rico's Operation Bootstrap, an economic development program, for example, US mainland businesses were attracted in droves to the island by tax incentives and the promise of cheap labor, which the government itself was willing to train. However, since minimum wage laws have extended to Puerto Rico, the island's labor force has become less competitive. As a result, some businesses have left the island for locations where people are content to work for less.

Fifth, Galbraith wants revisions in the international commodity organization and tariff protection that primarily protect the planning system. The major characteristic of the multinational corporation is that it extends its business over international frontiers by becoming a kind of corporate citizen in the host country. The corporation is thus able to avoid problems of international trade. In addition, price competition is excluded or minimized by what Galbraith calls "oligopolistic convention"[10] which means that General Motors can make and sell its automobiles in Great Britain and Germany. Volkswagen, Volvo, Datsun and Toyota, of course, have a big market for their cars in the United States, the center of auto manufacture in the world. A large American company that finds it can make its products cheaper in another country will sell these products under its own brand name in North America.

Although the executive of a large multinational corporation can take some satisfaction out of participating in a larger world of free trade, the trade union leader in America is justified in being concerned over the loss of jobs to lower paid workers in foreign countries. Galbraith states that the market system company does not enjoy the flexibility and ease in international business that the large planning system corporation does. He recommends that the interests of the market system company be protected by international agreement, which would stabilize prices and production. He also advocates the use of tariffs but admits that the major weakness in this approach is that tariffs often invite retaliation, which could produce serious consequences on the weakest firms.

However, Galbraith maintains, the use of tariffs cannot be excluded on ideological grounds if they strengthen the bargaining position of market system companies. Such exclusions would deprive them of protection which has become organic to the international industrial system.

Finally, Galbraith urges government support for the educational, capital, and technological needs of the market system. The large, modern corporation depends on the government to supply a qualified work force to fill its technostructure, to provide access to capital by the management of aggregate demand, and to make available technological innovation through military and aerospace programs that private industry can adapt to its own requirements.

Companies in the market system do not participate to any great degree in this governmental largesse. If a few companies receive some capital, qualified manpower, and technical assistance, they are provided these resources not as preferential but as compensatory treatment, according to Galbraith. He feels that government policy should be designed to reduce the unequal balance of essential resources for economic development between the planning system and the market system.

In addition, because the arts are organic to the market system but irrelevant to the fundamental goals of the planning system, Galbraith would prefer an increase in governmental support of painting, sculpture, theatre, and public television.

As admiring of the market system as Galbraith is, he nevertheless feels that it should not be "the employer of the last resort."[11] But it is now just that, according to his theory, because the market system pays lower wages. In short, people who cannot qualify for jobs in the planning system (which tends to pay more and provide better working conditions) settle for less agreeable, less financially rewarding work in market system companies. Galbraith's solution is to bring market system working conditions more in line with those of the planning system.

As the two systems are brought more closely together, however, some jobs will of necessity be affected. Galbraith's answer — shared by some, including Milton Friedman, on the right — is to establish a guaranteed income as a basic right to those who have lost jobs and cannot find another. Such unemployment income would be less than what one would make in a planning system job, yet high enough to ensure a decent standard of living. Alternative income would also prevent "involuntary self-exploitation"[12] by those who are self-employed.

To Galbraith, the old saw of artists starving in their garrets is not only inconsistent with the affluence of industrial society; it also denies the people's right to an improvement in their aesthetic and cultural environment. But just as important as the artist's right to survive and contribute to our enrichment, Galbraith, in wanting to strengthen the market system, is, in fact, seeking to increase free enterprise and stimulate competition. Although he may advocate democratic socialism, his economic and social philosophy is more supportive of the peculiarities and potential of each person's individualism than of those powerful segments of our society that exploit this theme to mask their own self-interests.

Galbraith states because of its group characteristics, the modern corporate technostructure is limited in its ability to use its money as a source of pressure on politicians and public policy, in contrast to earlier entrepreneurs who were able to do so. A prince in the Netherlands and some former leading political figures in Japan might argue this point with Galbraith. At home, more than a platoon of top-level American executives, members of the technostructure of large corporations, now live in disgrace because they engaged in the very kind of activity Galbraith minimizes in *The New Industrial State*. Bribing congressmen with brown bags stuffed with greenbacks was considered a necessary corporate expense in the early 1900s. Businessmen bought votes and legislation favorable to the industrial system.

In *The New Industrial State*, Galbraith writes about how difficult it is for salaried executives in the technostructure to bribe politicians the way the old-time entrepreneurs did because of the risks involved to the collective group. I asked him about recent disclosures of bribes being given to foreign and US politicians by such giant corporations as Lockheed. In this instance there were disclosures of corporation bribes to officials in foreign governments and bribes to our own politicians. How do these events coincide with Galbraith's view of the collegiality of the technostructure?

"I was surprised at the extent of bribery by big companies," he responded. "In *The New Industrial State* I said that people imagine that influence in Washington is wielded by little men going around with black bags filled with money, but that is actually exceptional. The real power is exercised by a symbiosis of purpose between the Air Force, for example, and its contracting companies. This symbiosis represents friendships and reciprocal favors of a much more subtle character. I certainly believe that the collective activities of managers in large corporations, the fact that so many people know about any single action, acts as a force for morality.

"But if I had to enter a defense for what obviously was an exaggeration, but not an error, it would be that these companies had to go to very great lengths to conceal their illegal activities," he went on. "These companies had to establish a subsidiary in the Caribbean in order to funnel money to somebody down there and then have him bring it back to the US in a satchel. This is a very complex operation. Second, it was probably much more serious in two classes of companies: oil companies and the weapons firms which live intensely political lives, as compared to Ford, General Motors, General Electric, or those firms whose relationship to the state is slightly more normal."

Large producers of weapons systems can mesh their goals with those of specific branches of the armed services. These shared goals create a symbiotic relationship between the Department of Defense and prime contractors in the planning system; each needs the other. Defense-oriented senators, congressmen, trade unions, and bureaucrats are all involved.

Though the entrepreneur in the market system wants to keep government agencies out of his business, the large corporation that depends on defense contracts puts out the welcome mat for public officials. This relationship is mutually congenial; ranking military officers and bureaucrats and executives sometimes share duck hunting and golf at private lodges. Of course, the "hog" in this instance is the American taxpayer.

Dwight Eisenhower's farewell presidential address warned Americans about the dangers of the military-industrial complex. He talked about how the interests of private enterprise and the military had combined into a powerful force that had the potential of significantly affecting the democratic way of life in America. If some East Coast liberal intellectual had made the same speech, it ʌould have hardly made the back pages of the paper, but Ike's last shot was a big one, and the blast from his verbal artillery continues to echo.

How did it come about that a Republican president, a close friend of big business, a military hero, and a soldier from his youth to his death would warn us about one of the greatest concentrations of power in the world?

"A whole generation of people who wanted to bring up the issue of allocation of resources during the cold war took refuge behind Eisenhower and used him as a kind of spearhead with that speech, which was written for Ike by Malcolm Moos," Galbraith told me.

"I was in Minneapolis in the late-sixties or early-seventies and had lunch with Malcolm one day. I asked him about the speech," Galbraith recalled. "He told me an absolutely fascinating story. When Ike wanted to make his last speech, Moos said to him, 'Why not talk about the concentration of power the military and the industrial establishment are developing? The American people should be warned that we are creating something that should be watched.' Ike said, 'That's a great idea!'

"Malcolm went off and wrote the speech and put in the sentence warning about the military-industrial complex. Ike read it and said, 'I think I'll leave that sentence out. I'm just leaving office and it's too controversial. I don't want to make everybody angry.'

"So Ike and Malcolm talked about it for a while, and they finally struck the sentence out. Malcolm left Ike's office to go home. He made it to the White House guard's booth when the policeman said, 'The president's office is calling you.' When Malcolm got back to the Oval Office, Ike was sitting at his desk, still looking at the speech, he said, 'Malcolm, I think it's a pretty good idea after all. I'm inclined to think that we'd better put the sentence back.' Much later, whenever Malcolm saw Ike again, the former president would always ask the same question, 'Malcolm, why do you suppose the warning about the military-industrial complex got so much attention?' "

I wondered if Eisenhower really understood what he was saying. "I wonder too," Galbraith said. "I think he saw the problem, but probably did not perceive the enormous impact that would follow his opening the subject up. At any rate, it was the most important statement that Ike ever made."

Galbraith makes sure that he is not misinterpreted about the nature of the American military-industrial complex. He acknowledges the existence of grounds for disagreement — perhaps more in the past than now. "No man who believes in liberty can accept a world that is forever half slave and half free,"[13] he writes in his chapter on "The Industrial System and the Cold War" in *The New Industrial State*. Although the two systems are fundamentally different, that of the West and that of the Soviets, both are, nevertheless, industrial systems, resorting to economic planning. This chapter also includes one of Galbraith's most interesting ideas.

Because the industrial systems of both the United States and the Soviet Union use planning to achieve their goals, there is an economic tendency toward convergence of the two systems. Although the differences between the two systems will continue to persist, they cannot be resolved in a war that could annihilate most of human life on this planet. Galbraith points out that the competition in the development and deployment of weapons is not necessarily benign, because there is always the chance that someone on either side will miscalculate and decide that war is the best possible option. The Cuban missile crisis, for example, during the Kennedy administration, is a grim reminder of how close the world came to the brink of war. Both the SALT talks and détente have been attempts by the United States and the Soviet Union to converge their self-interests rather than to exploit their differences.

As has been mentioned before, in *Economics and the Public Purpose*, Galbraith calls the industrial system of large corporations the *planning system*. The other half of our economic society, which is composed of thousands of small and medium business enterprises not large enough to create advanced technology and power through planning, he calls the *market system*. The main distinction is that, through planning, the large industrial corporation can eliminate or control most of the unpredictabilities of the market; small business, on the other hand, is totally at the mercy of the market's vagaries.

A walk through downtown Pittsburgh, for example, can provide a brief lesson in the differences between the planning system and the market system. Modern buildings belonging to or occupied by US Steel, Gulf Oil, and PPG Industries dominate the skyline.

These large, mature corporations are solid members of the planning system. Now, as you walk along the street, you will pass restaurants, bookshops, drugstores, furniture stores, antique shops, hairdressing salons, taverns, haberdasheries, jewelry shops, and boutiques featuring the latest in women's fashions. In the upper floors of some of the older buildings are print shops, employment agencies, graphic arts studios, and travel agencies. All these are examples of Galbraith's market system. Their individual contributions to the Gross National Product are not as significant in comparison to their giant corporate neighbors. But the market system's total contribution to the GNP is about equal to that of the planning system.

According to Galbraith, the sector of services is the special domain of the market system. He cites a paradox: When machines replace personal services, service enterprises increase. For example, computers are taking over more clerical tasks; computers now operate and even instruct other machines. Paralleling the increased use of computers is an increasing need for people to service and program them. While this situation expands the servicing and programming areas of large computer corporations, it also creates openings for smaller firms that offer quicker and better service to move in.

When Volkswagen was originally sold in America, two of its main appeals were its low price and its durability. In 1960, a Volkswagen sedan could be bought for around $1,600. But along with the automobile, the buyer also received a preventive maintenance booklet that urged the owner to bring the car back to the dealer for regular inspections. The inspection invariably included some degree of servicing and the replacement of one part or another. At that time very few mechanics knew how to repair or service the now-famous Bug. But the market system quickly responded to meet consumer needs; independent garages that specialize in fixing Volkswagens and other foreign cars soon proliferated.

By the same token, in the past, the servant class was not extraneous to the fabric of affluent life; it was the very substance of it. Today, live-in servants are as rare as whooping cranes. Even those who will come in for a few hours a day, once a week, are difficult to find. But the servant gap has not gone unnoticed by the market system. Catering services will provide a butler, waiters and waitresses, and clean-up people for anything from an intimate dinner party to a lavish wedding. In addition to renting a home or apartment, the affluent person can rent all the furnishings for it and an automobile complete with chauffeur to drive to work and around town.

That part of the industrial system composed of large, mature firms is characterized by a small number of sellers. Excluding European and Japanese firms, there are only four major domestic sellers of automobiles in the United States: General Motors, Ford, Chrysler, and American Motors. However, the dominance of the American auto market by General Motors and Ford is such that these two giants allow the existence of the other two firms in order to keep up the appearance of competition.

Steel, glass, processed foods, computers, aircraft, textiles, and petroleum are other industries that are dominated by a few large sellers. Galbraith refers to these few sellers from which most of our industrial production originates as legal oligopolies in contrast to illegal monopolies. American Telephone and Telegraph comes closest to being a natural monopoly, and with some justification. Telephone service in the United States is far better than the service provided by state-run monopolies in other countries.

Although federal antitrust laws were designed to break up monopoly power, they do not work. They only foster the illusion that the market system — and ultimately the consumer — controls the economy, according to Galbraith. The purpose of federal antitrust laws is to prevent collusion between sellers in fixing prices. The laws try to guarantee fair prices for all and to prevent prices that benefit only a few. Mergers and acquisitions are usually closely investigated so that the market power of the individual large firm is not inordinately strengthened in relation to other firms. Galbraith states that such governmental action only works to deny market power to those firms which do not have it. Moreover, he says that those oligopolistic firms that already have great market power are immune from the laws.

Certainly General Motors, Ford, and Chrysler executives do not have to meet in some remote hideaway to rig prices on new model cars. They have already studied each other long enough to set prices that serve their common interests. Their analysis of each other's pricing behavior is entirely legal. Smaller, weaker firms that deal with large buyers and need to develop countervailing power by getting together to control their prices face the arm of the law for collusion. Galbraith states that our industrial society penalizes the large number of smaller, weaker enterprises who use collusion to maintain market control, while accepting control exercised by large firms, which no longer need to resort to such collusion.

Galbraith's strictures on the institution of the corporation are numerous. In sum, many of his criticisms boil down to the proposition that corporations are run by managers who wield vast power and who are in no way responsive to the "public purpose." Furthermore, he says that the highly-paid executives who head these giants are often unequal to the task of achieving even their avowed purposes. In *The New Republic,* he comments on the pay received by Harold Geneen for running ITT in 1973 — $814,299 in salary and bonuses. Galbraith observes, "On performance he should be paying the company."

In many of his criticisms of the corporation Galbraith agrees with another observer of the industrial state, Peter Drucker. They concur that the running of corporations has slipped out of the hands of the owners to be taken over by professional managers. They agree that corporations wield vast power, and that they do not wield this power with the public good primarily in mind.

Then what is to be done? Here Galbraith departs from Drucker and from a great many advocates of the free enterprise system as it now operates. Drucker *(Concept of the Corporation)* acknowledges the power of the huge multinationals, but feels that the lust for power is inherent in human nature. If not given scope in one area it will emerge in another. While there are many things wrong with the way big corporations work, there is also great potential for good. For example, they are truly making the earth "one world" — although not in a way that is congenial to a lot of social reformers. Drucker rejects the notion of public ownership or control of corporations through governmental intervention. He insists that the first duty of the corporation is its own survival, and feels that this is proper and beneficial to our way of life.

Galbraith strikes out boldly to reform the corporation through liberal doses of state intervention. He suggests that when "the private stockholder disappears, the board of directors should be replaced by what might variously be called a board of public auditors or a board of public inspectors." This board would comprise perhaps a dozen members. A minority — say, four — would be selected by the management and include the senior executives of the firm. The other members — persons who have an instinct for promoting the public purpose — would be designated by government.

This body would not have operational authority, according to Galbraith. Its function would be that of a concerned monitor to maintain a continuing watch over the extent to which the purposes of the company diverge from those of the public. Its deliberations and findings would be public. He maintains that the great corporation is no longer a private institution and that the concept is no longer valid. Among the powers entrusted to the board would be the determination of top executive compensation.

Socialism? That is what many people call it, although Galbraith does not use the term in this context. His abiding view is that the corporation must be brought more closely into line with public law and purpose. To this end he admits no alternative to the introduction of the state into the conduct of what is now cherished as private enterprise.

Only in this way, says Galbraith, can the individual achieve a measure of control over the technostructure that now has so much power to run his life.

10
THE IRREVERENT DIPLOMAT — GALBRAITH AND FOREIGN POLICY

Since Galbraith had been an early supporter of John F. Kennedy and a member of his 1960 convention staff, it was expected that he would hold an office in the Kennedy administration. The post to which he was named came as a surprise to many. He was appointed ambassador to India, a position he was to hold until mid-1963.

I asked Paul Samuelson why Kennedy sent Galbraith to India. "Because Galbraith wanted to go. Oh, he wanted it so badly that he could taste it. On the other hand, Galbraith would have preferred to have been senator from Massachusetts for an unexpired term," Samuelson told me.

But why not Great Britain, or France, rather than India? "I'm not sure," Samuelson said. "Also, in those days, it was taken as axiomatic that you had to be extremely wealthy to be ambassador to one of those countries. But I think that India was an interesting ambassadorship from Galbraith's viewpoint.

"If he had wanted to be chairman of the Council of Economic Advisers under Kennedy, I think he could have had the job," Samuelson said. "But that position is the last thing Ken would want. However, I think if he had been offered the post of secretary of the treasury, he would have taken it, or the job of secretary of state. But that was not in the cards."

In December 1960, Kennedy told Galbraith he wanted him to go to India. Galbraith was pleased, but he asked Kennedy, "Would that be more useful than the Senate, with the prospect of bringing some decency back to Massachusetts Democratic politics?" Kennedy replied, "Yes. By a factor of five to one."

On March 17, 1961, Galbraith and Walter Heller, chairman of Kennedy's Council of Economic Advisers, went to the exclusive Occidental Club in Washington for dinner. The headwaiter took the two economics professors past a waiting crowd and said, "Your table is waiting, Mr. Ambassador."[1] Galbraith's pride in being called by his new title was quickly checked when he realized that the headwaiter had assumed that Walter Heller was Ambassador Galbraith.

At the Senate hearings on Galbraith's confirmation as ambassador to India, Senator Wiley, Republican from Wisconsin, asked him about his position on the admission of Red China to the United Nations. Galbraith says, "Then the shit hit the fan."[2] The standard answer any prospective ambassador should give, at that time, was "never, never, never."[3] Galbraith, however, suggested accepting China into the UN when the Chinese recognized the independence of Taiwan. Senator Lausche of Ohio jumped on Galbraith and wondered how long Galbraith had been harboring such thoughts. Senator Sparkman of Alabama saved Galbraith by saying that the professor's ideas were the same as those expressed by Henry Cabot Lodge.

During a breakfast meeting with Kennedy, the president asked Galbraith what he thought about a *New York Times* article that described his election memos as "sharp, funny, and mean."[4] Galbraith told the president that he didn't appreciate the newspaper calling him arrogant. "I don't see why. Everybody else does,"[5] said Kennedy. The president asked Galbraith how his family was taking the move to India. Galbraith told him that his young son Peter was reluctant to go. Kennedy said that perhaps a letter from the president to Peter Galbraith would be helpful. Galbraith quotes his letter in his *Ambassador's Journal.*

"I learn from your father that you are not very anxious to give up your school and friends for India. I think I know a little about how you feel. More than twenty years ago, our family was similarly uprooted when we went to London where my father was ambassador. My younger brothers and sisters were about your age. They had, like you, to exchange old friends for new ones.

"But I think you will like your new friends and your new school in India. For anyone interested, as your father says you are, in animals, India must have the most fascinating possibilities. The range is from elephants to cobras, although I gather the cobras have to be handled professionally. Indians ride and play polo, so you will come back an experienced horseman.

"But more important still, I think of the children of the people I am sending to other countries as my junior peace corps. You and your brothers will be helping your parents do a good job for our country and you will be helping out yourself by making many friends. I think this is what you will enjoy most of all."[6]

Galbraith was sworn in as ambassador to India on April 3, 1961. Five days later, the Galbraiths had arrived in New Delhi, where they received garlands of flowers from the Indo-American Friendship Society and various other groups. Galbraith describes one of his first breakfasts at the American Embassy: "I had asked for fresh fruit, a scrambled egg, and toast. I got canned grapefruit juice, a poached egg, and bacon. It takes some skill to spoil a breakfast — even the English can't do it. But our cook can. His bacon was what turned Islam against pork."[7] Later that month, Galbraith says, he had an "affluent attack of dysentery." His doctor told him to abstain totally from eating Indian food.

When Galbraith went to present his credentials to Prime Minister Nehru, he described himself as "the most amateur of diplomats" whereupon Nehru described himself as "an amateur prime minister."[8] Part of their conversation involved the Congo. Nehru felt that Americans had a misunderstanding about Patrice Lumumba, the Congo's controversial premier who was assassinated in 1961. Nehru told Galbraith that "Lumumba is not a communist and he probably doesn't know what communism is."[9]

In April, the Bay of Pigs invasion of Cuba was launched and fell flat on its face. Galbraith tells about a pro-Cuban demonstration at the Indian Chancery. Galbraith ordered that the gates be left open and that the leaders, if they wanted to present a petition, should be invited in. The demonstrators marched with red banners, some threw stones, and some called for Galbraith's resignation. After his staff had left the Chancery, Galbraith drove by the mob with the ambassadorial flag unfurled. It was hardly noticed by the mob. He says that he would have been more frightened had he left the building by the back door as one of his staff had suggested.

The *Times of India* reported that it was a sad thing to see Galbraith and Adlai Stevenson, then Kennedy's ambassador to the United Nations, covering up the pathetic affair in Cuba. Galbraith says that it was not America's finest hour; however, he felt fortunate that he did not have as much explaining to do as Stevenson. In one of his famous and frequent letters to President Kennedy (dated April 27, 1961), Galbraith wrote: "The last week wasn't the best in the history of the New Frontier, and I haven't found much comfort in contemplating your problems."[10]

There had been much pressure on Nehru "to give us the business,"[11] Galbraith goes on, particularly from enemies of the United States. "The Indians see protection . . . in the principle of nonintervention,"[12] he points out.

"We did not escape unscathed but it was no disaster. I kept our explanations simple and short; there is nothing worse than windy arguments. At a press conference, which came as these damn things always do on the worst day, I repeated you [Kennedy] and then contented myself running over our history of alleged misdemeanors in undermining Cuban despots as seen by the latter from the complaints of Spain to the present. Castro I made merely the last troublesome chapter on the list."[13]

In another letter to Kennedy, quoted in *Ambassador's Journal*, rather prophetic words, particularly in light of what later happened in Indochina: "I have reached two conclusions as a result of my concern with Laos and the Congo. These jungle regimes, where the writ of government runs only as far as the airport, are going to be a hideous problem for us in the months ahead. . . .

"The rulers do not control or particularly influence their own people; and they neither have nor warrant their people's support. . . . Most of all, we must not allow ourselves or the country to imagine that gains or losses in these incoherent lands are the same as gains or losses in the organized world, that of France or Italy — or India."[14]

During Vice President Johnson's visit to India, the American press lambasted him for giving a Texas yell in the Taj Mahal to test its famous echoing effect. Galbraith defends Johnson and says that the press was unfair. Guides demonstrate the echoes for tourists every day. In addition, Galbraith points out some papers put Johnson's yell in the same classification as a sacrilege in the Christian church. The Taj Mahal is a monument of a rich man's love for his woman, not a mosque. After Johnson returned to America, the prime minister told Galbraith that he liked Johnson and that he regarded the Texan "as an intelligent, down-to-earth, practical, political figure."[15]

One of Galbraith's stops on the way home was in Rome, and he took the time to visit St. Peter's. In one of the chapels he noticed a congregation of some forty priests, whom he describes as being overweight and wearing dirty surplices. While observing this scene, he thought that perhaps Pope John was too liberal. He felt that the next pope should be of the "spit-and-polish type"[16] and that Robert Kennedy should be brought to the Vatican to work the clergy into a physical fitness program.

Galbraith tells a story about meeting with the president in Washington, with one of the conferences being held while Kennedy took a bath. While Galbraith sat on the stool telling the president about some shady dealings, Kennedy in the tub would occasionally interrupt the conversation by turning on the hot water faucet with his foot. Then Robert Kennedy and one of his six children came in; Galbraith wondered if the boy had been cleared by the FBI.

Kennedy was disturbed by what Galbraith was telling him. "How do these things remain secret? In this town, the only things that are secret are the things I need to know,"[17] Kennedy said. The president then asked Galbraith how he liked being an ambassador. Galbraith said that it was easier than being in the White House. Kennedy commented, "Softer too, I imagine."[18]

When Galbraith got back to India, he wrote another letter to President Kennedy, specifically referring to the worsening situation in Vietnam. Galbraith again denigrated the State Department. "I hope, incidentally, that your information is good and I have an uneasy feeling that what comes in regular channels is very bad. Unless I am mistaken, Diem has alienated his people to a far greater extent than we allow ourselves to know. This is our old mistake. We take the ruler's word and that of our own people who have become committed to him."[19]

But there were moments of humor as well, and Galbraith describes one incident in *Ambassador's Journal*. At a dinner for the French ambassador on Bastille Day, two beautiful Indian girls "very much raised my morale. I am told that diplomats have not always been men of rigid virtue. A one-time US ambassador to India is the nearest thing yet devised to a male chastity belt. But one can still gaze wistfully."[20] In Calcutta, a reception held in Galbraith's honor was advertised in the newspaper near a picture of two half-naked girls.

On August 15, 1961, after a visit from Chester Bowles, a close friend and Kennedy's undersecretary of state, Galbraith wrote again to Kennedy: "In government people get boxed only when they won't kick their way out. I like Bowles. His only trouble is an uncontrollable instinct for persuasion which he brings to bear on the persuaded, the unpersuaded and the totally irredeemable alike. In my view, the State Department needs not to be persuaded but to be told.

"If the State Department drives you crazy you might calm yourself by contemplating its effect on me. The other night I woke with a blissful feeling and realized that I had dreamed that the whole goddam place had burned down. I dozed off again hoping for a headline saying no survivors."[21]

In September, he was back in Washington for meetings, which also included some at the State Department. "I am rarely so depressed as after a day in the Department. It is so large it crawls with bodies. And all energies are employed in arranging for so many people to live together,"[22] writes Galbraith.

One of his main reasons for returning to Washington was to arrange for a future visit by Prime Minister Nehru. It was during this visit that Galbraith proposed that Jacqueline Kennedy come to India. Galbraith called Mrs. Kennedy at the family compound in Hyannisport. She was so excited about the trip that she wanted to come to India the next month. But this was also a time of heightened tensions between the United States and the Soviet Union over Berlin, and Galbraith suggested that the Indian trip be postponed until the situation cooled off in Europe.

When Galbraith arrived back in New Delhi, he wrote his views on Berlin in a letter to the president, warning him about the Washington tendency to overcomplicate what Galbraith saw as a rather simple issue. The Russian buildup, as Galbraith saw it, may have had two aims — either to upgrade East German prestige, thus downgrading the American presence in West Berlin, or to deny US access and expel American soldiers. "If the first is their aim, things will be worked out. If they intend the second, we will have a nasty time — but I don't suggest it will be war except by accident, but there will be a lengthy trial of nerves and strength since we both are after the same thing."[23]

Galbraith attended a rather elaborate spectacle put on by the Maharajah of Mysore, in one of the greatest of the so-called Princely States. Galbraith looked at the royal female relatives and took note of their rich garments and the enormous number of diamonds, rubies, and other precious stones each woman wore. "Just an old piece from the South,"[24] said one of the princesses, when Galbraith admired her necklace of rubies and diamonds. He figured it was valued at about half a million dollars.

Nehru's visit to meet President Kennedy in Washington was rapidly approaching, and Galbraith was back again in "Foggy Bottom" to work out the details. Former President Harry Truman joined Kennedy and Galbraith for one meeting at the White House. Truman told Kennedy that although he liked Ike, he felt that Eisenhower would have remained a lieutenant colonel if it hadn't been for the patronage of General George C. Marshall. Galbraith says that also during this time in Washington, Maxwell Taylor and Walt Rostow were advocating sending American troops to Vietnam to do flood control work. The troops could work with shovels with one hand and deal with the guerrillas with the other. Galbraith says that he was frightened by the power Rostow was assuming.

Galbraith in *Ambassador's Journal* considers November 6, 1961, in Newport, Rhode Island, as the most interesting day in his memory. At about 10 that morning the presidential party boarded the *Honey Fitz* and sailed to the Newport Naval Air Station to meet Nehru on his arrival in the United States. The president, his family, and Galbraith had been staying at Hammersmith Farm, the home of Mrs. Kennedy's mother and stepfather. A military air transport plane carrying Nehru landed on time. He was accompanied by his daughter, Indira, the future prime minister of India. They returned to the presidential yacht and Nehru was intrigued at the sight of the mansions once occupied by America's very rich. During lunch Nehru was asked his opinion on what to do about Vietnam. He was against sending in troops, but agreed that some other alternative should be explored.

Later that day they all boarded the president's plane for the trip back to Washington. Galbraith says that while in transit Kennedy read one newspaper each minute. Nehru read the *National Geographic* and the *New York Daily News*, Indira looked at *Vogue*, and Jacqueline Kennedy read André Malraux. In Washington, they were met by the diplomatic community and high officials of the American government. Guns were fired in salute. The band played. And both President Kennedy and Prime Minister Nehru gave their formal addresses.

The next day, talks between the two heads of state began. As Galbraith describes their meeting, Kennedy was brilliant in his questions and comments while Nehru spoke in monosyllables. After the meeting, Kennedy and Galbraith walked on the lawn of the White House. Kennedy felt discouraged, thinking that he had done very badly. But Galbraith disagreed: "I fail to see how he could have done better."[25] A couple of days later at the suggestion of Galbraith, Kennedy and Nehru met privately and their conversations went better. After that meeting was over, Kennedy was happier and told Galbraith that he had caught some of Nehru's magic.

Nehru and Governor Nelson Rockefeller met at the Carlyle Hotel in New York City. Nehru later told Galbraith that Rockefeller was "a most extraordinary man. He talked to me about nothing but bomb shelters. Why does he think I am interested in bomb shelters? He gave me a pamphlet on how to build my own shelter."[26]

Galbraith returned to India by Saigon. He had suggested to Kennedy that it would be a good idea, and the president agreed. On his way from Washington to the airport, Galbraith met Angie Dickinson. As Galbraith described the incident, the movie and television star made a deep impression on him — not only her looks, but her humor and wit. The plane ride to the Coast went by too quickly for Galbraith. "I was heartbroken when Los Angeles came up under the wing and invited her to come on to Honolulu. She declined, and I kissed her tenderly, put her in a cab for Hollywood and got glumly aboard my flight."[27]

After his inspection of Saigon, Galbraith wrote to Kennedy. South Vietnam "is certainly a can of worms. I am reasonably accustomed to oriental government and politics, but I was not quite prepared for Diem."[28]

Galbraith felt that the US technical assistance program was jeopardized by increasing political unrest. Agriculturalists, for example, who were confined almost entirely to Saigon, were no longer of much use, he noted. And in another jab at his employer: "The ambassador there, a decent man who is trying to obey orders, has been treated abominably by the State Department."[29]

That year Leonid Brezhnev of the Soviet Union arrived in New Delhi, and the Galbraiths went to a reception for him. Brezhnev compared Galbraith to Peter the Great because of his size. Galbraith said that he didn't like being compared with a figure from the feudal system. Brezhnev retorted that Galbraith should not worry because Peter was a progressive.

On March 13, 1962, Jacqueline Bouvier Kennedy and her sister Lee Radziwill arrived in New Delhi. Galbraith refers to Mrs. Kennedy by the initials JBK. Nehru, the controversial Indian Defense Minister Krishna Menon, and hundreds of school-children greeted the two women. The visit of Mrs. Kennedy and her sister was considered "great fun"[30] by Galbraith. They went to see the colorful pageantry of the opening of Parliament and strolled through the Moghul Gardens. They also went to the Rajghat with roses to honor Gandhi.

After a series of glittering receptions and dinners in New Delhi, the party went on a sightseeing tour of the countryside. Wherever the party went, mobs of people and photographers were in excited profusion. According to *Ambassador's Journal*, Galbraith thought the mob scene was closer to a riot, even though JBK seemed to enjoy it.

Galbraith's assessments of the Indochinese situation continued to flow between India and Washington. Some key points from his April 4, 1962 memo to Kennedy are instructive, at least in retrospect:

"We are backing a weak and, on the record, ineffectual government and a leader who as a politician may be beyond the point of no return.

"It seems at least possible that the Soviets are not particularly desirous of trouble in this part of the world and that our military reaction with the need to fall back on Chinese protection may be causing concern in Hanoi."[31]

He strongly recommended political solutions to the Vietnamese problem — particularly a noncommunist government with a broad political base. Internal law and order are what South Vietnam needed, not increased military identification with the United States.

And his next words should have been heeded by everyone from Kennedy to Johnson to Nixon:

"We should resist all steps which commit American troops to combat action and impress upon all concerned the importance of keeping American forces out of actual combat commitment."[32]

In October 1962, India and China were engaged in a bloody border war. Fighting commenced between the two nations at the Thagla Ridge, a high mountain area in the border region with Tibet. Galbraith was in London at the time and had to cancel several lectures to hasten back to India. When he arrived in New Delhi, the military situation was going badly for the Indians, with the Chinese pushing them back on all fronts. Galbraith says that the Chinese were far more determined and stronger than the Indians. The Chinese objective was to take over territory on which they felt they had an ancient claim and then negotiate from strength. Galbraith's attitude was to reassure the Indian government that the United States was its friend, despite the harsh treatment the Americans were receiving through the rhetoric of the ascetic Defense Minister Krishna Menon. In addition, during this period, the Cuban missile crisis shook the world, and Galbraith had to explain the American position on Cuba again to the Indians. Galbraith wanted India to support the US position on Cuba in the United Nations, and the Indian leadership left Galbraith with the understanding that the Americans "could pretty well count on their restraint and UN support."[33]

The Russians, siding with the Chinese in the border dispute, urged the Indian government to settle the issue on China's terms. The Indians told Galbraith that they doubted that the Russians could hold back the Chinese. In addition, although the Indians needed a great deal of American assistance, they did not want a formal alliance. Neither did they want the United States to insist on inspecting the supplies they received, a procedure that would hurt Indian sovereignty. Galbraith replied that Krishna Menon had turned American public opinion against the Indians, and he informed them of the serious deficiencies of their weapons procurement system.

On October 24, Galbraith was informed that Krishna Menon was being sidetracked. In addition, the Chinese offered to stop fighting the Indians. Next there would be a conference between Nehru and Chou En-Lai, and the Chinese would pull back from their present position.

The Indian government rejected the Chinese offer. "It is rather cynical of the Chinese to take territory and then negotiate over it,"[34] writes Galbraith in *Ambassador's Journal*. At a press conference, Galbraith was asked about the Cuban missile crisis. He told the reporters that the Communists initiated the aggression by installing their missiles.

Two days later, the Chinese had advanced twenty miles south of the border. Four thousand Indian casualties were reported. Galbraith notes that most of these casualties were missing, rather than actual dead or wounded. At this point Galbraith was beginning to think that the conflict was turning into more than just a border dispute. The Chinese were now in position to move from the high mountains into the very plains of India. Pakistan, which was voicing support for the Chinese, was another big headache for Galbraith. Three Indian divisions were being maintained on their border with that country. On the plus side for the Americans, Indian disenchantment with Defense Minister Menon had grown to the point where it was expected that he would soon be sent packing.

Galbraith considers October 29 to have been the "last of the worst days."[35] He had received a letter from President Kennedy for Prime Minister Nehru offering the Indian government American assistance. When Galbraith saw Nehru, the prime minister told him that he had just sent President Kennedy and Khrushchev letters congratulating them on the peaceful settlement of the Cuban situation. Galbraith told Nehru that he was loved in the United States and that the American people would respond to his request for help. Nehru said that he needed the aid, and its source would have to be the United States. But he also added that he wanted to avoid irritating the Russians in the process.

The situation in India received worldwide attention and Galbraith had to hold off a flood of help that was offered but not needed. "Today's offering included a Marine Corps specialist on guerrilla warfare and a deluge of Congressional delegations for whom India has obviously become a place of interest and excitement,"[36] he writes. As the Chinese advanced, he wondered if their action in India was not creating a great deal of adverse international opinion. And on another day, he wrote, "One of the great problems of the world is that all crises are almost certainly handled by tired men."[37] By October 31, Menon had been fired and Nehru had taken over the defense ministry himself. In early November, Galbraith received word that the first air shipment of American weapons was on its way to Calcutta. He was impressed — he had only asked for the supplies four days before.

War creates all sorts of hardships for human beings. Galbraith personified the adversities of one Chinese shoemaker who had been born in India. Political tensions were making life impossible for him and his family of twenty. Galbraith hoped to get him a visa for a South American country.

Also in that November came the news that Richard Nixon had been defeated by Pat Brown for the governorship of California. "Another expendable politician was gone,"[38] Galbraith writes — somewhat less than prophetically — in his journal.

On November 13, 1962, Galbraith sent Kennedy another letter detailing the situation in India:

"Even he [Nehru] is now hoping only for friendly neutrality from the Soviets rather than active support. All his life he has sought to avoid being dependent upon the United States and the United Kingdom. . . . Now nothing is so important to him, more personally than politically, than to maintain the semblance of this independence. His age no longer allows for readjustment."[39] Galbraith's letter, in *Ambassador's Journal*, goes on:

"I think Nehru is still playing down our role to protect the sensitivities of the Soviets and perhaps, more especially, to protect his own feelings."[40]

In the same letter, Galbraith told Kennedy of yet more trouble brewing. The Pakistanis, he noted, were using the Chinese attack to press for Indian concessions in their own border disputes. American weapons shipments to India didn't sit well with the

Pakistanis, either. As Galbraith noted: "Their disappointment is understandable."[41]

Galbraith says November 21, 1962 was a day of panic in New Delhi. This was the first time he had witnessed a breakdown in public morale. There was talk that 500 enemy paratroopers were going to land in New Delhi. Other rumors had Menon in the process of being reinstated as defense minister. There were exaggerations about the actual extent of the Chinese advance into India. Galbraith suggested that elements of the US Seventh Fleet should be ordered into the Bay of Bengal and that the American airlift of supplies to the Indian troops fighting on the front should be restarted on a regular schedule.

On November 22, the morning newspapers reported that the Chinese wanted a cease-fire. They also wanted to withdraw. Nehru considered the Chinese offers genuine for two reasons: the anger of the Indian people (which Galbraith considered unmatched by their military effectiveness) and the rapid American response to Indian needs. Galbraith writes about meeting with a group of American newsmen who had come thousands of miles to cover a war only to discover that it was fading away. Some wanted Galbraith to advise Nehru not to negotiate with the Chinese. Others wanted to bring in American troops. That day the cease-fire took effect. It was not until Galbraith got to his office that he realized that it was also the American Thanksgiving Day.

In December Galbraith toured the military front. As he wrote to Kennedy, "As on all things having to do with the military, it is a great deal better to be observant and intelligent than to be professional, if you can't be both."[42] Although he was impressed with the Indian Army's training and discipline, Galbraith felt that the Chinese would have had the military edge if the fight had resumed. Indian equipment and tactics seemed particularly outdated.

After returning to the United States in the middle of December, Galbraith writes in his journal, "Everyone, I was assured, believes I handled the Indian-Chinese war in a masterful way. This does not, however, mean that I am universally loved. Rusk, I gather, continues to regard me as a major inconvenience in an otherwise placid organization."[43]

In July 1963, Galbraith resigned his post and left India. President Kennedy would have made him ambassador to Moscow if Galbraith had agreed to learn Russian. The offer tempted Galbraith, but the Harvard professor had had enough of Dean Rusk and the US State Department. It was time to go, to let someone else wear the black silk top hat of the diplomatic service.

When I asked Galbraith about India, Prime Minister Indira Gandhi was still in power, having imposed a dictatorial regime on that country. Galbraith declined to discuss Indian affairs in any detail; unusual for a figure who ordinarily is ready to offer comment on almost any subject. When India was mentioned, his eyes showed a fleeting hint of pain.

Galbraith stresses that his role as ambassador to India was not really very demanding. It allowed him to do a lot of writing, including *Ambassador's Journal.* Some of his most effective writing during this time was devoted to memoranda addressed to the president.

James Perkins, then vice president of the Carnegie Foundation, which had been funding Galbraith's work on what would become *The New Industrial State,* had told Galbraith that he could use his post in India to provide Kennedy with "literate" information on Asia. Galbraith's memos came back thick, fast, and literate — and full of darts at the "bureaucratic truths" the State Department uses to isolate itself from reality. His Mark Epernay (Galbraith's *nom de plume*) essays and *Ambassador's Journal* are witnesses to this constant and often amusing battle.

Sometimes Galbraith's darts at the State Department were caustic, as this memo from *Ambassador's Journal* illustrates:

"Rusk is an amiable Chairman of the Board, but not a leader. And he is singularly devoid of any desire to accomplish anything.

"Individuals are intelligent. But they are so numerous they cancel each other out.

"The senior officials preside but do not work. Thus telegrams and papers get drafted by cautious subordinates and approved by superiors. One should not dream of delegating even the first draft of an important cable.

"Finally, there is an endless faith in oratory and high-level representation. I have put in some fine cables on this. I have just noted in a telegram that they have now reduced letters from the President to Nehru to the level of Confederate money. The President will see and remember this."[44]

Even when Galbraith puts on his novelist's cap, he cannot resist jibing at the State Department. His best-selling novel, *The Triumph*, gives us a couple of glimpses of one of the agency's operatives, Worth Campbell, a rather pathetic man but with some redeeming features:

"There are men whom headwaiters recognize instantly as important. There are others, including many important ones, who invariably dine with the door of the men's room hitting their elbow and to the sound of running water. Worth Campbell, perhaps as a result of his rimless glasses, perhaps because he had need to look impressive only from behind a desk, was one of the latter. . . ."[45]

Later in the novel, Galbraith places Worth Campbell in Paris, and he is alone with the wife of a colleague in her bedroom after dinner and coffee: ". . . a very little later she invited Worth Campbell, with astonishing frankness, to remain and make love. She had no difficulty in discovering that he had at least contemplated the same possibility and commented colorfully on the same phenomenon. He escaped with no small pride in his self-discipline and a heightened awareness of the vulnerability of the basic design of men's pants. He never doubted that she had something more than sex in mind. He continued to be grateful for his self-control although not completely so."[46]

Galbraith's nonfiction and fiction make amply clear why some members of the US Department of State disliked him. Though some may reluctantly accept his expertise as economist and diplomat, the fact that he constantly deprives them of whatever machismo they may feel about themselves is more than most bureaucratic egos can stand.

David Halberstam in *The Best and the Brightest*, a popular book on Washington politics during the Vietnam era, writes about Dean Rusk's reactions to such presidential favorites as Galbraith and Schlesinger: "He [Rusk] worried about the liberals, he was one himself, although not too much of one: did they really understand the Communists, weren't they too likely to come to Washington just long enough to meddle in foreign affairs and fall victims to their own good intentions? Foreign affairs was something special, it was filled with pitfalls for well-meaning idealists."

Halberstam also quotes Galbraith about State Department bureaucrats: "We knew that their experience was nothing and that it was mostly a product of social background and a certain kind of education, and that they were men who had not traveled around the world and knew nothing of this country and the world. All they knew was the difference between a Communist and an anti-Communist. But that made no difference; they had this mystique and it still worked, and those of us who would doubt it, [Richard] Goodwin, Schlesinger, myself, and a few others were like Indians firing occasional arrows into the campsite from the outside."

Both Galbraith and Arthur Schlesinger, Jr., became outspoken critics of the Vietnam war. Early on they perceived the dangers of a massive United States involvement in Indochina, sooner and clearer than many of the people holding positions of power in the Kennedy and Johnson administrations.

"I didn't see it all that clearly until I was out of government," Schlesinger told me. "Ken saw what was happening quite clearly from the very beginning. Kennedy asked him to stop off on a couple of occasions in Saigon and send him a report about what he thought was going on, which he did. But the reason why these reports of Ken's were not acted upon was that the bulk of the national security establishment took another view. They were always under the delusion that with more military force they could win."

Galbraith contends that US foreign policy is made not so much to solve a particular problem as to appease the radical right in our country. Schlesinger said, "This is valid in certain points. His major concern is the extent to which foreign policy is made by a lot of people who are so committed to past policies that they cannot conceive of anything else, and do not have the courage to change. This is the extent to which foreign policy has become a function of the state of mind and the bureaucracy, the New York lawyer-banker type. This is conventional wisdom in the purest sense, because these people see the world as it was in 1950 rather than as it is now or will be in the future."

George Ball, undersecretary of state in the Kennedy administration, who is now a permanent representative to the United Nations, was asked what he thought of Galbraith as a diplomat.

"That's a funny combination of terms, isn't it?" Ball replied.

"Well, I mean his manner is not the most diplomatic in the world. I've known Ken in many different contexts over a number of years. Actually, during the period when he was in India, I thought he was extremely effective in establishing a close relationship with the prime minister [Nehru] on a common intellectual level — and this was a real asset in cementing relations between the Indian government and the government of the United States. I think Nehru had a great respect for him and was impressed with the fact that he was fully erudite and capable of dealing with the kind of abstractions that Nehru was fond of. In addition, Galbraith went through a very critical period in India because of the Chinese invasion of India over the mountain barriers.

"Galbraith had to come back to Washington and persuade the government to provide substantial assistance to India. And he did this effectively. We had our meetings at a very critical time; during the same period we were also talking with the British in Nassau. That conference was addressed primarily to British and American relations affecting the question of continuing our nuclear weapons arrangement with Britain, which was very critical for all of Europe. Galbraith met with President Kennedy and persuaded him to go ahead with that proposal.

"I would say that Galbraith was extremely effective in American government. If anything, from my point of view, he might have been slightly too effective. Nevertheless, there is no doubt that when he set his mind to achieve something, he was extremely persuasive. And he has the ability to mobilize the proper facts and make a very powerful argument.

"I would think that his tour of duty in India was a very successful one, and certainly the quality of his dispatches was somewhat more vivid than what we normally got. However, I am extremely prejudiced about Kenneth. He is one of my oldest and closest friends. I've known him for a very long time. So I tend to resolve all problems in his favor."

One of Galbraith's great accomplishments was the special bond of friendship he forged with India's complex and somewhat mystical prime minister, Jawaharlal Nehru. Nehru said of Galbraith in a speech in the Punjab, July, 1963, "He has done a wonderful job during his tenure in India. He has tried to inspire the Indian people to work harder, grow more, and to industrialize the country. I thank him and the United States Government for their help through these recent years." Nehru was not known for compliments.

Ambassador's Journal leaves me with the feeling that Galbraith must have enjoyed his role as a diplomat. "Oh, yes! It was an enormously good time," he said with joy in his voice. "However, the journal is misleading in one respect. It makes me appear to have been far busier than I actually was, because one only puts down one's activities. You never dwell in a journal on your idleness.

"During my time in India, fifty-five ambassadors were in New Delhi. And, other than the British high commissioner, who was busy for obvious reasons; the Pakistan high commissioner, who was busy for equally obvious reasons; the Russian ambassador, myself, and a few other special cases, the rest of the ambassadors represented one of the greatest exercises of disguised unemployment in all the world. The Brazilian ambassador, the Chilean ambassador, the Mexican ambassador, the Saudi-Arabian ambassador and the Lebanese ambassador would be lucky if they had five minutes of solid work a week.

"An embassy is set up like a state government. It will function with a good ambassador or with a bad ambassador — or with no ambassador at all. So, if you delegate all the administrative tasks, which I did, to people who could do them better — and if you do not worry about the sex life of the secretarial staff or the Marine Corps — you can have lots of time on your hands. The functions which require the attention of the ambassador, either in terms of ceremony or policy, could, most of the time, be disposed of in an hour a day."

I remembered seeing news photos of Galbraith out in the countryside with the people. "I did a lot of traveling because it was part of the theory at the time that it was good for an ambassador to get out and see the country, see the people, and be seen," he told me. "This was a doctrine that Washington promulgated and nobody ever examined it as to whether it amounted to anything or not. But it was an enormously agreeable form of education for the ambassador and not unduly expensive for the United States Government."

Galbraith undertook special assignments in Indochina. He was one of the first to warn about the growing danger of United States involvement in Vietnam.

If President Kennedy had lived, would he have kept the United States from becoming mired in the Vietnam War? "We were not into it when he died," Galbraith replied. "But we were deeper than some of us thought we should have been. This is a question I have always hesitated to answer. If you had asked Johnson in 1963, 'Mr. Vice President, are you going to get us involved in Vietnam, or would you advise it?', he would have said 'No!' If you had asked Kennedy the same thing earlier, he would have given the same answer as Johnson. All of us heard Kennedy say, 'I am not going to get involved in that kind of place.' My impression is that Kennedy would not have gotten involved in the way we eventually did. But what you don't know is how various pressures would have operated on him and how he would have reacted to them."

One of the most influential pressure groups was the New York foreign policy establishment. Galbraith describes its makeup and objectives.

"It can be called both the foreign policy and the East Coast political establishment. During the World War II and Marshall Plan years, a group of prominent businessmen, bankers, and lawyers played a very large role in the War Department. One of the captains of this group was John J. McCloy, who was assistant secretary of war under Henry Stimson. Another was the late William Draper, who was a senior military figure. There was also Paul Hoffman, who headed the Marshall Plan. When the war was over, these men returned to their law offices and businesses in New York City. All of them found their peacetime roles very dull. They went to the Council on Foreign Relations and nostalgically discussed their great days and what was currently happening in the world. They served on commissions in Washington. They became a kind of group of elder statesmen, and they were always available for special assignments. They loved to come to Washington to give advice and become in a way the nonofficial voice of the American people on foreign policy. Into this group also came David and Nelson Rockefeller and John Foster and Allen Dulles.

"This exclusive community remained very influential in American foreign policy through the 1950s and 1960s. Almost all of them, with the rarest exceptions, committed their prestige to the Vietnam war. And they also went down with the war. They all advised on it, urged it, supported it, and as it turned into an increasing disaster, their prestige went down with it. Very few from this group have spoken out on foreign policy since."

During the Vietnam era, many university students who lacked experience in foreign policy identified the issues of the war — and its pitfalls for the United States — and coalesced in political protests. Then how could the experienced members of the New York foreign policy establishment have been blind to its realities?

"Certainly they were men of experience," Galbraith told me. "But you would have to ask whether they were always men of great depth and insight. Much of the American foreign policy of the 1950s and 1960s was based on automatic anti–Communism. This was a notion of a homogeneous and monolithic Communism, and the conspiracy that went along with it. Most of this group accepted these premises. They assumed that the masses would rise up and support any set of rascals, no matter how corrupt, against the Communists. They expected this to happen in Vietnam and in Cambodia. But the masses in those places were not so obliging. So they weren't all that astute. This group of men had an intimate knowledge of Europe but they did not know Asia. Those of us who were familiar with Asia had a very different perception of that part of the world than the New York establishment did.

"One of the sources of our mistake in Vietnam was the Marshall Plan. The Marshall Plan itself was an enormous success of American foreign policy. At the end of World War II, Europe was threatened with disorder and possible takeover by the Communists and it was rescued by massive infusions of American money. This brought about a quick economic recovery and a quick rehabilitation of parliamentary institutions. Even in France, the Communists became one of the minority parties. Since the Marshall Plan worked in Europe, it was assumed that it could serve as a model for accomplishing the goals of American foreign policy in other parts of the world — such as Latin America, Africa, Asia, and particularly Vietnam.

"But the difference was that Europe after the war had honest, responsible leaders. Saigon did not. Europe had a structure of skill, discipline, experience in government and administration which the countries in Indochina did not have. Europe had a working class which had enough stake in society so that it was not genuinely in revolt."

In his writings, Galbraith mentions several different types of underdevelopment in the world. For example, his solution to Latin American underdevelopment is the overthrow of the ruling oligarchies through revolution. Is Galbraith advocating the kind of guerrilla activity Fidel Castro used to gain power in Cuba?

"I have great moral difficulty in ever urging violence for any purpose," Galbraith maintains. "I come from a pacifist background. My instincts are essentially nonviolent. To urge revolution can seem to be a kind of dry ascetic approach which has no particularly alarming sound. Yet, in its violent manifestations, it can be very painful to the participants. Having made that disavowal, one should not doubt that the main barrier to economic development in much of Latin America is the egregious maldistribution of wealth and power. In Latin America, the power has been monopolized by port traders, a few monopolistic firms, and the big landed oligarchies for whom economic development is neither necessary nor desirable. If one looks further and inquires where the most rapid economic development in Latin America has occurred, it is in Mexico, Brazil, and Cuba where the feudal power structure has in one way or another disintegrated.

"Development has come about much more peacefully in Brazil than it has in Mexico or Cuba. But development in northern Brazil, where you still have the old feudal land and social structures from colonial times, has been very slow. In southern Brazil, particularly in the Sao Paulo region, where that whole structure has broken down completely, you have had very rapid economic development."

Some people consider Brazil as an example of a nation where right-wing military control works. I asked Galbraith to comment: "After a certain amount of economic development, you can no longer have a monopoly of power by any one group. Trade unions come into existence. Intellectuals want more of a voice in running things. The small business community feels it must participate in the exercise of public power. This is the passage which Portugal and Spain are now in the process of making, and which will come about one of these days in Brazil.

"We think of parliamentary democracy as being the peculiar act of virtue of Americans and Northern Europeans. The fact is that it is something that becomes more or less inevitable when you reach a certain stage of industrial development. Then no group can have a monopoly of power. It has to be shared. The best way of sharing power is through some kind of parliamentary process."

Galbraith's years in India renewed and sharpened his interest in the enigma to the north — China. Years later — in September 1972 — Galbraith, Wassily Leontief, and James Tobin, each a past president of the American Economic Association, traveled to the People's Republic of China. In a sense, for Galbraith this trip was an ironic twist. In his Senate confirmation hearings to become ambassador to India, Galbraith had advocated a two-China policy. During the border dispute between India and China, Galbraith played a key role in getting the Chinese to back down by funneling massive American support in arms and supplies to the Indians. But what was even more ironic was the fact that his entry into China was made possible by a political figure whom he dislikes, President Richard Nixon.

That particular month was a key one for Galbraith to be away from the United States. His close friend Senator George McGovern was campaigning for the presidency against Richard Nixon. Even if Galbraith had remained in America, he could have done little to help McGovern. In retrospect, perhaps Galbraith's time was best spent in China. The trip also allowed him the opportunity to publish a journal of his trip — *A China Passage*.

On September 8, 1972, Galbraith, Leontief, and Tobin crossed the border from Hong Kong into the People's Republic of China. Their first stop was at the city of Canton, where they were met by a delegation from the Chinese Scientific and Technical Association. Galbraith describes Canton: "The older streets are arcaded like those of Calcutta but are wide and straight and — by New York standards — of cleanly elegance."[47] One studies the faces: everyone seems to be in excellent humor.

"I asked why people seemed to be working so hard and was told that it was because of Chairman Mao and the feeling that the country belongs to them."[48]

At one of their luncheons, the three professors decided that they would eat Chinese style. So they asked for chopsticks, and for their meal they received beef bouillon and lamb chops.

In Peking there were more warm speeches of friendship and cooperation. Galbraith writes, "But they [the speeches] are a long step from the warning of four or five years back about a billion Asian Communists debouching over Asia armed with nuclear weapons."[49] Then he becomes magnanimous in his remarks: "Fairly high marks must be given to the men who moved us on this path, meaning Messrs. Nixon and Kissinger."[50]

Galbraith wrote *A China Passage* before the Watergate affair unfolded; however, Galbraith does not deny Nixon's contribution to the improved relations between the United States and China — a contribution that only a conservative Republican president could have carried off.

Galbraith observes in *A China Passage* that Chinese economists were required to identify theory with practice, whereas American economists were divorcing theory from practice. And he notes, "On various occasions in the past I would gladly have exchanged the chairman of our department at Harvard for any available Chinese scholar."[51] After much sightseeing through imperial palaces, Galbraith had dinner at a restaurant that served him a meal consisting only of duck: duck hearts, duck wings, duck soup from bones, brown crisp duck skin, duck livers, duck tail. Galbraith says it was the most exquisite dinner he had ever eaten, and then comments: "Voltaire said he would not be pecked to death by ducks. For these ducks he should have made an exception."[52]

Galbraith and his fellow professors were taken to the Great Wall of China. Unfortunately, the visibility from the Great Wall was obscured by fog and drizzle. He noticed, however, that visitors had carved their names, countries, and the dates of their visits into the stonework of the wall — particularly a group of Albanians who had passed through, "all with a chisel that they evidently brought along for the work. Neither Nixon nor Kissinger is there, which is greatly to their credit. We did not look for Walter Cronkite,"[53] writes Galbraith.

On a visit to a Peking department store, Galbraith states that the markup cost is 13 percent, with a 7 percent net profit. In contrast, the markup in a US department store is much higher — around 40 percent. He also points to the advantages of the Chinese system of merchandising: no slow-selling expensive goods, almost no showing of styles, almost no fitting of clothes, very few returns of goods, no credit or credit cards, no green stamps, no advertising, no shoplifting, no elevators, no escalators. "The store would not do well in Westchester. It seems right for Peking,"[54] Galbraith writes.

At a textile mill he visited, 70 percent of the working force was women, working three shifts, six days a week. On Mondays the mill is closed — both for maintenance and workers' days off. There are no vacations as such. A developing country cannot afford holidays, Galbraith was told. One of the signs in the mill told the workers to "save every ounce of cotton, every inch of yarn, every drop of oil to serve socialist revolution and construction."[55]

On September 14, 1972, Galbraith gave a lecture at the University of Peking. Observing a display in the Archeology department, he comments, "I had not realized how much Peking Man resembles Mike Wallace."[56]

Galbraith's longstanding sinus condition has occasionally put him out of commission for brief periods. In Peking one severe sinus attack forced him into bed, and he missed going to the Temple of Heaven. Later he recovered enough to be interviewed by the *Toronto Globe and Mail*. The reporter, Galbraith writes in *A China Passage*, "was pleased to learn that I had been reared on the old Toronto *Globe* in a community in which no one risked an opinion until the *Globe* had spoken, except where basic truths had previously been published by the same paper. The accepted truths included beneficence of lower tariffs, prohibition of all alcoholic beverages, private enterprise, public ownership of utilities, an amiable attitude toward the United States, undeviating support of the Liberal Party, and an intelligently dubious view of aristocratic pretension in general and that of the British Royal Family in particular."[57]

On the train to Nanking, Galbraith awoke to stirring music coming from the corridor. Galbraith admired it and asked Leontief what the music was. Both men perhaps were surprised that Galbraith hadn't recognized *The Internationale.* In Nanking itself, a city of 2.3 million people, some 600 factories employed 400,000 people. When Chiang Kai-shek left the city before it was taken by the Reds, it had only 30 small plants employing 30,000. In this area the Yangtze River is one mile wide. The Chinese are very proud of a steel bridge spanning this distance, and sightseers are taken across for two and a half American cents. Galbraith was taken out to the suburbs to visit the Mausoleum of Sun Yat-sen, the founder of modern China.

Their visit to Shanghai took the professors to the Tsao Yang Number Two Middle School. A thirty-foot sign hung out in front proclaiming: "Welcome the American Economists."[58] One person who greeted him was "a girl of fourteen or fifteen, slender, with braided hair and a face of ceramic beauty."[59] Later Galbraith asked his lovely friend from the Red Guards which subjects the students liked best. She told him that the students liked all their subjects because they all served to create a better China. However, she preferred Chinese history because it "raised political conscious-ness."[60]

In his analysis of the Chinese economy in *A China Passage*, Galbraith ended with these observations: "As compared with the Eastern European economies or that of the Soviet Union, the Chinese economy sustains a far lower standard of living. . . ."[61] Although the Chinese living standard is lower and much more egalitarian, Galbraith felt that "very simply, the economy works better than in Russia and Poland."[62]

"Ever since Lincoln Steffens returned from Russia to proclaim (to Bernard Baruch), 'I have been over into the future and it works,' travelers to the Communist countries have been reluctant to risk hard conclusions,"[63] Galbraith writes in *A China Passage*. "When things went wrong, the skeptics remembered and rejoiced. One should not be craven. The Chinese economy isn't the American or European future. But it is the Chinese future. And let there be no doubt; for the Chinese it works."[64]

The very last sentences of *A China Passage* are Galbraithian gems: "For years I have been taking evasive action whenever I encountered a Harvard colleague whom I knew to have been traveling in some improbable place and who would wish to tell of his dreary adventures. I spot such people at the Faculty Club and sit at another table. I see them in the Yard and duck into Widener.

If they invite us to dinner, I develop a sinus attack. They know what I've done. There is now no one, absolutely no one, who will want to listen to my China odyssey, which, unlike the annals of my friends, is really interesting. How sad! I should have foreseen that I would one day need an audience."[65]

Is war between the United States and the Soviet Union inevitable? According to Galbraith, the Soviets once thought so, as did many Americans. In *The Age of Uncertainty* Galbraith cites five factors that changed such beliefs on both sides: Khrushchev's leadership, the Cuban crisis, the war in Vietnam, sharp divisions within the Communist world itself, and the inability of the human mind to "accept persuasion that is in conflict with evidence."[66]

Galbraith considers Khrushchev one of the decisive men of our time. After Stalin's death, Khrushchev made significant changes in Soviet society. He denounced Stalinist terror, lessened the people's fear of their government, allowed more debate within the system, made the intellectual and cultural life of the country more liberal, and stated that in an atomic war it would be difficult to tell the difference between the ashes of Communists and capitalists. His theme to non–Communist countries was peaceful coexistence, and he traveled widely to sell this idea.

Khrushchev once told Nehru that Stalin "had made the name of the Soviet Union a stench in the nostrils of the civilized world. His task was to see that this was changed,"[67] Galbraith writes.

"Nothing in the Cold War years was more striking than the incapacity of the scholarly personnel of the CIA for talented falsehood,"[68] Galbraith writes in *The Age of Uncertainty*. "Perhaps this was not surprising. They had been well brought up in good families, had gone to good schools, and had been hired on the basis of character and intelligence. So they were without experience in sustainable mendacity."[69]

The Cuban missile crisis followed the Bay of Pigs. In *The Age of Uncertainty*, Galbraith points out that during the latter crisis, American generals threatened the Communists with nuclear destruction and expected the American people to accept this kind of action with patriotic fervor. Some of President Kennedy's advisers urged a "surgical air strike"[70] against Russian missile sites in Cuba. Others, notably Adlai Stevenson, George Ball, and Robert Kennedy, felt that there must be an alternative and argued for restraint. Galbraith recalls going to the theater with President and Mrs. Kennedy after the crisis. Kennedy told Galbraith that during the crisis he received a great deal of reckless advice. "The worst, he said, was from those who were afraid to be sensible."[71]

Galbraith acknowledges the massive economic power wielded by weapons manufacturers. Galbraith sees their power in terms of magnitudes: the amount of money spent on several supersonic bombers could build a modern mass transportation system in almost every city in the United States. "There is a chance that, with passing years, the economic question will not be what will take the place of military spending. Rather, it will be how military resources can be economized to make way for the other, more urgent claims of an increasing classless consumption. The economic pressures will be for agreement on arms limitation, not against it,"[72] Galbraith argues.

Soviet scientists and other intellectuals who might promote convergence, peaceful competition, and an expansion of human liberty without abandoning the social benefits of communism, are held in low repute — sometimes even exiled or imprisoned. In the United States, it would be unjust to say that the industrial system is heavily dependent on the manufacture and sale of weapons because the members of the technostructure are bloodthirsty or thrilled by the spectacle of war. Certainly patriotism and a desire to have a strong defense to protect what freedom we enjoy are, without a doubt, worthwhile motives. But, according to Galbraith, their real motives are rather pragmatic: the US-USSR arms race provides the greatest amount of money to the industrial system. This money supports the planning which brings about the successful achievement of industry's goals without much interference from outsiders.

But the United States and the Soviet Union are not the only countries with weapons to build and sell; Great Britain and France also compete with the United States. And there are eager buyers all over the world — developing nations and new industrialized nations without weapons manufacturing of their own. Selling weapons to whomever will buy them, regardless of political ideology, is one of the richest games in the world. No wonder so many industrial nations play it.

11
GALBRAITH
IN GOVERNMENT
AND POLITICS

Galbraith has been involved in Democratic politics for most of his life in the United States. His first political job was as deputy administrator for the Office of Price Administration under Franklin D. Roosevelt. He was the principal organizer of the wartime system of price controls, and he headed this operation until 1943.

Later Galbraith was a director of the US Strategic Bombing Survey which went into Germany after World War II to study the effects of Allied bombing. He was one of the first observers to point out the degree to which Nazi Germany — far from being a model of fighting efficiency — mishandled its war effort. Galbraith called attention to the fact that Germany went to a full war-production basis only after the war was, in effect, lost. At the time he said, in a *Fortune* article, "The simple fact is that Germany should never have lost the war it started"; the reasons he gave for Germany's failure were undermobilization and overconfidence.

There were other political offices; there was the award of the Medal of Freedom by President Harry S. Truman. Galbraith, who had been attending Democratic conventions since 1940, was active as a partisan politician, serving as a speechwriter and adviser for Adlai E. Stevenson in his unsuccessful races against Dwight D. Eisenhower in 1952 and 1956.

However, Galbraith's deepest and most influential involvement in politics began with the arrival on the national scene of John F. Kennedy.

A portrait of President John F. Kennedy is among the photographs and political cartoons that decorate Galbraith's Harvard offices. Kennedy is seated, looking relaxed and confident. It represents Galbraith's active participation in the Kennedy administration. Had there been no Kennedy or Camelot, obviously Galbraith would still have made his mark as an unorthodox economist and a famous writer. But his contributions to the Kennedy administration — as speechwriter, economist, adviser, diplomat, and friend — helped to increase his international reputation.

Galbraith's association with the Kennedys dates back to his friendship with the late Joseph P. Kennedy, Jr., when the oldest Kennedy brother was a student at Harvard. Later, as a leader in the Democratic party, Galbraith was an early and enthusiastic supporter of John F. Kennedy. He encouraged Kennedy to run for the presidency, helped develop some of his ideas in domestic and foreign affairs, and helped write a few — only a few he says — of the late president's speeches.

Galbraith worked with Theodore Sorensen on Kennedy's inauguration speech. On Inauguration Day itself, Galbraith sat close to the podium where Richard Cardinal Cushing of Boston "began by exhorting God and ended by instructing Him,"[1] Galbraith writes in *Ambassador's Journal*. During the cardinal's speech the podium caught fire. John Steinbeck, who was also on the podium, said to Galbraith that he had his own conversation with the Almighty and that God said to Steinbeck, "I hadn't realized there was anything much going on in the United States until around noon, and then I received one hell of a blast."[2]

When Galbraith went to the White House to discuss the State of the Union speech with the new president and his advisers, Kennedy took him by the arm and showed him where Ike's golf shoes had poked innumerable holes in the office floor. One day in February a heavy snowstorm kept Galbraith in Washington. During a long conversation, Arthur Schlesinger, Jr., revealed that he was unhappy about his post at the White House. Galbraith says that the matter was eventually resolved, but that it confirmed his belief that no sane man would go into a staff job in Washington. He felt that people should get their power from the jobs themselves, a line responsibility, rather than from the person above. A job must not be one where the president wants to see a particular individual but one where he *must* see him.

Galbraith recalls that the Navy-run mess was one of the most pleasant things about the White House, where the food was both good and properly served. He mentions that the conversation at the White House was much the same as at the Harvard Faculty Club, mainly because it involved the same people. One of Kennedy's unexpected pleasures, according to Galbraith, was in reading the FBI dossiers on the people he selected for his administration. Kennedy told Galbraith that the documents would keep everyone from public life if their contents were revealed.

Paul Samuelson was also one of President Kennedy's economic advisers. He told me, "Galbraith has often had influence, but on the other hand, it would be very difficult for a learned scholar to document his influence or lack of it — such as in the Kennedy administration. He was constantly writing to the president. And he was always coming back to Washington and disagreeing with the president's other economic advisers. By the way, Kennedy liked Galbraith. People like me were just advisers. People like Ken were friends. But Kennedy liked some of Galbraith's economic ideas — and he thought a lot of them were awful."

Economist Walter Heller recalls Galbraith's role during the Kennedy administration, when Galbraith tried to put his theories into political reality: "I think back over some of our old battles. You always think back with amusement coupled with whatever annoyance or disagreement you had with him.

"It was our battle over the tax cut, in 1963, when he kept coming back from India and insisting that public needs were so great that we had no business cutting taxes. The reality of the situation was that Kennedy was knocking his head against a brick wall in the form of Congress, trying to get expenditure increases as the only way to get the economy moving again," Heller said. "This was something he had pledged himself to do and cutting taxes was vitally necessary to accomplish his goals. But Ken's long shadow kept falling across the scene at the White House — arguing for expenditure increases. Sure, in our hearts, we all wanted them. But in our heads, we knew we couldn't get them."

The last entry in Galbraith's *Ambassador's Journal* is dated

November 26, 1963. On Friday, November 22, Galbraith was in the New York office of Katherine Graham, the head of *The Washington Post* and *Newsweek,* when a staff man suddenly entered her office and said, "I think I should interrupt. President Kennedy has just been shot in Dallas."[3] Later, television and radio announcements broadcast the news: "The president of the United States is dead."[4]

In *The Ambassador's Journal,* Galbraith makes these observations of President John F. Kennedy: "No one knew the President well. In a sense no one could, for it is part of the character of a leader that he cannot be known. The rest of us can indulge our moments when we open the shutters to our soul.[5]

"But he carried his armour lightly and with grace and, one sometimes thought, with the knowledge that having it without escape, at least it need not be a barrier before his friends and associates. He surprised even friends with the easy candor with which he spoke of touchy problems, half-formed plans, or personal political dangers. Without malice or pettiness, he contemplated the strengths and weaknesses of high officials and influential politicians. He was constantly and richly amused by the vanities of men in high places. He freely discussed ideas the mention of which would make most men shudder. No president ever said so much to so many friends and acquaintances and so rarely had to disavow or explain. . . .[6]

"Like all men of deep intelligence, he respected the intelligence of others. That was why he did not talk down to the American people. . . .[7]

"Knowledge is power. But knowledge without character and wisdom is nothing, or worse. These the President also had in rich measure. I suspect, in fact, that few men in history have ever combined natural ability with such powers of mental self-discipline."[8]

Kennedy's death by no means ended Galbraith's activities as a politician. At the 1968 Democratic convention he was a floor manager for Eugene McCarthy, and, in 1972, as he says, "a McGovern archon."

In an *Esquire* article (1960), Caroline Bird writes, "To Galbraith, politics is more than an exhilarating and sometimes literally exhausting release of personal aggression. It is an art form particularly suited to intellectuals because its material is ideas — at least for Democrats, he would add."

Galbraith observes that "the United States is the only country that ever converted politics into a spectator sport. The whole political process in the United States has become a great fascinating game that attracts an enormous amount of interest and invention. If the casting is good, the people involved will range from very intelligent to very ridiculous. And the show, in consequence, is very much enjoyed. In order to maintain the enjoyment and to maintain the extraordinary amount of employment for people working for the press and television, one has to invent great political moves and strategies, and to analyze these whether they exist or not."

Any nation's economic policy ultimately rests with its political leaders and their advisers. How does Galbraith view American presidents' roles in setting economic policy? "Economic policy is not likely to be a favorite field of activity for any president," Galbraith told me. "It is a dull subject, and it involves dull people coming in with contentious positions which are hard to reconcile. Determining the difference between the right policy and the wrong policy is not a matter on which the president can easily reach into his own experience and then make the necessary decisions. Economic decisions being unpleasant as compared with those in the more glamorous areas of foreign or military policy, it is often hard to get the president's attention."

Diplomacy in foreign affairs is the handmaiden of politics. With his great interest in and experience with politics, I wondered why Galbraith never sought elective office himself. Several years ago, in Massachusetts, his name would occasionally surface as a possible candidate for governor or senator, and then within a short time it would fade out of the political spotlight. Perhaps at this point in his life kissing babies and shaking hands at factory gates would be a bit too much for him, even as energetic as he is. On the other hand, at the opposite political pole, S.I. Hayakawa, in his seventies, defeated the incumbent in the 1976 California senatorial race. Does Galbraith harbor any desire to run for office?

"In the past I would hear recurrently that I would run for the Senate. I always permitted that discussion to continue just long enough to reward my vanity. I thought of it seriously in Massachusetts only once. And that was to run against Ed Brooke [Senator Edward Brooke, Republican from Massachusetts and the only black US Senator]. However, I was restrained for a variety of reasons, including the terrible thought that I couldn't beat Ed."

Is there anything positive about the Republican party, I asked. "Oh, sure," Galbraith said. "I'm basically in favor of the two-party system in America — but with the liberal Democrats in power."

When politicians seek election or reelection, they seem to come out of hiding in Washington to meet the voters. They are typically photographed shaking hands with a blue-collar worker or housewife, trying to give the impression that they are in touch with ordinary people. Once they win office, they disappear until the next election. I asked Galbraith what he thought of the quality of the US Congress.

"I would emphasize one thing in this age of self-flagellation and self-criticism, and that is that no institution in my lifetime has improved so much as the Congress of the United States. An absolute world of difference separates what the Congress was like in the 1930s when I first came to Washington, and what it is today. Today's representatives and senators are far better in quality. They have better educational backgrounds. They are, on the whole, much more professionally competent and far more honest. And, they are far less given to rhetoric and demagoguery.

"The typical southern senator forty years ago was someone like 'Cotton' Ed Smith, a man from the boondocks of South Carolina. He had been in the Senate for almost half a century. He combined a certain legislative cunning — a great knowledge of the legislative process — with the greatest collection of ingrown rural prejudices you can possible imagine. Furthermore, his personal hygiene was deplorable. He would begin a hearing by pulling a plug of tobacco out of his pocket, putting the plug in his mouth and sending great streams of tobacco juice flowing onto the floor. The witnesses appearing before him had to move their feet constantly to avoid the flood."

During our interviews, in 1976, Galbraith and I talked about Jimmy Carter's astonishingly rapid rise in national politics. I asked Galbraith if he thought that Americans would find it difficult to accept a leader who speaks with a southern accent.

"Oh sure, there's no question about it. Until very recent times, the one legitimate form of race prejudice in the United States was against white southerners. It still operates to some extent against rich Texans.

"When I was president-elect of the American Economic Association, I had occasion to put on a program dealing with southern regional development. The meetings that year were held in New Orleans in the homeland of a black friend of mine, Vivian Henderson. I put Henderson in charge of a program which had to do with economic problems of the South, not with the issue of race. I called Vivian up after a few weeks and asked him how he was getting on in selecting speakers. Henderson said to me, 'Do you realize what the most oppressed minority in our association is? It is American economists who are also white professors in the South.'

"The main strength of the Democratic party lies in the fact that its adherents feel that they have automatic access to it. It is not so much the party of the left, although it tends to be. If you want to express yourself, you can always find a home there. It is where the Irish went. It is where the Italians went. It is where the Jews went. It is where the Spanish-Americans have gone. And the most extraordinary proof of the fact is that the Democratic party, identified in the past with black oppression, has become in the end the place where the blacks can express themselves."

Galbraith went on to characterize the differences between the Democrats and the Republicans. "The Democratic party is basically made up of a great aggregation of people seeking a voice in the political process. I think the Republican party is essentially two things: people who have made it, and people who identify with the protection of earned affluence. In addition, it is the party of people who view themselves having over the years earned the right out of present or past service to the country to speak for the character of the country and its virtues. It is a kind of Daughters of the American Revolution mentality which gives them the feeling that they were meant by their heritage to speak for the natural American virtues. This right to speak excludes eastern intellectuals, blacks, Orientals, Latin-Americans, European ethnics, and the rest of the great mass of people who compose the Democratic party, or even those who compose the liberal wing of the Republican party. This is a problem which Nelson Rockefeller faced. I'm certainly prepared to defend Nelson against the charge of excessive liberalism.

But Nelson Rockefeller has been around too long. He also knows too many people who collect modern paintings and abstract and slightly communistic art. Nelson isn't really considered to be a good custodian of the American virtues. And he is so perceived by the conservatives of his party.

"I believe there is something which explains the differences between the relative cheerfulness and the avidity with which Democrats embrace the idea of government and the fear and distaste with which Republicans generally regard government. Democrats see it as an avenue to the achievement of the changes they seek. The Republicans and the conservatives see it as the source of inevitable defeat."

Many politicians today are trying to avoid the liberal label and the American public seems to be moving toward the right. While acknowledging that shift, Galbraith does not believe liberalism is being ejected because its solutions are perceived to be too costly, too inefficient, and essentially unequal.

Galbraith said, "The Republicans in office had the singular capacity of attacking government as being incompetent and then proceeding to make it so, which is a great tactical advantage. Also in the United States the voice of the privileged class is so much more articulate that it is regularly mistaken as being the voice of the masses. This mistake is made even by liberals. We have had so many complaints from the rich about taxes and about the regulations to which corporations are subject that liberals have come to imagine that this must be the voice of the people at large.

Although his *The Age of Uncertainty* considers many of the social and economic crises of the past, Galbraith says that humanity can point to two centuries of impressive achievements. In Ricardo's time, poverty was accepted as part of the natural order of things. Today millions of people live relatively affluent, comfortable lives. Human beings have walked on the moon, sent scientific instruments to other planets, pumped oil from the ocean's depth and the Arctic tundra, created impressive communications devices such as the telephone and television, invented computers which can do the work of people and teach other machines to work, and eradicated many serious diseases.

Galbraith maintains that social existence is a process whereby solutions produced more problems to solve. In addition to wanting solutions to problems, Galbraith says that equally as important are the mechanisms by which problems are solved, those of democratic government.

The power struggle between the United States and the Soviet Union can be shifted away from weapons to scientific and engineering competition, Galbraith believes. The key factor in this shift is that the magnitude of the competition must be sufficiently large in scale, have great technological complexity, and cost an immense amount of money.

Although the substitution of scientific competition for weapons competition makes sense, and may actually evolve in time if tensions continue to relax through disarmament action rather than mere discussion, the Soviet Union, nevertheless, continues to be a dictatorship of the proletariat.

"Only on rare occasions do you find the average man has a chance to make himself heard. I remember hearing of an incident in 1962 when Edward Kennedy first ran for the Senate. He was shaking hands outside of a factory in Worcester, Massachusetts. At that point in the campaign it was being held against Ted that he didn't have a great wealth of experience for the office. At the factory gate this old man with a rich Irish brogue came up to Kennedy and shook his hand. He said, 'Well, Teddy, me boy, I have read in the newspaper that you have never done a day's work in your life.' Before Ted had a chance to reply, the old man told him, 'Let me tell you something. You haven't missed a thing.' "

Galbraith feels that we do not make proper use of senior politicians in the United States: "In many ways the Canadian counterpart of the House of Lords deserves much more attention than it is given. The great problem in all countries is what to do with retired politicians. A novel could be written on the terrible darkness into which a politician descends on the day he is defeated or retires. One day the lights shine on him; he is at the head of the parade. Next day all is dark."

I offered that this is true of generals, as well. "But generals can always go to work in industry; it is far worse for former ambassadors, if they can't write books," Galbraith replied. "But it is worst of all for a politician whose life has been spent depending on public adulation.

"The British system, through the House of Lords, gives a man a highly fraudulent title which allows him to listen to debates a few times a year and have some symbols of continuing importance. That is good. But, the arrangement is weakened by the fact that these former political leaders go to the House of Lords in association with the hereditary peers, who give a rather depraved and sometimes illiterate aspect to that legislative body. However, most of the hereditary peers do not go to the House of Lords anymore anyway.

"The Canadian system is ideal. When people have finished political service, they are appointed to the Senate at a handsome salary. The title senator is quite good as well. And, if they wish they can even do some work of one sort or another. It's a fine arrangement. Any aged or inconvenient politician can always be made a senator."

CHAPTER **12**
TREND
TO THE
RIGHT

I s Galbraith's brand of liberalism dying in America? Is there a trend to the Right? The mood of the American public seems to be moving in that direction. And the new breed of Democratic politicians, such as President Carter and Governors Brown (California) and Dukakis (Massachusetts) appears at times to be more at home with conservative values than with liberal ideology à la Galbraith.

Historian Arthur Schlesinger, Jr., discussed this trend with me. "I don't feel beleaguered by it," Schlesinger said. "I doubt that Ken does either. If you only look at the polls, people now tend to identify themselves as conservatives rather than as liberals. But if you ask them specific questions about the role of government, they generally are in favor of more positive government action in solving specific problems. I think you have to distinguish between the symbolism of the trend and its substance. The substance of liberalism is inevitably going to move our society toward liberal solutions."

I raised the same question with William F. Buckley, Jr., whose conservative credentials are impressive. "Well, I wish it were definitely so. I don't think it is. Galbraith is dogmatic about his central addiction to the uses of government, and he is able to swing around and adopt this thesis or another thesis depending upon what he considers to be the most saleable nostrum of the day," Buckley replied.

But how can one account for the fact that there seems to be a movement to the Right in the United States, while at the same time there is a trend toward socialism through the rest of the world? "I think there you have a genuine paradox," Buckley told me. "Irving Kristol says that paradoxically even as socialism has become theoretically discredited, its forms continue to encroach. And the reason they do, I think, is most easily understood in purely human terms. If you fail to make the kind of progress that your ideological conceits tell you that you've got to make, you do not characteristically show the kind of humility you should. When Gomulka, Poland's former chief of state, briefly permitted private agricultural planting in his country, in 1956, the harvest went up by 65 percent in two years. Whereupon, he promptly outlawed it."

But Galbraith feels that the American system and the Soviet system have, in fact, reached a point of convergence because the goals of both bureaucracies, in their use of technology and planning, are somewhat similar. Galbraith also stresses that we should not be swept up by the exaggerated dangers of Communism that conservatives frequently and emotionally stir up.

"I think that the Soviet Union with a Gross National Product which is 35 percent of ours and which spends $140 billion on strategic weapons is up to something," Buckley said. "The fact of the matter is that they do not want to wage a nuclear war, even a successful one. They want something else. They want to dominate the politics of the world. And they think that they can do it by the presence of this kind of force and by acts of diplomacy. It seems to me the indications are, more than at any time in the past 15 years, that the Russians are succeeding with this."

In Galbraith's article, "The Economic Problems of the Left," in the February 1976 issue of *The New Statesman,* he calls socialism the "dustbin of capitalism." "Public ownership is for those industries where private enterprise has one of two characteristics: either its performance is no longer tolerable or private capitalism is no longer profitable.

"There is now no industrial country in which private enterprise provides good housing, good medical care, good hospitalization, good public transportation, at prices that people of modest means can afford," Galbraith writes. "These happen to be the industries — housing, health care, transportation — that are difficult to do without. So in all countries they have been taken over, in greater or less measure, by the state."

Galbraith holds that a continuing series of "booms and busts" are inevitable and can be effectively controlled only by permanent wage and price controls. Paul Samuelson — himself a leading authority on Keynes — disagrees. He believes that the United States has a mixed economy consisting of an energetic free enterprise sector and a strong government sector, the latter often involving itself to the detriment of the private sector and the general economic well-being of the nation. Samuelson maintains that the consumer is sovereign in the marketplace, that the consumer's needs and wants determine what products will be made and sold, that the American economy is subject to the free play of economic forces, such as competition, and that it is not controlled by any Galbraithian-like "planning system." Moreover, Samuelson believes inflation can be stopped by cutting government spending and balancing the budget. Samuelson feels that contemporary economic thought has moved beyond Galbraith's theories.

During an earlier "trend to the Right," the McCarthy era, Galbraith, although a left-winger of some prominence, was not drawn into the inquisitions of Senator Joseph McCarthy in the early 1950s. I asked him why this was so.

"Well, I suppose, it was partly owing to caution. In the 1930s, I was concerned with the technical matters of my field, agricultural economics — the branch of economics furthest removed from Marxism. And, while Marx greatly influenced my thinking, I had never made the political commitment to socialism or communism. I was always a New Dealer, a reformer. I was always politically a Democrat. However, I'm sure the FBI dossier on me is quite considerable [he has since obtained it and it is] and, I have had numerous associates who were, at one time or another, Communists.

"I followed two rules during the McCarthy era. Where others were passive, I would react aggressively by attacking the people who attacked me.

"That was one rule. People will think twice if they know they are going to be hit themselves in return. The other was never to conceal anything. You only became vulnerable if you tried to cover something up, with it then being discovered.

"In the mid-1950s, a little after the peak of the McCarthy period and just after I had published *The Great Crash*, I was called to testify before the Senate Banking and Currency Committee. While I was testifying, the stock market slumped. Homer Capehart, a senator from Indiana, reacted to my testimony by saying that my undermining of the stock market was probably Communist-inspired. He dug out a pamphlet which I had written at the end of World War II for the National Planning Association. I had written something to the effect that one of the great weaknesses of the non–Communist Left in Europe was that it didn't have the same reputation for redressing grievances as the Communist Left had. By selective pulling out of quotes, Senator Capehart was able to extract from my pamphlet a mildly impressive endorsement of Communism.

"I responded with a powerful attack on him. By a great bit of good luck, this pamphlet was the result of a speech I had given at, of all places, Notre Dame University. And by a second piece of good luck, shortly after Capehart unleashed his attack on me, I happened to be at a meeting at Purdue University, also in his home state. So, I held a press conference there, and I followed the rule that nobody who is under attack of this sort should be too modest. Any senator who didn't know my views, which were part of modern American history, had no business representing the state of Indiana. As you can imagine, this got considerable play in the local papers.

"It went pretty much as I hoped," Galbraith recalled to me. "Capehart retreated and apologized. He wasn't a malicious figure. But he did suffer certain intellectual handicaps.

"I was always a little puzzled when in 1952, McCarthy attacked the people who were with Stevenson when he ran for president. He attacked Arthur Schlesinger, Jr., Bernard DeVoto, Archibald MacLeish and others. But he never attacked me. This neglect was rather damaging to my prestige."

I wondered if McCarthy were afraid of him. "In 1953, McCarthy told a Boston newspaperman named John Harriman, 'I'll have to do something about this university of yours up at Harvard.' Harriman asked, 'You mean people like Schlesinger and Galbraith?' 'No,' said McCarthy. 'I want people who are politically more innocent than they are.' "

But McCarthy had damaged the careers of many individuals who genuinely feared him, and their fear was one of the reasons why they did not reveal their past. If some of them had been as strong as Galbraith, might they have survived McCarthy, I wondered.

"I'm not suggesting that I was strong," Galbraith replied. "All of us after the 1952 campaign looked forward with real concern to the forthcoming attack. The Republicans came in after this long period of Democratic rule, and I was fairly active in the Democratic party. I had several months of uneasiness expecting that I would be one of the considerable number of liberals who would now come under fire. It wasn't something that I was particularly looking forward to. I gave a lot of thought to how disagreeable it would be. But, by the time the attack came, which was later, I had gotten myself in hand, so that I was able to hit back, and eventually with some pressure. Non-concealment was very important here. The atmosphere of the late 1940s and the 1950s was such that a large number of liberals tried to deny their past. That led others to think that it was wicked, criminal. They set themselves up for the attack.

"I don't know whether Alger Hiss was guilty or not," Galbraith told me. "But let us assume that the first time he was asked about Whittaker Chambers, instead of denying their relationship, he had said, 'Certainly I knew Whittaker Chambers. We were all active members of the Left. Those were my views, and I was closely associated with people of similar views in the Department of Agriculture. I had great sympathy for the Soviet experiment.' If he said things like that the whole case against him would have been deflated." Galbraith said, "Liberal intellectuals worry about their particular stock in trade, which is their freedom of speech and thought. I do. I wouldn't like to live under a form of government where I could not express myself.

"The conservative property owner worries about his possessions. You have here a natural alliance which is formidable. No one should ever doubt that the much larger objection to Communism is that Communists are not thought to be overly friendly to private property."

He chastizes liberals for siding with conservatives in wanting to cut taxes. Galbraith feels that the "rational liberal" will resist tax cuts that might at first appear to benefit the poor. He challenges liberals to attack the loopholes in the present tax system, loopholes that are advantageous to the rich and that maintain the condition of inequality. For one who is considered to be a pillar of the liberal establishment, Galbraith is often caustic about liberals. He has, for example, referred to liberals as "summer soldiers," who flock to Washington when there is an administration that they like. When the excitement diminishes, he said, the liberals go back to the campus, or to journalism, or the law. "On the whole," Galbraith observed, "conservatives are more stable."

"The Left must never be beguiled by the economists' claim that through some combination of fiscal or monetary magic, there can be price stability and full employment while leaving prices and income to the market. If that were possible, the formula would have been found before now. Let us not forget that there is no vested interest greater than that of the textbook economist in the market," he told me.

Galbraith insists on what he sees as the critical distinction between indigenous nationalist Communist movements and what used to be called the monolithic international Communist conspiracy. For example, in an interview published in *Playboy* in June 1968 he noted that we have assisted nationalist Communism in Yugoslavia, and that many felt it should be encouraged in Poland and Rumania. Why, then, he asked, should we fight it in Vietnam? He said, "What we are concerned with in South Vietnam is an indigenous nationalist movement. The Communists are concerned with this movement, certainly; they are even paramount; but the movement has strong nationalist roots . . . it's giving us trouble because the Viet Cong has managed to associate itself with the patriotic and national sentiment of a very large proportion of the people there."

His distaste for the cold war has fortified prevailing impressions of him as a left-winger. In the same 1968 interview he expressed his views on where he felt US foreign policy had gone wrong: "First, it relied excessively on the mystique of military power. Second, it had the vision of a united, international Communist conspiracy, just at the time the Communist world was breaking up and giving way to the stronger force of nationalism. Third, it was rigidly and narrowly anti–Communist. Far too many issues were decided in accordance with whether they seemed to advance or impede the cold war with what was called the Sino-Soviet bloc. And fourth, it terribly exaggerated the possible American role in bringing about desirable social change in other countries." All of these errors, Galbraith added, came to focus in Vietnam.

Before it was fashionable, Galbraith pointed to dangerous tendencies being fueled by cold war emotionalism. He commented in 1968 on what he called the "James Bond mystique" within the CIA: "the notion of the highly masculine adventurer who can bring off perfectly fabulous coups. These people must be watched 24 hours a day. Indeed, if at all possible, they shouldn't be hired." It should be added that Galbraith was by no means condemnatory of the CIA: "There have been some impossible people working for it, but, in the main, it has been composed of careful, diligent, hard-working men. My own experience with the CIA is that, given strong leadership, it is responsive, loyal and responsible." Galbraith's comments on the "James Bond" tendencies within the organization appear prophetic in the light of the revelations of recent years.

While Galbraith's prevailing image is that of a consistent leftist, hard-line left-wingers have denounced him as a closet conservative, an adroit defender of the status quo. In the final analysis, much of his thinking may be attributable less to ideology than to pragmatism; a dedication to things that work. He has said that there are countries in which revolution is therapeutic, but that the history of the United States mainly is one of successful reform. "This being so, I have an unabashed commitment to reform. If reform works, revolution becomes unnecessary. So the reformer *is* in some measure a defender of the status quo."

CHAPTER **13**
WHAT
CRITICS THINK
OF GALBRAITH

While making his ideas and theories widely known, John Kenneth Galbraith has become one of the most controversial thinkers in the fields of economics, sociology and politics. His intense involvement in key issues has helped to make him famous, though hardly beloved by some of his colleagues. He seems to find jousting with his peers and enemies both highly stimulating and a call to generate more action. Like General George Patton, who loved war because he was able to be his preferred self in the midst of angry armies, Galbraith savors intellectual battle and the discursive victories he has won over those he considers his vanquished. However, according to some of his critics, Galbraith's armor is thin — vulnerable to well-timed and well-placed ideological and pedagogical puncturing.

Despite their philosophical differences, Galbraith and William F. Buckley, Jr., the conservative editor of *National Review*, are friends. Commenting recently at length on Galbraith's predilection for wage and price controls, Buckley stated, "In an interview with an English newspaper, Ken had to admit that fifteen years ago he and his colleagues at Harvard proceeded on the assumption that they really had all the answers to all the important economic problems. Now he recognizes that they don't.

"His admission wasn't an expression of humility, though. Humility isn't one of Ken's specialties. The fact is that an awful lot of things happened to the economy which none of that gang predicted. Milton Friedman stitched together a great deal of economic data, the force of which persuaded practically the entire economic profession that the old Keynesian mix was wrong. In that sense, I think Galbraith is beleaguered. There aren't many economists around now who say that you can reduce inflation by the simple fiat of controlling prices and wages.

"Galbraith continues to have in common with liberals a belief in the numinous powers of the federal government," Buckley added. "But he is rather more dogmatic on this point than most liberals. This doesn't mean that he goes around picketing the White House for the president to nationalize our basic industries, because he is prepared to roll with the historical situation and to seek government intervention when he finds that it will either be most useful to him or most deadly to the capitalistic system.

"In that sense, one would think of Galbraith as being to the left of Walter Heller and Arthur Schlesinger, Jr. But it is true that in America there has been a considerable disillusionment with that part of liberalism that fancied itself as having redemptive answers for America's problems. The liberals discovered that such answers were really not available to the extent that government sought to enhance the quality of American life, which it wasn't able to do. Peter Drucker in *The Age of Discontinuity* said that there are only two things which the public sector can do better than the private sector. One is to inflate the currency. The other is to fight wars. I cannot imagine that a war in South Vietnam fought by the private sector would be less efficient than the war fought by the public sector.

"I think it is significant that Galbraith now calls himself a socialist, which he didn't before. This doesn't mean he wasn't essentially a socialist before, but now it is a terminological change, and it distinguishes him from the nonsocialist liberals," Buckley told me in his *National Review* offices.

Paul Samuelson believes that Galbraith is naive in succumbing to the inevitability of bigness and power. "Galbraith," Samuelson argued, "thinks of large corporations as being absolute monarchs. And the whole economics profession thinks of them as being constitutional monarchs operating with some system of checks and balances. But when Ford tries an Edsel, it can lose half its shirt. Plenty of firms lose their *whole* shirt. Every one of those big monarchs is invading each other's territory. Galbraith may have invented the term 'countervailing power,' but he ignores the most important countervailing power of all. That is a Lever competing against a Colgate. No, he simply exaggerates the influence of planning that the Fortune 500 corporations do."

Does Samuelson mean to imply that Galbraith is more of a utopian than a realist? "Galbraith is an artist, in the sense that he doesn't let his vision get cluttered too much by reality," Samuelson told me. "He is always looking for an interesting hypothesis. He is actually terrible with anyone else's ideas. His research is always selective. There are no Ph.D. theses written on Galbraith's ideas because they are not researchable hypotheses. In short, his ideas are never stated in a way that you can determine their correctness."

From Galbraith's native Canada there come some negative comments offered by none other than Prime Minister Pierre Elliott Trudeau. When Trudeau clamped strong controls on the Canadian economy to control inflation, Galbraith was identified by many as the source of the prime minister's thinking. In a *Fortune* interview, Trudeau declares that he was by no means a strong devotee of Galbraith: "I'm inclined to say, 'Who's Galbraith?' I've read two or three books by him. I've met him a couple of times socially. I find he is a delightful writer and thinker. But in terms of economics, you know, I spent two years studying with Schumpeter and two years studying with Leontief and if you want to know who is permeating my economic thinking you'd be better to think in terms of Leontief and Schumpeter. . . . When a job isn't being done by the private sector, I have no ideological hang-ups about the government stepping in and doing the job . . . [But] in my view the proper role of government is to make policy decisions and not to administer the private sector. So, if there is any preconception in my mind it is on the side of private enterprise." It is interesting to note that Joseph Schumpeter was a staunch advocate of free enterprise and that Wassily Leontief, though a Keynesian, is not a strong promoter of wage and price controls. And regardless of what Prime Minister Trudeau says about his casual acquaintance with Galbraith, the system of controls he installed in Canada bears the Galbraith stamp.

An opinion of Galbraith's ideas on wage and price controls is expressed by Alfred L. Malabre, Jr., News Editor, *Wall Street Journal:*

"I find particularly bizarre Professor Galbraith's continuing advocacy of some form of wage-price controls as a means of combating inflation. Such a notion has never worked and never will — unless the country is at war and patriotism is running very high, or unless we are willing to refashion our economic arrangements into some form of ironclad dictatorship in which a vast army of wage and price controllers, commanded no doubt by Professor Galbraith, runs our lives for us. Today's inflation doesn't reflect the absence of controls, or any sinister collusion between big unions and big corporations. It reflects an overly rapid expansion of the nation's money supply and, generally, a proclivity of our political leaders to overspend and overstrain the capacity of the nation's economic resources."

Yet another view of Galbraith is expressed in a review by Robert Heilbroner in *The New York Review*, June 29, 1967.

"The authors of a recent textbook found it useful to include as a student exercise a quotation from 'an economist serving as American ambassador to India,' instructing the student to 'Explain why every sentence of that quotation — except the third and fourth — is wrong, nonsensical, or irrelevant.' A colleague of mine, discussing a list of books that might be useful for a graduate seminar in Political Economics, simply shrugged off *American Capitalism* and *The Affluent Society* as works that serious people could not take seriously."

While Galbraith has come under heavy fire from conservatives, he has by no means enjoyed accolades from the Left. The Marxist Paul Sweezy, a leading US radical economist, writes a highly critical review of *Economics and the Public Purpose* in *The New York Review*, November 15, 1973. Sweezy says that Galbraith's "picture of a more or less homogeneous 'market system' confronting a handful of giant corporations is fanciful in the extreme." While there are many small enterprises which are victims of the system, "there are also plenty of winners who are by no stretch of the imagination in Galbraith's planning system. To name only a few of the more important categories is to reveal how extensive and significant the phenomenon is: small and medium-sized corporations in manufacturing and trade, locally-based construction firms (nearly the whole construction industry), large farmers and ranchers, real estate owners and operators, owners of radio and TV stations, local bankers, professionals (especially doctors and lawyers)."

Not all are winners, says Sweezy: "But literally millions of them are in no sense victims of the system; on the contrary, many are among its chief beneficiaries. To put them in the same bag with the owner of the corner grocery store makes so little sense that one must assume it has an ulterior motive. And in Galbraith's case, I believe the ulterior motive, probably unconscious on the part of the author, is to further confuse the picture of the power structure in US society."

To seek a friendly opinion, I asked Arthur Schlesinger, Jr. if Galbraith's perceptions of our economic reality would become obsolete. He replied, "This is a risk anyone takes. If you were not prepared to take risks, you would never say anything at all. I do not believe that Galbraith's main propositions are now either obsolete or fully accepted.

"There was a great division between Theodore Roosevelt and Woodrow Wilson in the 1912 campaign. Roosevelt thought that big business was inevitable and that its bigness had its advantages. He felt that the bigness could be reconciled with democracy by having the national government stronger than the economic power of business. Galbraith, in that context, is in the tradition of the new nationalism of Teddy Roosevelt."

I asked Schlesinger for his opinion about Galbraith's description of the large corporation's impact on industrial society. "Ken Galbraith has argued that the great organization is far from being a kind of phony creation but that, in fact, it is an organic necessity in our society. Ken feels that the great organization, whether public or private, is a dominant feature of all industrial societies, be it that of the United States or the Soviet Union. And that it is an illusion to suppose that ideas derived from a market economy can prevail outside the rather limited sectors which the industrial state or planning system controls.

"Another point which I think is very important, which liberal economists understand, is the extent to which inflation is an inevitable byproduct of this system of economic concentration. With Galbraith, prices of the planning system are administered. They are not set by the free play of market forces. Inflation is a more serious problem than depression because we know how to stop depression. You can always stop depression by increasing government spending," Schlesinger told me. "Strength is rooted in the realities of a situation. We cannot go on fighting recession by inflation or fighting inflation with recession. We need some form of stability. I think that Ken's emphasis on administering stable prices as against the notion of indefinite inflation is correct."

Another of Galbraith's distinguished critics is Professor Milton Friedman, a highly acclaimed spokesman for the free enterprise system and the 1976 Nobel Prize winner in economics. In a speech devoted to the single topic of John Kenneth Galbraith and presented before the Institute of Economic Affairs in London, Professor Friedman told his audience, "Some of my best friends are Galbraithians, including John Kenneth."

Professor Friedman finds a paradox: Galbraith is convinced that his ideas are correct but even his most ardent followers are unable to provide hard evidence that his theories can work in the real world. Friedman acknowledges that Galbraith made a "serious attempt" to justify his position on wage and price controls in *The Theory of Price Control,* but he considers Galbraith's analysis wrong.

The Affluent Society discusses the theory of social balance, which, in the case of the United States, describes the massive expenditures for the purchase of private goods in contrast to the small investment made in upgrading and expanding public services. *The Affluent Society,* according to Professor Friedman, is "denigrating to the tastes of ordinary people." He feels that it was a slap at people who liked automobiles with excessive tailfins in contrast to those who bought costlier compact cars. Increased energy and automobile costs have obviously made this Galbraithian issue a relic of the conventional wisdom of the past. Professor Friedman drew on the words of that immortal free-enterpriser Adam Smith to comment on Galbraith's penchant for increased government spending for public services:

"It is the highest impertinence and presumption in kings and ministers to pretend to watch over the economy of private people and to restrain their expense either by sumptuary laws or by prohibiting the importation of foreign luxuries. They are themselves always and without any exception the greatest spendthrifts in the society. Let them look well after their own expenses and they may safely trust private people with theirs. If their own extravagance does not ruin the state, that of their subjects never will.

"There is no art which one government sooner learns of another than that of draining money from the pockets of the people."

Friedman is also critical of Galbraith's theory of countervailing power. In certain industries where individual companies exercise little power by themselves, large unions are able to force their position with considerable power — for example, the influence of The United Mine Workers on relatively small coal operators. The Teamsters Union is another example of countervailing power of labor which did not come into being to offset the power of monopolistic corporate interests. Rather, it grew because the private enterprise sector was in fact dispersed, allowing the workers to operate a cartel for the benefit of themselves and their employers.

Professor Friedman considers *The New Industrial State* to be Galbraith's most ambitious book. Friedman says that in *The New Industrial State* Galbraith discards his theory of countervailing power and, instead, finds that power is concentrated within the technostructure. One of the main goals of the technostructure, according to Galbraith, is to maintain its own security within the corporation by controlling every aspect of its existence from the purchase of raw materials and supplies to the selling of its products and the creation (manipulation) of wants to their present and potential new customers. As a result of the planning system's power, the free market as such exerts very little influence on the economy. Friedman takes issue with Galbraith over the idea that the giant corporations have as great a control over their destinies as Galbraith maintains that they do. He says that the poor stock market record of such large defense-oriented corporations as Lockheed or General Dynamics reveals their inability to control their own destinies.

Because Galbraith champions a wide spectrum of liberal causes there is the tendency to assume that his ideology is egalitarianism. I feel that Galbraith is an elitist in a meritocracy, where acceptance into an elite is based on an individual's merit and talent. Professor Friedman has his own definite views: "Galbraith has always seemed to me a twentieth-century version of the early nineteenth-century Tory radicals of Great Britain.

". . . . the Tory radicals expected and thought it appropriate that

190 PERSPECTIVES ON GALBRAITH

the masses would accept the dominion of the aristocrats over their values and beliefs, because they would accept that the aristocrats were seeking the welfare of the masses.

"I believe that Galbraith's view is essentially the same. He knows that his values are superior to those of the masses and he thinks that if the masses are properly instructed by enough of his books, they will come themselves to that view and will ask him and his fellow intellectuals to take charge."

Professor Friedman continues by saying, "I object to being ruled by either the natural born aristocracy or by a meritocracy, but if I were to be ruled by either it seems to me that aristocracy of birth is much the less evil. . . ."

Many reformers, and Galbraith is not alone in this, have as their basic objection to a free market that the free market frustrates them in achieving their reforms, because a free market enables people to have what people want and not what the reformers want," said Friedman in his London speech.

William F. Buckley's *National Review* has long kept tabs on John Kenneth Galbraith and his ideas. Colin Clark, a leading Oxford University economist, reviewed *The Affluent Society* in a *National Review* article, "The Horrible Proposals of Mr. Galbraith." Like Professor Friedman, Clark takes issue with Galbraith's emphasis on meritocracy, "a new order run by a new class of planners." Clark writes, "The 'new class' is to represent a 'class' in the full sociological meaning of the word, i.e., something more than a group of men who follow similar occupations and live within similar ranges of income. They are to constitute also a group who will mix with each other, rather than with other people, for purposes of culture and recreation, will marry into each other's families, and will bring up their children to share their tastes and occupations." Clark feels that Galbraith is attempting to assemble a society or class of people similar to that of Edward VII's England, with its distinctive delineations of class. The Oxford economist says that Galbraith's "new class" will take for granted that it is the exclusive custodian of culture.

In Galbraith's view, public services are lacking because an excessive amount of money is spent on private goods. Clark, on the other hand, believes that social imbalance is not so much caused by a lack of money but by the incompetence and corruption of politicians. He also blames businessmen who make "under the table" deals with corrupt politicians, a practice that evades social responsibility and perpetuates poor quality public services, such as a polluted environment. Clark chides Galbraith's perception of the role and power of advertising in economic life and finds no justification for condemning manufacturers and merchants who sincerely feel that they have "something new and useful to offer" consumers and who use advertising to make their products and services known. He distinguishes between manipulative advertising that sucks in people to buy what they do not need and informative advertising that stresses benefits and new features but leaves the ultimate decision as to buy or not buy to the consumer. Clark believes that advertising in the United States is more informative than manipulative, though he admits that the power of the Madison Avenue huckster is increasing particularly in merchandising politicians.

Of course, both *The Affluent Society* and Colin Clark's review were published in the late 1950s. Now, in the late 1970s, much of what both wrote about advertising appears to have become conventional wisdom. The Watergate scandals, the energy crisis, and the generally poor economic situation have dampened the trend to sell image instead of substance — whether of politicians or products. Impulse buying of cars, cosmetics, and even candidates for office has been replaced, to a large extent, by a more intensive public search for the true value in things and in persons and how that value relates to the actual cost. Although no economist is currently predicting a 1960s boom in the near future, if anything approximating affluence should come again for the general public, the economic waters for manipulative advertising will again be at a more congenial temperature. The question to be answered will be how much actual power does this form of advertising have in the present economy and over contemporary consumers, as distinct from the consumers of the late-1950s and of the 1960s?

At the end of Colin Clark's review, he senses that Galbraith too perceives some weaknesses in his "new class." Clark writes, "Professor Galbraith himself does not seem to be under any illusion about human nature on this score, or about the sin of sloth. . . ." In fact, he uses Galbraith's own words, "The ancient art of evading work has been carried in our time to its highest level of sophistication; in the universities its practice has the standing of a scholarly rite. The art of genteel and elaborately concealed idleness may well reach its highest development in the upper executive reaches of the modern corporation." And Clark offers, "In face of these sad but undoubted truths, is not Professor Galbraith afraid that his 'new class,' his graduated unemployment compensation and his protected monopolies will soon degenerate into a world in which there are as many idlers as there are men working to support them?"

Galbraith, however, took up this issue later in *The New Industrial State.* He points out that enough people will always prefer to produce an income above that provided by the state. And he maintains that although the state will maintain an individual's survival at a level of dignity and above the current welfare denigration, most people will work to produce more income to meet increased desires for higher quality goods and services. The flaw in Galbraith's theory here is that there is no guarantee, unless it is imposed by the state, that the individual will go to work to satisfy heightened expectations. Instead, the individual may have the power, in coalition with others, to force the state to provide what he or she desires from the public trough.

A more recent *National Review* article, "On Professor Galbraith's View of America" (June 1976) by William Peterson, a member of the faculty of Ohio State University, presents Galbraith's strong point, "his successful popularization of his ideas." Peterson uses *Money: Whence It Came, Where It Went*, as well as his more famous books to state his case that Galbraith lacks substance.

Critics such as Peterson often attack Galbraith's talent to write — the area of competence I feel is most sacred to him. Moderate views are difficult to find; readers feel as intensely about his prose as his ideas.

Peterson believes four prime factors form Galbraith's "careful didactic style" in most of his books:

1. "The staple point is that everything is easy."

2. "As a corollary, then, writers, who make demands on their readers, who cultivate the belief that they are in privileged association with the occult, are behaving like a 'doctor or witch doctor,' manufacturing complexities in order to 'gain prestige, esteem, and pecuniary return.' "

3. "When everything is made easy, boredom may set in unless the text is spruced up. Every ten pages or so."

4. "But in order to produce *haute vulgarisation*, as even the editors of *Esquire* know, one must maintain a Serious Purpose."

The comments of Dr. Paul M. Sweezy, one of America's leading Marxists and good friend of Galbraith, illustrate some of the ambivalence Galbraith generates: "No one understands better than Ken Galbraith the fraudulent nature of orthodox economics, as evidenced in a whole series of post-Second World War books from *American Capitalism, The Affluent Society, The New Industrial State,* through to *Economics and the Public Purpose.* In this respect he stands in a long and honorable tradition of dissent going back to the populists and the muckrakers at the turn of the century and including the various types of institutionalists who owe at least part of their inspiration to Thorstein Veblen, the greatest and most neglected social scientist this country has yet produced. I think I speak for most of the growing number of self-styled radical economists who make up the membership of the Union of Radical Political Economics (URPE) when I say that as a critic of economic orthodoxy we consider Galbraith to be one of us.

"But then there is the other Galbraith who thinks it is possible to patch up the system of monopoly capitalism to make it work tolerably well as a promoter of the 'public purpose.' Here we have to part company with him. The books listed above, taken in chronological order, contain plenty of evidence that the system has been working progressively worse for the whole postwar period, and of course there is absolutely no reason to suppose, from the perspective of the 1970s, that it is going to do anything else for as far ahead as anyone can pretend to be able to see. I wonder if Ken Galbraith is ever going to admit this and join with those of us who consider the patching up of capitalism to be as fraudulent as its neoclassical apologia? I would like to pay him the compliment of believing that he is capable of it," said Sweezy.

In reviewing *Economics and the Public Purpose,* for *Book World,* Bernard D. Nossiter, author and correspondent, offers this interesting observation: "Galbraith's private joke, of course, is that he pretends to be a radical and in fact is deeply conservative. So conservative that he would not only preserve more or less intact the great private and public bureaucracies that now rule our lives but even replicate them in areas where they do not now exist."

Obviously, others have thought that Galbraith is a closet conservative. An Englishman, Ralph Miliband, writing in 1961, questioned Galbraith's concept of political power: ". . . for what? Professor Galbraith has no serious answer to that question. For all the verbal iconoclasm and the seeming dismissal of 'conventional wisdom' and orthodox economics, there is too much here of apologetics and obfuscation, too little genuine probing, too ready an acceptance of the 'logic' of the system, too cramped a view of its contradictions, too much underlying intellectual and political timidity, notwithstanding the self-conscious *enfant terrible* posturings, for Professor Galbraith to speak seriously to the American condition, or to those who seriously seek to change it. For such people, *The New Industrial State* has little to offer, either by way of diagnosis, or of prescription. What it does offer is a further demonstration of the limitations both in diagnosis and prescription, of a type of liberalism which constitutes not an alternative but a variant of that conservatism which Professor Galbraith claims to condemn."

Calling Galbraith a conservative is a neat and convenient rhetorical trick, designed to draw attention to the critic and to get the hackles up on the back of the victim. Even that nimble master of rhetorical jousting, William F. Buckley, Jr., probably wouldn't even imply that Galbraith was a conservative. Galbraith's self-description — a nonviolent man who would like to see reform take place within an intelligent and democratic process — certainly is not extreme enough for those on the far Left who desire a more rapid and radical transformation of our economic society.

Rudolf Klein, writing in *Commentary* magazine on *Economics and the Public Purpose*, takes issue with Galbraith's view that corporations spend huge sums of money to "brainwash" consumers. Klein contends that Galbraith himself may be "brainwashed" by Madison Avenue's claims for its own products. "For one of his most irritating habits is to present himself as the one man who sees the truth behind appearances — who can distinguish (like the Marxists) between false and real consciousness or (like the Freudians) between rationalizations and real motives. If one disagrees with him, one therefore stigmatizes oneself as conventional in thought and conformist in one's views; if one agrees with him, one becomes part of the select band of those who are not deceived by the 'socially convenient virtues' and who sees them for that they are — the values propagated by the planning system in order to further its own purposes. Irritation is compounded by the fact that Galbraith is right to question conventional wisdom, then spoils a good case by his intellectually arrogant assumptions about the motives of other people."

Klein offers the possibility that it is within the self-interests of the technostructure to conform its activities with that of the general public, instead of exploiting people into consumer-slaves. Klein states that the technostructure may, in fact, be giving people the goods they actually want.

Galbraith is always criticized for not being specific enough and for not providing sufficient documentation to back up his ideas. Klein is among these critics: "Galbraith tends to be contemptuous of those who dare to ask for such precision;" he recognizes, however, his contributions: "Galbraith's ideas are too influential to be treated as nothing more than entertainment. It would be a pity if he continued to take the view that oversimplification is the soul of wit, and that neat generalizations are an adequate substitute for sustained, rigorous argument."

Professor Charles H. Hession's 1972 book, *John Kenneth Galbraith and His Critics,* is an analysis of some substance that attempts to present the strengths and weaknesses of Galbraith's ideas. Professor Hession finds what he feels is a flaw: "Galbraith's relative neglect of the element of culture in his analysis is illustrated in his discussion of the goals of the industrial system. In the course of his treatment, he makes the surprising statement that 'the acceptance of economic growth as a social goal coincides closely with the rise to power of the mature corporation and the technostructure.' Perhaps I am misinterpreting what Galbraith means by 'acceptance of economic growth *as a social goal,*' but I find it hard to reconcile the general import of the sentence with my understanding of American history. From the days of Alexander Hamilton to those of Andrew Carnegie and Henry Ford I, there would seem to have been wide acceptance of the desirability of material progress for the nation. From Comte to Herbert Spencer, progress was not only an ideal to many nineteenth-century Europeans, it became almost a scientific law. Americans as a 'people of plenty,' to use David Potter's expression, were the most progress-intoxicated of all. The relative abundance of our economic environment contributed to optimism and the faith in progress. In this sense, 'growthmanship' is a relatively old characteristic of the American way of life that much precedes the advent of the mature corporation."

I asked Dr. James Howell of The First National Bank of Boston about Galbraith's concept of social balance and his contention that American citizens and corporations could afford to be taxed more to pay for increased public services.

"I think there is a need for social balance in our society," said Dr. Howell. "But I feel that it is a question of how you achieve it. The most troublesome part of achieving social balance is that the deliberate attempts to achieve social balance have been in the hands of states. The federal government has done a fair amount in this area but the federal government has always given the option to the states with regard to income redistribution beyond what the federal government would deal with. Medicaid is a good example. The federal government mandated eleven items that had to be taken by all states and gave them an option of up to twenty-one. States which were interested in pursuing social balance went ahead and took all the options . . . states such as Massachusetts, New York and California. That works out very well and a liberal can't criticize that, but a banker can then say 'Well, that's fine, but what happens if industry moves out of the state and people don't?' Galbraith may be right with regard to his theory of social balance in concept but the way it is implemented causes a terrible dislocation of where industry goes and people stay."

I mentioned to Dr. Howell that Massachusetts is a classic example of this condition: where industry has either failed to expand or left the state and where the state has traditionally been a leader in the provision of public services. New Hampshire has a reputation for having low taxes and providing the minimum amount of public services; according to Galbraith's philosophy such states are in acute social imbalance.

Dr. Howell described a recent research project: "The Campbells (Colin D. Campbell and Rosemary G. Campbell), a husband and wife team of economists from Dartmouth, did a study on the delivery of government services and what one gets from government for tax dollars in both Vermont and New Hampshire. Vermont and

New Hampshire are alike in many ways, with some exceptions; they are almost kissing cousins except that Vermont is a very high tax state and New Hampshire is a very low tax state. After about six or eight months work, the Campbells wrote a report that reached two conclusions. Their first conclusion was that the delivery of some key public services in Vermont was not qualitatively superior to that in New Hampshire. Second, they concluded that if you want to give state government more money, state government will go ahead and spend more money, and that you will get diminishing returns on the quality of services you are attempting to deliver. There are probably no two states in the country where you could make that kind of comparison. I guess what this all means is that the Campbells have raised some questions and we can't just put them away. What it will probably call for is another five or ten years of research but there has been a major crack in the pot here in terms of the argument that more spending necessarily fulfills the social contract to those who need it.

"If you want to pick a state that has tried to do everything to achieve social balance with almost total disregard to its economic base, it is Massachusetts," Dr. Howell added.

Across the Charles River from the First National Bank of Boston is the office of Professor Robert Solow at the Massachusetts Institute of Technology. Having once written a critical review of *The New Industrial State*, Solow says that although Galbraith was very annoyed with it, they are friends again. In "The New Industrial State or Son of Affluence," in *Public Interest*, Solow wrote, "Professor Galbraith makes an eloquent case for big-thinking, and he has a point. Little-thinking can easily degenerate into mini-thinking or even to hardly thinking at all. Even if it does not, too single-minded a focus on how the parts of the machine work may lead to a careful failure ever to ask whether the machine is pointed in the right direction. . . ."

I asked Professor Solow how could Galbraith continue to push for his system of wage and price controls in the face of American opposition? Business and labor reacted quickly and negatively to Carter's pre-inauguration trial-balloon mention of controls.

"Ken Galbraith, like any liberal-minded economist, likes to see a more prosperous economy than we now have. He would like to see less unemployment, even more production, although he has his doubts about some of that. Why can't we have a more prosperous economy? The answer that is always given is 'Oh, well, if you try to pump the economy by spreading purchasing power around, you will run into inflation.' That's what everybody says. This poses a problem for the liberal-minded economist because we would like to have the prosperity. On the other hand even privately if some of us don't happen to think that the inflation is as bad as some of the people complain, it is still *the* obstacle. Then it is very handy to have something you can say. And what you can say is, 'If you are worried about the inflation, it would be far better to have wage and price controls even though they are somewhat inefficient and they may make messes in some markets, but that is going to be considerably less than the cost of running the economy at half speed as we have been doing for the last two or three years.' That does give you an answer to the people who say, 'No, you can't have prosperity because the price level will start to rise.'

"The fact is that serious wage and price controls are not a realistic, political thing. Everybody, business and labor, is against them. And I think deep down Ken knows this. But you have to have some answer to the inflation bogey, and one answer you can give is controls. However, if I thought there was only a choice between what was Gerald Ford's economic policy and wage and price controls, I would opt for the controls. Because as damaging as the controls would be, they would not nearly be as damaging as having Ford and Greenspan for close to three years. The Ford and Greenspan method of managing the economy didn't give a damn about the level of employment. I don't think they were even interested in the trickling down method of stimulating the economy. They were sacrificing everyone's economic welfare for an ideology. However, I don't think the choice is between wage and price controls and Ford and Greenspan. I think the more routine methods of expanding the economy still have a lot of mileage right now, and the need for controls is not clear. But at any case . . . you are not going to have them. They serve the purpose for Ken, who must know that you are not going to have them, of giving him an intellectual argumentative way out of the inflation bind."

I mentioned to Solow that Galbraith considers tax cuts to be ineffectual in stimulating a sagging economy and that the money should be spent in creating new jobs from the public sector.

"That's an area where I think Ken lacks knowledge and understanding. The lowbrow professional knows rather more about that than he does. First of all, everybody agrees that temporary tax reduction is less effective in stimulating the economy than permanent tax reduction. Many people agree that you can get substantial mileage from even a temporary tax reduction. The notion that a large part of those tax reductions go to the rich simply isn't true. The rich are very rich but there are not very many of them. The tax credit, however, does go to people who have very definite consumption needs, those in the median income level.

"I, like Ken, believe that job development and direct government spending are important. But people say, and quite justly, that the federal government cannot spend money quickly and efficiently. You need planning and you need time for planning for public projects. Ken would like a great deal more federal expenditures instead of tax reductions . . . but he is not going to get it. It is not politically viable. In the Kennedy period, Ken was a pain in the neck. He was opposing the Kennedy-Johnson 1964 tax reduction because he wanted instead an increase in expenditures. Kennedy was allergic to an increase in expenditures and so was the Congress. The choice was tax reduction or zilch, and Ken was a fifth wheel at that time. I too would have liked a bigger budget from Kennedy and would have been prepared to give up some of the tax reduction for more expenditures but it wasn't going to happen."

I told Solow that Galbraith was very critical of Walter Heller with regard to tax reductions. "You should hear what Heller has to say about Ken," Solow replied. "Ken, at that time, was prepared to sacrifice the reality of some stimulus to an underemployed economy for ideology. Not the ideology of Ford and Greenspan — a much better ideology — but I think he was prepared to sacrifice reality for the appearance. Ken is not a numbers man and I feel that the numbers are almost everything in this business."

I asked Professor Solow what he felt about Galbraith's place in history. "I think Ken will be remembered as an historian and a philosopher, but I don't think he will be primarily remembered as an economist. Economics is becoming more and more a technical subject like dentistry. Ken is not going to strike the future as a great dentist."

Even his critics will agree.

CHAPTER **14**
GALBRAITHIAN VIEWPOINTS

We can learn something about an individual by listening to his opinions of other people. Galbraith has known many prominent persons over his long career. He is usually willing to size them up in pithy and sometimes sardonic terms.

Here is a sample of Galbraith on people he has known. Perhaps it is appropriate to begin with Milton Friedman. Galbraith said, "Milton has a brilliant and not invariably misguided mind. There have been things on which we have been in agreement. We were both very active in promoting the idea of a volunteer army and we served on a committee to bring it into being. We attacked the idea of selective service as being both an unprincipled form of coercion in a democracy and a device by which you persuade people who are poor — namely the young — to serve in the military at less-than-going wages in order to keep down the burden of paying for defense on the part of the affluent.

"We all owe Milton Friedman thanks, as well, for the most important single reform of the last twenty years. It is his idea of a minimum income, which he presented as a negative income tax. If this idea had come from anybody but Milton Friedman, it would have been quickly dismissed as being ridiculously radical. However, coming from him, the very logical notion to secure everybody a minimum income gained wide acceptance almost immediately. Nixon proposed it. So did George McGovern. It will probably happen some day."

At another point Galbraith observed, "Milton Friedman had been giving advice to the Chilean government to apply what he calls the shock treatment to the nation's economy. Well, that sounds quite benign, not very painful, just a little jolt. A shock treatment doesn't sound very serious. But, it is, when you find that in Chile it amounts to an unemployment rate that comes up to between one quarter and one third of the labor force and an inflation rate at 200 percent or 300 percent a year. My radical friends have been objecting to Friedman's advising the junta. They shouldn't. The best way to get rid of the Chilean junta is to have it advised by Milton Friedman."

He next commented on his colleague Paul Samuelson.

"Paul Samuelson has taught a whole generation their economics," Galbraith told me. "No one in our time compares with Paul as a teacher. He had the courage and the imagination, in the years following World War II, to see that the pre-Keynesian ideas were dead. He took the great step of moving economic instruction into the world of Keynes. His has been an enormous achievement.

"It does not detract from his achievement to say that Paul Samuelson has been anchored to his textbook. As a result, he has tended on occasion to defend the old ideas rather than to embrace the new ones. Paul has paid the price of keeping an anchor into ideas which he probably himself recognizes have to be modified."

Galbraith expressed high admiration for Gunnar Myrdal, the Nobel-Prize-winning Swedish economist: "Gunnar is the greatest living figure in economics. [He] never touches a subject without illuminating it. He is not a man who builds orderly systems, but he has an enormous capacity for seeing reality in any subject he takes up.

"His book The American Dilemma is a classic on the racial problem in the United States. Nobody has spoken as authoritatively on the problems of the developing countries of the world, or has seen so clearly that the capacity of government and the nature of economic development were intertwined with poverty itself."

Galbraith also expressed his opinions about various presidents. "There is a very great difference between individual presidents and their personal feel for economics," Galbraith told me. "In the case of Nixon, I accept that he was essentially a rather lazy man and very much interested in the panoply and perquisites of being president. When somebody talked to him about the speculation going on against the lira, he surely did say 'Screw the lira!' John Kennedy, by contrast, liked economics. He wanted to understand it. He found the issues interesting and he liked the terminology.

"This was equally true of Lyndon Johnson. I don't think that Johnson was intellectually stimulated by economic issues, but he had an instinctive feeling for them. Perhaps, in this respect, even more than Kennedy, Johnson had, over his lifetime on Capitol Hill, absorbed the basis for economic judgments through his pores. Kennedy received his knowledge of it out of books and from his colleagues. Johnson was able to get the same knowledge by osmosis and by being a leader in the Congress for such a long time," Galbraith continued.

"I am sure that Eisenhower's span of attention on economic issues was extremely brief. Harry Truman was perhaps, in this respect, a bit more like Johnson. Again, Truman was the product of his experience in Congress." President Hoover was a man well trained for the presidency, according to Galbraith, but he could not face directly the dire economic problems of the depression. Franklin Delano Roosevelt, on the other hand, "hated having anything to do with economics," even though his social welfare policies and the associated spending appeared to ease the terrible suffering of the depression.

"In the 1952 campaign we were depressed with Adlai's views about economics," Galbraith went on. "I'm not suggesting that they were comparable with, for example, Alan Greenspan's, because Stevenson had a compassionate view of society. He wasn't a follower of Ayn Rand. But Stevenson's views were firmly grounded in the nineteenth-century ideas of Edwin Kemmerer and Harley Lutz, who were his teachers at Princeton. After the 1952 campaign was over, knowing that he was again going to be a candidate in 1956, we conducted a special seminar on economics for him once every few weeks. Stevenson came, listened, read the papers and we had a very good discussion. But, the next time we would see him, he would say, 'Well, we certainly must get on top of this economic problem.'

"Stevenson had a reputation for being a brooding intellectual. Kennedy had the reputation of being a stylish, practical politician by contrast. In fact, John Kennedy would read ten books to Stevenson's one. Kennedy devoured books. Stevenson would be lucky if he read a book a week. I remember going down to see Kennedy in Palm Beach and taking with me a new volume on Sir Robert Walpole. I gave the book to him at dinnertime along with some other books I had brought for Jackie. He read it overnight and the next morning wanted to know what modern figure could be compared with Walpole and to discuss numerous other details about him. I had to confess that although I had brought him the book, I hadn't read it."

John Kenneth Galbraith's distaste for Richard Nixon is well-known. Writing in the *Boston Globe*, August 18, 1974, on the occasion of Nixon's resignation, he said, "Someone, I promise you, will say that the fault lies deeply within ourselves. Well, the hell it does. It lies with Richard Nixon and the people who voted him into office."

Galbraith recalled that Nixon's public career began when "young Dick, after having been turned down sometime previously by the FBI, showed up in the lower reaches of the Office of Price Administration of which I was then an unadmired archon and asked for a job. Thus he was launched on the public payroll. A bad mistake."

In summing up Nixon's career, Galbraith said, "He was a pious fraud in the deepest meaning of that phrase which is to say that whenever he was caught in public falsehood, personal peculation or any other dereliction, he assumed a mood of righteousness and complained that his enemies were having at him again. Yet he was rarely so described in public."

In London, Galbraith discussed various aspects of diplomacy and world affairs with me. Our discussions touched on the last few secretaries of state. "Kissinger is by far the best," said Galbraith. "Both Dulles and Rusk kept the cold war going. Kissinger had the imagination to see that a conflict must ultimately be destructive. And if the initiative is taken, particularly by a conservative administration, right-wing reaction can be muted. For example, we had the moves toward better relations with China and the Soviets. These were moves which the Democrats should have taken but which they were afraid to take.

"Kissinger is also diligent. The nicest thing for a secretary of state to do is to sit in Washington and engage in conversations. You can always have useful talks if you are the secretary of state. Secretary Rusk was a great man for useful talks. So was Secretary William Rogers. However, it's much more difficult to travel to the Middle East and then commute back and forth from Cairo to Damascus to Jerusalem. The secretary has to know how to deal with people who have a built-in beastliness of character. He has personally to know them well, to appreciate them, to retain their confidence, and to work out some sort of an agreement with them. Henry was able to do all this.

"I have a very one-sided view of Rusk, as he would be the first to suggest. Kennedy came into office with a very narrow margin of support. He had to have the backing of the New York foreign policy establishment. Kennedy also believed that foreign policy was something that he had to dominate. Kennedy's first choice for secretary of state was William Fulbright. Robert Kennedy persuaded his brother against Fulbright because the senator was a southerner and had generally supported southern policies against blacks. His appointment would be taken as a slap in the face of black Africa. This was a bad mistake. Fulbright would have been the better choice. He had by far the best and most sophisticated grasp of foreign policy in our time.

"Stevenson was another possibility. But there was a difference in style between Stevenson and Kennedy. Kennedy was never completely comfortable with Stevenson. I am not sure of this, but my impression was that Kennedy was afraid that Stevenson had his own constituency and that he could appeal to his own power base in the event of a disagreement.

"The third possibility for Kennedy was Chester Bowles. But here again there would be a difference in style. Bowles would have made an excellent secretary of state. He was able to inspire confidence. He was a fine negotiator. And he had good relations with senators and congressmen. But Kennedy passed over all three of his obvious choices — something that often happens when you're dealing with people you know well. By not knowing the faults of the people you don't know, you see only their virtues. This was the case with Dean Rusk. The virtue of Rusk was that he had had years of experience in the State Department. He was the head of the Rockefeller Foundation and a senior figure in the foreign policy establishment. But he was also a cold warrior, with a damaging tendency to trust the military. On the other hand, it has to be said that Dean Rusk was completely loyal to both Presidents Kennedy and Johnson. Rusk never doubted that when the president spoke, that was the final word on the matter."

In *Economics, Peace and Laughter* Galbraith includes an essay on Eisenhower which first appeared as a review of the general's papers in his role as commander-in-chief of Allied forces in Europe. Galbraith's remarks about Ike were very complimentary. I had been somewhat surprised; it seemed out of character for him to praise a Republican, a former Republican president. "Very few people have ever read those papers. You cannot read them without seeing what a superior administrator Ike was in his prime.

"In later years I had dinner one night with his brother, Milton Eisenhower, an acquaintance from our agricultural days, and then president of Johns Hopkins University. At dinner, Milton was commenting on my review of his brother's papers and he said, 'There are two things that we always knew about Ike, but there is great difficulty in persuading anyone they were true. One was the meticulous attention he gave not to the details of administration so much as to the selection of people. As a general he deeply distrusted generals. He would not appoint one without the most careful examination and consideration as to whether the man was the kind to whom he could delegate responsibility.'

"This," Galbraith noted, "explained the very high quality of his command during the war and also the varied personalities of his generals, as different as Montgomery's and Patton's. Ike's only concern was with their competence, which was enormously high as compared with that of the World War I generals." He went on to recall Milton Eisenhower's account of Ike's meticulous attention to literary style. His press conferences were noted for his assaults on the English language. But Ike was proud of his writing, of the fact that, when with MacArthur, he had composed some of his more purple passages.

Galbraith continued, "One must bear in mind two things about Ike. First of all, he had the built-in laziness of most generals. It is a profession which emphasizes idleness as a form of therapy; the military call it physical fitness. Second, he is most remembered for the way he eased himself through the presidency, rather than for his greater achievement, which was keeping Patton, Montgomery, and the others aware that Hitler was the enemy, not each other."

I was interested in Galbraith's opinion of another great world leader of recent times, Winston Churchill. I asked him if, like Franklin D. Roosevelt, Winston Churchill had been rescued by World War II and thus was able to achieve an honored place in history.

"First of all, I wouldn't make that comparison," said Galbraith. "Roosevelt was a towering figure on the American scene before the war. Had there been no war, he still would have been reelected in 1940. The 1940 election was fought mostly on domestic issues. However, in Churchill's case there is no question that he was rescued by the Second World War.

"On the other hand, Churchill had been rescued many times before. He was rescued after his strange campaign in the Dardanelles. And then he reemerged to power in the 1920s as a Tory chancellor of the exchequer. He was a disastrous chancellor. Churchill was responsible for the worst single mistake in English history, that of returning the country to the gold standard. What you have to say about Churchill is that among all modern politicians he was an extremely high-risk operator. He never weighed actions in terms of his own personal safety.

"If the United States hadn't come into the war, and if Germany had continued to concentrate on Great Britain, he could well have been regarded as the same kind of disastrous figure that he was after his campaign in the Dardanelles.

"Churchill was a great artist in the use of the English language, particularly in his early writings. His book, *The Roving Commission*, also called *My Early Years*, can still be read as one of the most expressive accounts of a man's youth. He makes it come alive, and he is very funny. He tells, for example, of going to Cuba as a young officer. At that time, nobody from his class at Sandhurst had experienced war except for serving on the Indian frontier. Churchill was anxious to see combat. He and one of his colleagues accompanied the Spanish Army in Cuba. He describes marching across an empty canebrake. The sugar cane had been removed by the rebels, who were shooting from the jungle. To demonstrate Spanish valor, the soldiers felt it necessary to march across the open field. Churchill and his friend had to do likewise. Churchill writes this marvelous sentence, 'For the first time, I began to take a thoughtful view of war.' "

In 1976, after a close primary battle with former California Governor Ronald Reagan, Gerald Ford had won the presidential nomination. Former Texas Governor John Connally, once a Democrat, played a prominent role for the Republicans. I asked Galbraith what he thought about Connally's future influence on American politics.

"I think John has seen his best days. His speech at the 1976 Republican convention at Kansas City was billed as one of the great moments of that affair. It would be hard to think of anyone who more completely blew it than John when he attacked the Democrats. He caused people, even the most retarded Republicans, to say, 'Well, he's well qualified to do that because he's spent his whole life as a Democrat.' He also made the mistake of emphasizing every point in his speech at the maximum decibel level. It all came out as a long harangue. Barry Goldwater, whose views are no more compatible with mine than those of John Connally, spoke with varying emphasis, with sincerity, and a quiet charm which was infinitely more persuasive. Most people watching the convention got the feeling that Connally was a disappointed man. John is a man who struggled for the main chance. But John's idea of the main chance isn't all that good. Any man who joined the Republicans in the last months of the Nixon administration has an instinct for the *Titanic*."

But Galbraith recognizes Goldwater's reputation for integrity and candor. Because Galbraith is a superstar among American liberals, I was interested in his thoughts on Goldwater, a superstar of conservatives.

"Barry Goldwater is a nice man who in his 1964 campaign for the presidency was led into an unrealistic position on the issue of social security. He also gave the impression that he was trigger-happy about bombing Vietnam. In retrospect, Barry Goldwater didn't propose anything that Lyndon Johnson's advisers didn't eventually persuade him to do. In my opinion, Goldwater is a civilized man with high principles."

In the waning days of Richard Nixon's administration, the former president's chief assistant, General Alexander Haig, emerged as a figure who held together the shreds of a White House tearing itself apart. I asked Galbraith if the country was fortunate to have a man such as Haig on the scene in those final days and hours of administration chaos.

"No. We would have survived," Galbraith answered. "It took Alexander Haig a long while to wake up to the moral deficiencies of Richard Nixon. There are certain men, as I.F. Stone once said, whom history treats with a yawn. In the case of Haig, I believe that history is already doing so."

Along with Dean Acheson, Averell Harriman has exerted influence on contemporary American foreign policy. Galbraith knows them both well. "You are talking about one of my closest friends over the greatest length of time. Harriman is a man of great intelligence, character, and durability. He has given a decent image of the United States to the world, and he has a deep commitment to peace.

"Averell Harriman has been both the severest critic and the closest friend of the Soviet Union. He is incapable of detaching himself from responsibility. Regardless of whether the Democrats or Republicans are in power, he continues to have this deep sense of concern for maintaining peace. He has had the durability to stay the course and to stay with the problem."

I asked Galbraith if the United States still had statesmen of the quality of Dean Acheson and Averell Harriman in our government.

"I'm sure they exist and in a greater number than before. But as time passes and as government becomes more complex, we become governed more by bureaucrats than by individuals.

"World War II, for example, was a time of great individual leaders like Stalin, Hitler, Mussolini, Roosevelt, De Gaulle, and Churchill. In recent times, history has thrown forward people like Gerald Ford, who function only as part of an organization. This phenomenon is particularly true in domestic affairs. However, there is still some room left for initiative in foreign affairs."

Galbraith has always been fascinated by General Charles de Gaulle: "He was the head of a government without a country, almost without an army, in London during World War II. He attempted to protect French prestige and French tradition. This was a very difficult position for him and almost certain to cause friction among the other Allied leaders.

"Like Konrad Adenauer, who restored the self-respect and the prestige of the Germans after the war, De Gaulle did the same thing for the French. He conveyed an air of grandeur, which he combined with a deep capacity for feeling what the French people wanted. One has to read De Gaulle's memoirs to see the depth and variety of his thought and also to see that he was a stylist and writer in the manner of Churchill. Churchill has a much greater reputation as a writer, but De Gaulle also had a remarkable gift of self-expression."

I told Galbraith that perhaps the world was better off in not having any more of these so-called great leaders in power. "It's much more comfortable, and safer," Galbraith replied.

I mentioned that I was puzzled by the public's continued fascination with Adolf Hitler and the Third Reich. One would think that the world would want to forget Hitler and yet each year new books about him are published.

"Those who write about Hitler dwell little on his motivation and too much on events. There does seem to be a fascination with a man whom no one is obliged to defend and in whom no one can find any virtue, for that matter, any great intelligence. As long as he had overwhelming power, he was brilliant. When he had to deal with adversity, he was a fraud.

"I became aware of this in 1945 when I discovered how deficient German mobilization and civilian management had been. Nazi leaders believed they could build up munitions supplies, use them up in a short campaign, and, even as the campaign was underway, return to civilian production. The number of servants for the affluent in Germany did not decline during the war. German factories did not go into multiple-shift operations. The high Nazis were incompetent militarily and also in running the civilian affairs of the country."

I asked about Canada's late Prime Minister Lester Pearson, who moved Canada toward a greater sense of her own national identity, away from being an appendage of Great Britain.

"Mike Pearson was a man of charm and intelligence," Galbraith commented. "And though he came up through the ranks of the civil service, he had a great aptitude for party politics. (He was one of the pioneer figures in the Canadian foreign service.) Partly through the force of his personality, he was a man who placed the negotiation position of Canada for the first time on a parity with that of Great Britain, the United States, and France. So for the first time when other countries were discussing an issue, Canada had to be included in the deliberations."

Dean Acheson and Galbraith were associated for a number of years. "Dean had his good and bad periods. His bad periods were in the early days of the Roosevelt administration, when he was in the Treasury Department. He was at odds with the administration because he was in favor of hard money and the gold standard. Dean recognized in later years that his stand had been reactionary.

"In the war and postwar years, Dean was the focus of the liberal element in the State Department. We all regarded him as the center of our circle. He was one of the great innovative figures of the Marshall Plan, and it still has to be decided whether in fact he had more to do with the plan than General George C. Marshall did. I suspect that he had quite a hand in Marshall's Harvard speech, which gave the plan its theme. But in his later years he hardened into a very resistant cold warrior. We served together in the Democratic Advisory Council. He was chairman of foreign policy, and I was chairman for domestic policy. In those days the rest of us spent our time softening down Dean's declarations of war. He repeatedly criticized Dulles for being soft on Communism.

"Dean Acheson was an enormously interesting man, with an extremely well-educated mind, who wasn't very receptive to ideas from lesser mortals. And that is why he got frozen into a cold war posture in his later years. He also made no pretense about his lack of knowledge of the Third World. He was very much the European in his outlook. In consequence, he was particularly open to the erroneous thought that the long arm of Moscow was everywhere.

"He was a man of supreme and, one can say, excessive self-assurance. He was a godlike figure who always sought to impress his ideas on other men. Dean Acheson never thought other people were worth the bother. When somebody accuses me of being an elitist, I always mentally deny it and say that I am not quite that much like Dean Acheson."

The conversation then turned to William F. Buckley. "I am very fond of Bill Buckley," said Galbraith. "He is a very kind man, and few people understand this about him. He is enormously well read. He has a wide-ranging set of ideas and an extensive vocabulary. He has a good sense of repartée. When I am with Bill, I never have to stop to think. When he states a proposition, I know it is wrong, and then I can safely disagree."

He and Buckley worked together on television during the national political conventions of 1972 and 1976. Galbraith found it a great pleasure. "Our participation on the *Today* show was handicapped by the fact that we needed more time than the morning television show format provides. We could not fully develop any topic. I doubt if we will do that kind of thing again."

While Galbraith was ambassador to India during the Kennedy years, the United States had serious problems with Cuba, notably the Bay of Pigs invasion and the missile crisis. Since the end of the 1950s, the United States has had Dwight Eisenhower, John F. Kennedy, Lyndon Johnson, Richard Nixon, Gerald Ford, and Jimmy Carter as presidents. During that time Cuba has had but one chief of state, Fidel Castro.

"Fidel Castro has certainly earned his place in the world, when you consider what Cuba was like before he came to power," Galbraith told me. "Cuba had a corrupt government in which a large percentage of the land was under foreign ownership or in the hands of predators. Even the Mafia interests in Cuba were probably better than the local despots who controlled the island before Castro. It had a large, half-starved, rural population as well. Castro brought off a social revolution, certainly at some cost to those who left. To those people who remained, he brought a sense of participation in the day-to-day affairs of their own country."

I asked Galbraith about the late J. Edgar Hoover. How was Hoover able to retain his great power for almost forty years?

"Fear," said Galbraith. "There was an uneasy fear on the part of everybody who came into government that he would have adverse material about them. This has to be coupled with the fact that Hoover built a strong, efficient organization. If the FBI had been a sloppy, lousy police force, Hoover wouldn't have lasted. It was a combination of what he could do to hurt somebody, plus the efficiency of the organization, that created this sense of fear.

"I don't think he was a very effective propagandist for himself, except that he worked at it all the time, and wrapped himself up in patriotism and the flag."

The top man at *Fortune* magazine was Henry Luce, the legendary founder of *Time, Life,* and *Fortune* magazines. Galbraith has many fond memories of Luce and his five years as a *Fortune* editor: "Luce had two important qualities as an editor. He was extraordinarily curious. Luce wanted to know everything. He would be walking down a street, and Luce would look up and see a window with a private detective sign. He would then wonder what kind of work detectives did, how they operated, what the legalities of their business were, what kind of lives they led. Before you knew it, he'd ask twenty questions about detectives, not one of which you could answer. Then he'd say, 'Let's have a story on those fellows.'

"The other thing about Luce was that he had a gift for the essential. Something that's unneeded is worse than useless. When the reader encounters filler he quits. It takes some effort when you are in the theater to walk out. But it takes no effort whatsoever to put down a magazine. Luce was also a highly competent businessman. He kept a close watch over the circulation of his magazines. If an enterprise wasn't making its way, Henry either cut it away, or he sold it."

The grand old man of today's American labor movement is AFL-CIO President George Meany. Some observers believe that Meany, not the president of the United States, runs the country. I asked Galbraith what he thought: "George Meany is a tough, very honest, and, what very few people realize, an amusing man. I think he has served the American labor movement very well.

"He was more rigidly anti–Communist, particularly on the stance he took on the Vietnam War, than I was — in fact, we were at opposite extremes. I didn't have sympathy for the position the AFL-CIO took on that war, and they had even less sympathy for the position I took."

At one time Ronald Reagan was a liberal Democrat; he and Galbraith co-founded the Americans for Democratic Action. Now that Reagan had lost his bid for the Republican nomination for the presidency and had returned to his ranch in California, I asked Galbraith his opinion.

"Ronald Reagan made the transition from being a left-wing liberal to being the hero of the Right. I suppose the transition was caused by the frequently piquant combination of conviction and pecuniary reward. After his movie career was over, he became a lecturer for General Electric. General Electric doesn't pay people to lecture on socialism or even liberalism.

"There was a difference between Reagan's rhetoric and his practices as governor of California. In his speeches as governor, he was antiexpenditure, antitax, and antiuniversity. But in practice, during his administration, taxes and expenditures went up. And the universities survived. If he had really started to crack down on all the public services of California, Reagan wouldn't have remained as governor.

"In running for the presidency, there was a certain flexibility which allowed him, among other things, to select Senator Richard Schweiker of Pennsylvania as his vice presidential candidate, a man who had a nearly perfect score in the ADA."

Once Galbraith touched briefly on André Malraux, one of the great contemporary French writers and a minister in Charles de Gaulle's cabinet: "Malraux has an imaginative capacity for inventing personal history. I read him with enjoyment.

"Some friends of mine have felt that there was a considerable difference between Malraux's impression of his personal history and what actually happened. This is a good process. I've thought of someday writing my memoirs but I'm going to wait until everybody who is in a position to contradict me is either senile or dead."

CHAPTER **15**
WORLDWIDE CLASSROOM

One spring day in 1976 as I was walking with Galbraith in London, we stopped at the Queen Victoria Memorial in front of Buckingham Palace. A group of English schoolgirls approached, clutching illustrated worksheets. Pointing to her worksheet, which depicted the imperial scene before us, one of the girls asked me, "Can you tell me what's symbolic of the Empire here?" I volunteered that it was the statue of the late queen, which represents the monarchy as a binding force for the nations of the Commonwealth.

Galbraith quickly broke in, "No! No! That's wrong!" He pointed to the streets radiating from the Victoria Memorial and to the metallic letters fastened to the stone pillars flanking the mall. They spell out the names of countries that were once part of the largest empire the world has ever known. Gratefully the girls filled out their worksheets with Galbraith's information. He was back in the role of teacher, a role he had filled at the University of California (Berkeley), at Princeton, and at Harvard University.

Galbraith has played many roles, often simultaneously. There is one part, however, in which he is always in character — that of educator. He has the great teacher's art of weaving a point or a moral into even the most casual conversation.

He has formally retired as a member of the Harvard faculty, but he maintains an office on campus in the Littauer Center of Public Administration. The *Harvard Crimson* once called the location of Galbraith's office the best kept secret at the university — especially from his students.

His presence at the school is still very much felt. The president of a nearby university once told me that "Harvard needs Galbraith just as much as Galbraith needs Harvard." The doors leading to his office suite are unmarked, and the rooms themselves are rather small. Andrea Williams, Galbraith's administrative assistant for the past eighteen years, and one of her aides Emmy Davis, work in one room; another secretary is across the hall. Among the decorations in Galbraith's office are photographs of famous friends and political cartoons. There is no desk as such; a comfortable Eames chair is next to the telephone.

Harvard, of course, has been home base for Galbraith since 1949. "Harvard was a great place in the 1930s and to some extent in the 1940s," said Galbraith. "It was the place to which the Keynesian Revolution came in the United States and from which it passed to the rest of the country. Harvard was also the preeminent place where the practical men from Washington and the academic community of the university came together to discuss economics. But I have never made any secret of the fact that the happiest years of my academic life were spent at the University of California at Berkeley. I have always regarded the University of California as the greatest accomplishment in university education in this country."

Galbraith adverts time and time again to the importance of education as an element of social balance. He sets a high value on the role of the educator; but he is under no illusions about general acceptance of that valuation. Once, commenting on the fact that his old friend Michael Kalecki had been removed from his public posts in Poland and relegated to teaching, he remarked, "The government's assumption was that nobody can do much damage teaching. It's the same belief we have in the United States."

He is critical of the many facets of education today.

Education throughout the United States is compulsory until age 16. However, because public education is most typically a local responsibility, the quality of education can vary greatly — from state to state and from community to community. Indeed, in large cities, the quality of educational services may vary even from school to school.

One useful way to measure the quality of educational services is by the amount of money a community, or a state, spends on that essential service. Using money as the yardstick, affluent communities by and large provide better educational services than poor communities. Galbraith has stated many times that a quality education is one important step in eliminating insular poverty.

"The high school is the weakest part of our educational system. It has always seemed to me that high school is the time when the case for discipline in the schools is very strong. Unfortunately, there is usually not enough discipline then. But one has to recognize that the school environment is only one part of the educational process. The family has a lot to do with it; the defects and shortcomings of a family are self-perpetuating."

Could some of the problems of education rest with young people themselves, who tend to resist the process, regardless of how good or bad it is?

"I suppose every generation since the beginning of time has regarded children from the age of 10 to the age of 20 as being rather ghastly. The adults are probably right. We have been a bit too inclined to relax our educational standards. I once said that every move students make for educational reform ends up in a lowering of educational standards. I look with great discontent on this decline in our universities, and the even greater decline in our high schools."

Continuing education is becoming more widely accepted, both by those who wish to upgrade their occupational skills and by those who desire to investigate new areas for the pure pleasure of learning.

Galbraith believes that the public should invest in continuing education and assure that it is available in every community. However, he wouldn't put any social pressure on adults to use it. There comes a time in life when a person would rather go to a football game or watch a murder mystery on television than take conversational German at the local high school.

Galbraith looks to the educational and scientific elites to scrutinize foreign policy and its relation to the industrial system. He feels that this elite has an important obligation to become involved in changing the present economic structure.

The American industrial system encourages public expenditure in those areas which will benefit it, such as defense, highways, air safety, space exploration, harbor development, bridge construction, communications development, and particularly, education, which supplies it with qualified people. However, the system resists, according to Galbraith, those public expenditures which either hamper its usual way of operating cr which do not directly contribute to its goals.

With regard to his own education, and particularly the Cambridge experience, I asked Galbraith if it were important for a student of economics to study in England.

"It was once," Galbraith replied. "I am not sure that it is anymore. Although if one is going to study outside of the United States, Oxford and Cambridge are still the places one should go. I would say that more than any other country, the United States has maintained discipline in its universities. Although this discipline has slackened a bit, our universities still make students work. We have resisted the student concept of reform, which always results in having them do less work. In my own courses, I always rejected the 'pass or fail' system, though I never thought my courses were particularly difficult, and neither did my students. In Europe, but to a lesser degree in England, there has been a lowering of standards. If one had to name the fifty best universities in the world in terms of the quality of teaching, research, and facilities, forty would be in the United States or Canada.

"It has been impossible for me to be in Switzerland or in France without having people ask me to help their children get into Harvard. Forty years ago, the affluent French family would never have thought of sending their children to universities in the United States. Now I cannot go through Paris without having someone come up to me and say, 'You know, Mr. Galbraith, the Sorbonne is a wonderful place, but do you think my child could get into Harvard?'

"I said in *The Scotch* that I have always known that students did their best work when an element of terror was involved. Hounding students to death is not quite necessary. But the hope of excellence must be balanced or reinforced by the fear of failure."

The students of the 1960s rejected history as being totally irrelevant to the present or the future. Galbraith didn't blame the students. "I do blame my colleagues for yielding on that point. The students had some justification for their attitude. The history of economic thought, for example, is usually taught by the least inspiring professors. The fact that graduate students did not find this area of knowledge interesting should not surprise anyone. However, I am not entirely exempt from responsibility on this. The history of economic thought has always interested me very much. But I have never taught it. I always found it more convenient and interesting to teach whatever I was working on. But one should not be guided on student preferences on these matters anyway.

"One thing you can be certain of is the impermanence of student interests," he told me. "At Harvard, for example, within the last decade, there has been student opposition to the Vietnam War, which might have been partly motivated by the draft. There was opposition to ROTC. There was the commitment to civil rights, women's rights, educational reform, and the campaign of George McGovern. Anyone who expects an enduring commitment from students has no sense of history. On the other hand, every one of these bursts of student interest has had some permanent effect on our society. And some of them were very brief, such as their concern with the environment."

I asked him to evaluate himself as a teacher. "I tried to make my lectures interesting and informative. I was never much of a success in the intimate guidance of students on their work, papers or what they had heard in class. It was said that the location of my office was the best kept secret at Harvard. This may well have been true. I had a conflict between instruction and the kind of writing I wanted to do. I never made any secret of the fact that I got the greatest satisfaction and the greatest sense of self-expression from my writing."

Galbraith has, of course, another constant dimension — that of widely-known public personality. Wherever he goes, people stop and stare at him — a phenomenon enhanced by the fact that, at six feet eight inches in height, he towers above the crowd. Not as familiar to the public as a leading actor or sports figure, he is enough the superstar to enjoy public adulation without the danger of being mobbed. Indeed, his renown may be given yet another dimension. His satiric novel about the American foreign service, *The Triumph*, may be made into a film. "Seeing my name in lights at the movies is something I could easily forego, although I would really like to see *The Triumph* produced — and certainly before Bill Buckley's novel is turned into a movie."

These two facets of Galbraith — teacher and public personality — came together in 1976.

In 1975 and 1976 Galbraith filmed a series of television programs for the British Broadcasting Corporation about the history of economic ideas and their consequences. Public television stations in the United States started carrying the series in May 1977. *The Age of Uncertainty* sums up Galbraith's personal view of the past two hundred years. "I have always believed that the distinction between good economics and bad economics is a sense of history."

According to *London Daily Telegraph* reviews, "Considered simply as an economic and sociopolitical view of the last two centuries, *The Age of Uncertainty* is without equal in the history of television. . . . There is never a minute of the series that is uninteresting." Galbraith's television series explores the last two hundred years of social thought and political economics.

From the formulation of classical capitalism by Adam Smith to such current concerns as the state of our cities, the arms race, and the modern corporation, Galbraith traces economic life with film, location footage, rare archival material, graphics, drama, and, of course, his own words.

Galbraith says that the modern era of uncertainty began with World War I. Social structures that had developed over centuries fell apart. The privileged position of the nobility and the rich was shattered. The disintegration of the old order began in Western Europe, where it was least expected.

In 1914, the "territorial imperative"[1] dominated the ruling structure of Europe. Rulers suspected each other of coveting territories and peoples that would strengthen their wealth and power. All the major nations of Europe — France, Germany, Austria, Russia, and Great Britain — had highly developed plans for war, plans that would quickly put millions of armed men in strategic areas.

Galbraith says that in 1914 there was a "stupidity problem" among European generals, who held their rank by virtue of social position, family background, and tradition. Intelligence was not a requirement for generalship: "Both the rulers and the generals in World War I were singularly brainless men,"[2] Galbraith writes in *The Age of Uncertainty*. World War I resulted from what he calls a "rogue reaction"[3] to the territorial imperative — the suspicions it caused, the threat of putting millions of men to arms under stupid rulers and generals.

The Second International tried to form an agreement between all the workers in Europe to unite and protect themselves against mobilization through parliamentary power and strikes. The general strike, in which workers in all occupations stopped their labor in protest, was considered to be the ultimate weapon against the policies of the capitalistic and ruling classes. Its organizers theorized that a general strike would stop a nation's economic life and therefore, its ability to wage war.

However, when mobilization was decreed in Germany in 1914, the German Social Democrats, the country's strongest labor party, supported war preparations. Almost one-third of the German workers put on uniforms and began drilling. In France, instead of resisting the war effort, the workers cheerfully donned their uniforms and shouldered their rifles.

Although the British were concerned about Germany's growing naval strength, there were no plans for mass mobilization. In Russia, the militant Bolsheviks among the Social Democrats in the Duma protested against war, but were quickly arrested.

Although the workers had power in Germany, they had almost none in Russia. The Russian peasant was important only because he was needed in the ranks of the army as cannon fodder.

In the television episode "Lenin and the Great Ungluing,"[4] Galbraith says that Lenin was far more a revolutionary than Marx: "Marx wrote; Lenin led. He remains the revolutionary colossus who stands astride a whole age, the point of reference still for the long, slowly moving lines beside the Kremlin Wall."[5]

Lenin watched the developments in Europe with great interest from Poland. In that summer of 1914 he was forty-four years old. Lenin was the second revolutionary in his family — his brother was hanged for attempting to assassinate Czar Alexander III.

Galbraith recalls his visit with an elderly Soviet man who had known Lenin. Galbraith had pictured Lenin with the tidy appearance of an accountant. When he asked the old man the source of Lenin's leadership, he replied simply, "When Lenin spoke, we marched."[6]

Though Lenin was a follower of Marx, he was not a slave to the German philosopher's ideology, according to Galbraith. Contrary to Marx, Lenin maintained that a successful revolution results from a closely knit group of disciplined and committed individuals. While Marx expected industrial workers to lead the revolution, Lenin believed in the peasants of Russia. He promised them land if they agreed to form the basis of the socialist state. During the war, Russian peasant soldiers opted for taking land confiscated from their former masters, instead of fighting for their weak-willed czar.

In August 1914, the police arrested Lenin at his Polish summer retreat on charges that he was a Russian spy. Lenin spent a short term in jail before he and his family were permitted to go to Switzerland.

According to Galbraith, Switzerland then was the revolutionary capital of the world. Geneva rents fell in two categories: one for people who went to bed at night and the other for Russians who spent all night debating their cause. During his stay in Switzerland, Lenin was supported by money sent from Russia. He spent long hours in the library developing his pamphlets — a weapon of revolution. Another revolutionary tool was the conference.

An important conference was held at Zimmerwald in September 1915. Thirty-eight revolutionaries, including Lenin, Trotsky, Zinoviev, and Radek, came from eleven countries, posing as birdwatchers. Lenin stressed that the workers were not each other's enemies; rather, they had enemies in common, their rulers.

In spring 1916, another conference was held at Kienthal, at a time when soldiers were being slaughtered by the thousands. Galbraith makes this comparison in *The Age of Uncertainty*: 154,000 British and French lives were lost in an attempt to gain six miles on the Somme in 1916, and 270,000 French and German soldiers lost their lives at Verdun the same year. In contrast, in World War II, France was liberated at the cost of 44,000 Allied dead.

One night in the winter of 1917, Lenin and his wife were dining at their home in Zurich when a friend burst excitedly into the room with the news that revolution had broken out in Russia. The moment had come at last. The Swiss socialist Fritz Platten arranged with the German government to transport Lenin and members of his entourage across Europe in a sealed train for protection. There were twenty people on the train, including Lenin's French-born collaborator-mistress. Lenin arrived in Petrograd on April 3, 1917, and took power in October.

Galbraith says Lenin's most significant accomplishment was in consolidating power after seizing it. He brought the Russian Revolution from anarchy and civil war to dictatorial authority within five years. But there were also failures, particularly Lenin's inability to understand the complexities of constructing a socialist economy and the problems of planning and managing a socialist society. The bureaucratization of socialist management astonished and depressed Lenin. It strained his physical and mental energy until his death in 1924.

In the book version of *The Age of Uncertainty,* Galbraith is at his readable best. Galbraith maintains that the Scotch and the Jews have dominated the study of economics starting with Adam Smith, the founding father of economics. Smith, a Scotchman born in Kirkcaldy on the Firth of Forth in 1723, is considered the patron saint of free enterprise.

Smith studied at Oxford and returned to Edinburgh to lecture on English literature. At Edinburgh, Smith became a lifelong friend of the philosopher David Hume. In 1751, Adam Smith was named a professor of philosophy at the University of Glasgow.

The American colonies attracted Smith's attention. Galbraith believes that Smith learned a great deal about the New World from his contemporary Benjamin Franklin, who spent many years in England. In 1763, Smith left the university to tutor the wealthy Duke of Buccleuch, and together they set out on the Grand Tour of Europe. Smith visited the home of Voltaire, near Geneva. Like Voltaire, Smith was a man of reason; religious belief or emotion had no role in solving problems. Only relevant information was to be brought to bear in the reasoning process. And Smith's ability to assimilate and apply available information allowed him to open new paths of knowledge and therefore become a pioneer of thought, Galbraith says.

In France, Smith came in contact with the Physiocrats, whose philosophy was based on the premise that agriculture was the source of all wealth. At Paris and Versailles, Smith met and was impressed by François Quesnay, physician to Louis XV and friend of Madame de Pompadour, whose *Tableau Economique* was a quantitative approach to describing how the main parts of the economic system worked.

Also in France, Smith became friends with Anne Robert Jacques Turgot, the comptroller-general of France and a founder of the science of political economy. Turgot and his colleagues believed that the burden of taxation should be distributed more equitably, which would require limiting the state's power. Turgot attempted to control the extravagance of the king's court, much of which was subsidized by taxing agriculture. Turgot failed, Galbraith writes in his book, because "the privileged feel that their privileges, however egregious they may seem to others, are a solemn, basic, God-given right. The sensitivity of the poor to injustice is a trivial thing compared with that of the rich."[7]

Years before the French Revolution, Smith returned home to write his great book. In 1776, the year of the American Revolution, Smith published *An Inquiry into the Nature and Causes of the Wealth of Nations,* in which he proposed that the wealth of a nation was the result of individuals pursuing their own self-interest. By serving his self-interest, the individual contributes to the common good. According to Smith, the individual is guided by an "invisible hand" — a far better alternative than the visible, authoritarian presence of the state that inhibits or prohibits the free actions of individuals.

Adam Smith also described modern assembly-line production. Specialization results in a more efficient utilization of labor, he felt. As Smith described the manufacture of pins: "One man draws out the wire, another straights it, a third cuts it, a fourth points it, a fifth grinds it at the top for receiving the head: to make the head requires two or three distinct operations: to put it on, is a peculiar business, to whiten the pins is another; it is even a trade by itself to put them into the paper. . . ."[8]

According to Smith's calculations, by dividing the work among ten men, 48,000 pins could be produced each day, with each of the ten men contributing his labor to each pin. However, if one man performed every operation in manufacturing pins, he would probably produce only one pin per day — or, if he were particularly fast, as many as twenty. Assembly-line methodology is the basis of today's industrial society. The concept hasn't changed since Adam Smith's time; it has only become more sophisticated.

One benefit of increased production resulting from the division of labor is the ability to expand markets. This led Adam Smith to reject tariffs and other restraints to free trade. He believed in the greatest possible trade of private goods in the largest possible market. Smith further believed that free trade resulted in more individual freedom. Smith's vision of free trade was not limited to the

British Isles; his vision was worldwide and is still actively pursued by today's multinational corporations.

But behind every freedom lurks a threat. In Adam Smith's concept of free trade, the threat was — and is — government, which has the power to set tariffs, permit monopolies, and impose taxes. Adam Smith saw another threat to free trade — businessmen themselves. He once observed that "people of the same trade seldom meet together, even for merriment and diversion, but the conversation ends in a conspiracy against the public, or in some contrivance to raise prices."[9]

Smith was opposed to what are now called corporations. He wrote that stockholders "seldom pretend to understand anything of the business of the company; and when the spirit of faction happens not to prevail among them, give themselves no trouble about it, but receive contentedly such half yearly or yearly dividend, as the directors think proper to make to them."[10]

About corporate directors, Smith wrote, "Being the managers rather of other people's money than of their own, it cannot well be expected that they should watch over it with the same anxious vigilance with which the partners in a private co-partnery frequently watch over their own. Like the stewards of a rich man, they are apt to consider attention to small matters as not for their master's honour, and very easily give themselves a dispensation from having it. Negligence and profusion, therefore, must prevail, more or less, in the management of the affairs of such a company. . . . Without an exclusive privilege joint-stock companies have commonly mismanaged the trade. With an exclusive privilege they have both mismanaged and confined it."[11]

Galbraith feels that if Adam Smith were brought back from the grave to attend gatherings of the United States Chamber of Commerce, the National Association of Manufacturers, or the Confederation of British Industries, he would be amazed to hear his name used in extolling the sanctity of the free enterprise system. Galbraith also feels that today's executives would be appalled that Adam Smith would condemn their actions as being directly opposed to free enterprise.

Smith, who died in 1790, spent his last years as commissioner of customs in Edinburgh. After Smith's death, the English statesman

William Pitt canonized him as a prophet: "Smith's extensive knowledge of detail and depth of philosophical research will, I believe, furnish the best solution of every question connected with the history of commerce and with the system of political economy."[12]

Galbraith states in *The Age of Uncertainty* that Adam Smith offered "a view of how the economic system works."[13] Smith contributed two seminal ideas that continue to absorb the attention of economists and governments: the labor theory of value and the reality of a continuing population explosion. These ideas were adapted by two of Smith's close friends, David Ricardo and Thomas Malthus. In fact, Galbraith contends that Ricardo is Smith's only rival for the title of founding father of economics.

David Ricardo was a Jew, a stockbroker, and a member of the British Parliament. Thomas Malthus, an English clergyman, left the pulpit in pursuit of other interests. Throughout most of his life, Malthus taught at Haileybury, a staff college for the East India Company.

In *An Essay on the Principle of Population*, Malthus theorized that population increases geometrically while the world's food supply grows arithmetically. As a result, there always will be more people than food to feed them. It is famine, war, or other catastrophe that checks the growth of population. While Adam Smith was an optimist, basing his hope for man on the freedom of the individual to pursue his self-interest, Malthus and Ricardo were both pessimists — indeed, it could be said that they gave economics its title of the "dismal science."

While Malthus concerned himself with unrestrained growth in human population, Ricardo viewed the masses in terms of workers fiercely competing for jobs and food. As a result of competition, the population would be reduced to grinding poverty barely above the survival level. Ricardo believed the struggle to survive was man's fate. Accordingly, he felt that workers should receive only that which was necessary for survival; anything more would be damaging because it would tend to elevate the worker's hopes. This short-term rise in expectations and money would only encourage the worker to have more children, the result of which would be to wipe out his meager success. Ricardo's theory also took in governments and trade unions, neither of which he felt should try to emancipate people from poverty, which, after all, was their fate.

Galbraith emphasizes that Ricardo was not cruel. To Ricardo, the world was cruel; he was merely acknowledging its inevitable reality. Nevertheless, Galbraith points out, Ricardo's theories did provide people of wealth and privilege with a convenient rationale for avoiding a social responsibility.

One of Ricardo's contemporaries was Jean Baptiste Say, Adam Smith's French interpreter and creator of Say's Law: "Production always provides the income to purchase whatever is produced. What is saved is also spent, but in a different way, thus ensuring purchasing power."[14] Ricardo speculated that depressions resulting from a shortage of purchasing power were inevitable, and that any economy would occasionally have serious problems. Galbraith notes that those who accepted the possibility of a shortage in purchasing power in the time when Say's Law was accepted were guilty of crackpot thinking. It was not until John Maynard Keynes, who died in 1946, that the theory of the shortage of purchasing power became accepted as gospel.

In the eighteenth century, Ireland suffered a grim human tragedy. Between 1780 and 1840, its population had doubled and nearly doubled again to eight million. (In contrast, approximately six million people live in Ireland today.) During those decades the staple of the Irish food supply, the potato crop, also increased. But much of Ireland's farmland was owned by absentee landowners living in England. As the population grew, so did the need for land. And as the demand for land grew, so did the rents that the landlords could command. So the Irish sold their grain to pay the rent and then, to survive, ate the potatoes they grew. "Starvation might conceivably be survived. Eviction for nonpayment of the rent meant there would be nothing to live on forever,"[15] writes Galbraith.

Between 1845 and 1847, when the Irish potato crop was devastated by parasites, the Irish desperately needed food. Charles Edward Trevelyan, head of the British Treasury, argued that trade would be paralyzed if the government interfered with the profit of free enterprise by giving away food. Trevelyan believed that the natural laws of economics were at work — that men, women, and children were starving in Ireland had no meaning. In 1846, he wrote in a letter, "Being altogether beyond the powers of men, the cure has been applied by the direct stroke of an all-wise Providence in a manner as unexpected and as unthought of as it is likely to be effectual."[16] Millions of Irish found their way out on the ships sailing to the United States and Canada. The bleak theories of Malthus and Ricardo seemed remote in the New World. Indeed, land in the United States and Canada was both cheap and abundant, and both countries welcomed a growing population.

The new immigrant was free, unbeholden to either landlord or employer. If he didn't like where he was and what he was doing, he could freely move on. Contrary to Ricardo's theories, the incomes of workers got progressively better. There was enough food and work for everyone. Galbraith states that these immigrants were producing more food in a year's time than their mothers and fathers had seen in all their lives. In addition, Irish-American construction crews were building the transportation systems that would make this food available to all the people of the world. The famine in Europe forced the migration of thousands of people to North America to survive. Galbraith says that these immigrants then "solved the world's food problem, at least for a century."[17] Ricardo and Malthus would have been astonished.

From the time of the early economists to the present, the poor have been subject to intensive study. Scientists have wanted to know the reasons for poverty. Is there something deficient in poor people's breeding and their environment that keeps them — and their children and their children's children — poor? Galbraith, for his part, maintains that the one class of people that has been neglected by scholars is the rich. A poor family often will freely let the sociologist observe its living habits. The rich, however, are far more loath to share their privacy and their life styles with anyone but their peers. Charles Darwin and Herbert Spencer, according to *The Age of Uncertainty*, are the two major apologists for explaining scientifically why the privileged are the privileged.

Charles Darwin's doctrine of natural selection gave the rich a new rationale: They had survived because of their superior strength in adapting to their environment. The phrase "survival of the fittest" belongs to Herbert Spencer, who acknowledged his debt to Darwin: "I am simply carrying out the views of Mr. Darwin in their applications to the human race. . . . All [members of the race] being subject to the 'increasing difficulty of getting a living . . .' there is an average advance under the pressure, since 'only those who *do* advance under it eventually survive;' and . . . 'these must be the select of their generation.' "[18]

Galbraith maintains that Spencer's ideas were well suited to American capitalism and the new capitalists it bred. Because wealth was assumed to be the result of natural superiority, no one, not even the government, could question it. Being wealthy was even more enjoyable because it indicated that one was also superior. Spencer did not believe in private or public assistance to the poor because such action was dangerously harmful to the continued development of the favored race. He defended his view: "Partly by weeding out those of lowest development and partly by subjecting those who remain to the never-ceasing discipline of experience, nature secures the growth of a race who shall both understand the conditions of existence and be able to act up to them. It is impossible in any degree to suspend this discipline by stepping in between ignorance and its consequences, without, to a corresponding degree, suspending the progress. If to be ignorant were as safe as to be wise, no one would become wise."[19] To Spencer, charity was a bad thing for those who required it and a virtuous expression of nobility for those who administered it.

Spencer's philosophy won such devotees among American intellectuals as Yale professor William Graham Sumner, considered by Galbraith to be the "most influential single voice on economic matters in the United States in the second half of the last century."[20] It was Sumner who said, "The millionaires are a product of natural selection. It is because they are thus selected that wealth — both their own and that entrusted to them — aggregates under their hands. They may fairly be regarded as the naturally selected agents of society for certain work. They get high wages and live in luxury, but the bargain is a good one for society."[21]

The building of the railroads in North America catapulted many people into great wealth. Contractors, real estate agents, shippers, and, of course, the owners, all got rich. But for the Irish, Chinese, and other immigrant laborers, building the railroads represented the other side of the coin: hard work, low pay, injury, disease, and often death. It was quintessential human exploitation. But the railroads were built and vast fortunes were made. Galbraith points out that the railroad attracted scoundrels who used Spencer's theory of natural selection to their own advantage.

Cornelius Vanderbilt, king of the New York Central Railroad, according to Galbraith, was committed to robbing the public, whom he scorned.

Galbraith distinguishes between those who robbed their stock-holders and thereby lost their reputations with the public and those who robbed the public and thereby — ironically — found their reputations enhanced in the public's view. To the latter group Galbraith assigns the Vanderbilts, Rockefellers, Carnegies, Morgans, Guggenheims, and Mellons. These people made their money by producing goods and services as cheaply as possible, stamping out competition, and selling what they produced for the highest prices they could get. They also began family dynasties of impeccable and distinguished reputation, which helped to convey the impression that they were "God-fearing men."[22]

There is much more, notably Galbraith's insights into the career and thinking of John Maynard Keynes, who we have discussed elsewhere in this book. *The Age of Uncertainty* is Galbraith using many facets of himself — his wide-ranging interests, his commanding presence, his fame, his humor — to do the thing he loves best: to teach. In this medium he was able to address himself to a worldwide classroom containing millions of students. He made the most of the opportunity.

16
MAN
OF
STANDING

There is so much to John Kenneth Galbraith — physically, professionally, intellectually — that it is impossible to obtain a comprehensive view.

I spent a great deal of time with Galbraith. Some of that time was spent sitting — in his office or in his study — but some of it was spent walking. Andrea Williams, Galbraith's administrative assistant, had warned me about what she called his "death marches." Galbraith loves to walk, and loves to talk on a variety of subjects while he walks. A companion is hard-pressed to keep pace and listen at the same time. Once Galbraith took a woman friend for a stroll around his country house in Newfane, Vermont. Like a mountain cat who knows every inch of his terrain, he strode down a steep trail running alongside a waterfall. His companion, struggling to keep up with his speed and length of stride, came tumbling down after him. She suffered only a few bruises, but to her, "death march" is an apt description of a Galbraithian walk.

Here — culled from conversations in study or office or on "death marches" through London or the Vermont countryside — are some kaleidoscopic impressions.

* * *

Galbraith is six-feet-eight-inches tall. As you walk with Galbraith through the streets of a city, people stop and stare. Some recognize him; others cannot recall the name right away, but they know they are looking at someone of consequence. When he visited Peking there was great concern at the hotel about how to accommodate his unusual height. The resourceful Chinese put two beds together and he was able to sleep without contortions.

Galbraith takes great pride in his height. In his *Ambassador's Journal*, for example, he tells about talking to General de Gaulle at the reception for heads of state after President Kennedy's funeral: ". . . the world belongs to tall men. They are more visible, therefore their behavior is better and accordingly they are to be trusted. He (De Gaulle) said he agreed and added, 'It is important that we be merciless with those who are too small.' "[1]

* * *

Galbraith's Scotch-Canadian background, with its overtones of Calvinist convictions, might suggest that he believes in a degree of predestination in an economic sense — that some nations and individuals are preordained to be rich, others poor.

"I've always been suspicious of ethnic stereotypes, and particularly as they apply to the Scotch," he maintains. "Much of the ethnic identity of the Scotch was established by John Knox, and the rest of us were never as bad as that.

"I certainly do not believe in predestination. I am a strong economic determinist," he told me. "I consider myself a reformer rather than a revolutionary. I have always put my faith in the idea of change from within which has continuity with the system and does not involve a radical break with the past. I cured myself of a commitment to predestination when I left the Old School Baptist Church at Wallacetown, Ontario. As a matter of fact, that church provided a great therapeutic effect; it cured me of all commitment to formal religion. I cannot to this day go into Notre Dame or St. Paul's without a positive sense of fear that I am going to be trapped there forever.

"I remember a few years ago, I went to a memorial service for Senator Wayne Morse. I walked into the National Cathedral in Washington, and I immediately felt a sense of fear and alarm. I thought Wayne was doing it to me even though he was dead. When he was alive, you could be sure of an enormous lecture on what you should believe and do. But it was still the old fear of churches. I think Stonehenge wouldn't give me the same trouble."

* * *

Galbraith usually spends some time at his Newfane, Vermont farm every summer. Many academics have Vermont homes. Both Milton Friedman and Arthur Burns have residences in the state.

Putney, Vermont, is a short drive from Newfane, the hometown of former US Senator George Aiken, who once remarked that the town is "the intellectual center of the world. It's where people from Harvard come to get the rust rubbed off."

Galbraith's study at Newfane is bright with memorabilia — colorful rugs, a battered Japanese military bugle, several Russian peasant dolls, a photo of Galbraith and Jacqueline Kennedy in India, books and newspapers, easy chairs, and a fireplace.

I first went to Newfane to interview Galbraith in 1975. I found that he has a special arrangement for receiving visitors at his secluded eighteenth-century retreat. I went into the local general store and told the woman at the counter that I was calling the Galbraiths. She handed me the phone and I dialed the number Andrea Williams had given me. Emily Wilson, the Galbraiths' housekeeper, surrogate mother for their children, and a member of the family for over thirty-six years, asked me to pick up some groceries and papers she had ordered on my way up — another ritual for the Galbraiths' guests.

I asked Emily how she had liked living in India. She told me that she loved every minute of her time there. I then asked her how she felt about seeing all the poor people and their suffering in that country. Emily Wilson is black, and she told me in no uncertain terms that there are still a lot of poor people and suffering in the United States. A warm and open person, Emily Wilson stands a little under five feet and she sprinkles her language with salty terms, especially when the topic is on how she perceives the rich "ripping off" the poor. Emily told me that when she was with the Galbraiths in India, beggars would come to the back door, she would give them articles of her clothing, and had to be restrained in her charity so as not to give everything away.

Mrs. Galbraith is a strikingly handsome woman, a good deal shorter than her husband. Kitty Galbraith's eyes are her most striking feature. They are large and dark with an unblinking intensity. On the one hand, her gaze is coldly analytical; on the other hand, her gaze doesn't make you feel uncomfortable or uneasy. One can never forget Ken Galbraith's height; one can never forget Kitty Galbraith's eyes.

It was at the Newfane farm that the Galbraiths helped to launch Senator George McGovern's 1972 campaign for the presidency. The Galbraiths had invited over two-hundred people to attend a reception for the senator at the farm. Kitty Galbraith told me that she prayed that it wouldn't rain because she wouldn't know what to do with the people if they all showed up. Fortunately, fair weather prevailed; all the people who were invited came. Of his times with Galbraith in Vermont, Senator McGovern said, "Galbraith and I have had for quite a while a fine institutional arrangement — a long weekend each summer at Newfane. Often, Arthur Schlesinger and former Oklahoma Senator Fred Harris would drop by. On those occasions at Newfane, I've had the best discussions with Ken — on economics, politics, and international affairs."

* * *

On a Vermont visit, during interviews for this book, Galbraith stood by the living room fireplace and told me about filming *The Age of Uncertainty* television series. The last episode, "A Weekend in Vermont," is a free-swinging forum on the future of capitalism, democracy, and foreign policy. Galbraith debated the prospects of the industrial West with Katherine Graham of the *Washington Post*, Arthur Schlesinger, Jr., Edward Heath, the former prime minister of Great Britain, Gyorgy Arbatov, director of the Institute for the Study of the USA/Canada of the Academy of Sciences in Moscow, former Secretary of State Dr. Henry Kissinger, and others.

In addition to the BBC crew, Kissinger was accompanied by Secret Service men, Vermont state troopers, and the local sheriff. Galbraith told me that the Secret Service was concerned about Kissinger's safety because the fields and woods around his house offered many hiding places.

One day, Kissinger sent a Secret Service man to nearby Brattleboro to pick up the latest batch of dispatches and cables. When he returned, Kissinger opened the thick folder and read the first dispatch with a worried expression. "Damn it! They're shooting in Lebanon again," he said. A sheriff's deputy sought to assure Kissinger of his safety: "Don't you worry about it, Mr. Kissinger. That shooting is nowhere near here. It's way across the border in New Hampshire."

* * *

Galbraith's capacity to travel constantly is astonishing. I wondered how he was able to keep up the pace. "I think traveling is much easier than working. I've always liked traveling. So does my wife. I did a lot of flying during the war with lousy pilots and terrible airplanes. That cured me of any uncertainty or uneasiness when I get on a plane run by a civilian pilot and a civilian organization. I used to get very tired flying with the military. Everyone did.

"The key to travel is to see an airplane trip as a long period of relaxation. And I try to avoid any extended conversations. I got on a plane one day, coming back from Hawaii, and I settled down for several hours of rest. A stranger sat beside me, and said, 'Professor Galbraith, I want to talk to you about some of your egalitarian views.' I found myself facing the prospect of a long defense of myself when what I really wanted to do was to read, do some writing, and relax. I used one of my formulas for getting rid of this type of person. I said to him, 'That's something which you can't discuss on an airplane.' He gave me a puzzled look and moved away. Everyone once in a while during the trip he would look at me with a bemused expression. But he didn't say anything more to me.

"The other great problem with air travel is the talking pilot. When you're taking off from Boston to go to San Francisco, he is the man who tells you that you are passing over Connecticut and then gives you a two minute lecture on the geology of the Berkshire mountains. Then he really goes into detail when you fly over Albany and the Finger Lakes. There are various ways of handling the talking pilot. A friend of mine has a solution. He takes an airline envelope and puts a dollar into it, along with a little note which tells the pilot, 'In return for services rendered in the form of this payment, would you kindly maintain silence, except for routine announcements.' The dollar always comes back with an angry response. If the pilot doesn't stop his lectures, my friend sends in five dollars. That usually does the trick."

*   *   *

Galbraith cherishes some of the surprising encounters he has on his travels. He talked about one characteristic conversation:

"In 1969, I was in Los Angeles for a political meeting just at the end of my term as head of the ADA [Americans for Democratic Action, an ultra-liberal political action organization which he and Ronald Reagan helped to found]." Galbraith went on, "It must have been a very light day in the news business because I had a press conference with among others a *Los Angeles Times* man who said, 'Mr. Galbraith, do you think that we will ever have another crash like the one we had in 1929?' I said, 'Oh, sure.' He knew I had written a book about it. I then said, 'The only question is when it will come.' The next day, the *Times* had a headline across its early edition saying, *Galbraith Predicts New Crash*. It got out on the news wires and a friend of mine saw it and sold all of his stocks right at the peak of the market. I didn't know anything about what he had done but then the great slump came and the stocks went down. He called me and said, 'To what would you like me to give some money?'

"I said, 'What do you mean?'

" 'I saw that news story of yours and I sold everything I had, and now I'm way ahead of things. I want to know what your favorite charities are so I can make a contribution.' "

*   *   *

In 1968, with Mohinder Singh Randhawa, Galbraith wrote *Indian Painting: The Scene, Themes and Legends*. He once told me that this was his favorite among all his books. (He has so described several others from time to time.) "I'm one of the eight or so experts on Indian art in the world," he said. Then he added, "It's a highly noncompetitive field in which to excel."

*   *   *

As twilight approached one day at Newfane, I happened to remark to Galbraith that some of the best times of his life were still ahead. "I wish that were true," he said with a heavy sigh. "I think that is excessively optimistic. Nobody should ever suppose that getting old is that agreeable. The only advantage I can see is that, after a certain age, women treat your advances with understanding rather than with repugnance."

On our "death march" in Vermont, we crossed some open land to the rear of his house and entered the woods. In previous generations the land had been cleared for farming, and Galbraith pointed to the stone walls the early inhabitants had built as they cleared the land. The stone walls were covered with brush. Trees, intertwining vines, and lichen penetrated the brush that covered the gray boulders. There was very little machinery available when this land was first cleared and the stone walls were put up. Their construction represented enormous physical labor, as well as skill. Most of the forest in Galbraith's area is not original growth and has a somewhat scrubby look in places. However, it was early autumn and the maple leaves were turning yellow, scarlet, and orange. By the time the peak color would reach Newfane, Galbraith would be off again. I sensed that he savored every moment of the air and the scents from the forest.

As we walked, Galbraith commented on how the population of Newfane and surrounding communities had shrunk during the past hundred years. He said that the Civil War monument in the center of town listed a great many names of local men who had fought in that conflict. The World War I monument had fewer names and those listed for World War II were even fewer. The monuments were an unusual but effective comment on the decline in a town's overall population.

We walked along what appeared to be a narrow path. With his walking stick, Galbraith thumped the ground, and a solid sound came from underneath the accumulation of pine needles, leaves, and dirt. He said that there was gravel underneath, that we were walking on what once had been one of the main roads.

We came to a small clearing in the woods, and Galbraith was surprised to find that we had a pond to cross. The pond had not been there the last time he walked through this area. We quickly saw the unmistakable signs of the beaver all around us. The only way to cross was over the beaver dam itself.

The beaver is one of nature's finest engineers and builders. This one, in the southern hills of Vermont, had done its work well. We walked over the dam without displacing one stick. On the trail, we stopped to admire a sluiceway the beaver had built to send lengths of cut timber down the hillside and into the pond. Galbraith remarked that the beaver must indeed be endowed with a higher form of intelligence.

As we were coming close to his house, I wanted to get Galbraith's comments on one more influential figure, the French author and founder of *L'Express*, Jean-Jacques Servan-Schreiber. Servan-Schreiber, although not well-known to most Americans, made his literary impact on this country with his book *The American Challenge*. Unlike many Frenchmen during De Gaulle's reign who considered Americans and any aspect of American culture to be condemned and highly inferior to the French, Servan-Schreiber criticized his countrymen for being self-satisfied with their mediocrity and he upheld American technological development as a challenge to which the French must respond in order to compete in the modern industrial world. But in *The American Challenge* he was not patting the Yankees on their heads as being good boys. He said the economic unification of Europe was both urgent and the only solution to counter the increasing danger of American industrial colonialism. As leader of the Radical Party, Jean-Jacques Servan-Schreiber attempted to become president of France, but failed in his attempt. Jean-Jacques Servan-Schreiber wrote another book, *The Radical Alternative*, which had an audience in the United States; and coincidently the American edition has a foreword by John Kenneth Galbraith. In his foreword to the book, Galbraith writes, "The most literate, most discussed, most abused, and quite possibly the most interesting political leader in modern France is Jean-Jacques Servan-Schreiber. After making a name for himself as an opponent to the dead-end French policy in Algeria, then building a publication empire comparable in magnitude (if not in viewpoint) to that of Henry Luce, then in his *The American Challenge* writing one of the great, best-selling economic and political tracts of modern times, he has plunged into French politics. His aim is to rejuvenate the French Radical Socialist Party, the custodian of the greatest (as we would say) liberal tradition in French politics but, in modern times, moribund in both spirit and program."

My question to Galbraith about Servan-Schreiber was very basic: What has happened to him? Like a comet in the European sky, he flashed brilliantly across and disappeared.

"He is a very close friend of mine and so is his brother Jean-Louis. He tried to revive the Radical Party, which has fallen on evil days, and which is probably impossible to revive. He was not able to build-up the kind of political trust that a center party leader has to have. He became perceived as somewhat of an unpredictable figure, instead of one of certainty and stability. The French wanted a centrist politician in the form of an old, established figure."

I told Galbraith that Servan-Schreiber probably had a little too much panache for the French. He agreed with my observation.

We were now crossing the broad open field in front of Galbraith's house. All of a sudden, Kitty Galbraith, dressed in jodhpurs, ran out of the house and started yelling at us. We couldn't make-out what she was trying to tell us, but it seemed like a warning of some sort. When we finally reached her, she said, "Julie got loose and I was afraid that she might attack both of you. She hates men."

I was startled and asked who this Julie was. She pointed down the road and there was this magnificent chestnut-colored horse giving us the once-over. The horse seemed undecided about charging at Galbraith and myself or returning to munching the tall grass growing by the roadside. So, without further hesitation, we retreated into the safety of the house. Mrs. Galbraith told me that the horse when very young was mistreated by its former owner, a man, and the animal continued to carry an intense grudge against those of the male gender.

After tea, it was again time to leave the Galbraiths. The next time I would see them would be after this manuscript was finished, in Cambridge for a preview screening of some of the segments of his BBC television series. He said he was quite pleased with his performance in these shows.

As I stepped out of the door, I turned to Galbraith and said that our next "death march" should be at his place in Switzerland. He agreed and extended a warm invitation.

EPILOGUE

My first memory of Galbraith is when I was in the Swedish Parliament some years ago and he arrived to see me with this long, scraggly, skeletal scarecrow body. It almost shocked me, his length. He is a very delightful friend. He doesn't conceive his high opinions about himself, that he is right against the others. Yet always he succeeds by some sort of self-avoiding irony that makes him sympathetic to you. He's one of the least pompous men I know, particularly if he has not too large an audience.

Fundamentally, of course, even when Galbraith is changing his opinions on various issues and focusing them in different directions, he has always stood up against conventional economists — the school sect of conventional economists that you find in almost every university, even more in England or Sweden than in America. That is, the sect of people who keep ignorant about not only what is written in other social sciences, but also about life, about what is actually happening around them. They quote each other, read each other and no one else.

Galbraith is tremendously important as a man who is constantly challenging that conventional type of economist — even during this period of reaction not only in America but in the whole Western world. He's been very effective in bringing people to feel skeptical of what they are thinking. He writes for the broad public instead of other economists who mostly write for each other and, of course, he has at his service his wonderful style. He could just as well as Churchill become a Nobel Prize winner in literature.

One sees his natural gift when he goes outside his field and writes about his Scottish forebears in Canada. I think *The Scotch* is a wonderful book even though it's not among his economic treatises.

He's moving the direction of American ideals a little more toward the direction of Swedish democracy. For example, he always decries the lack of money given for public consumption.

Galbraith has the courage to stand for his opinions. That sometimes is missing in America. I was visiting some minor university in America and we had a faculty luncheon. Someone said to me, "How lucky you are to publish a book like *Challenge to Affluence.*" "My God," I said, "it took me exactly a month and a good secretary to write it. Why shouldn't I do it?" "Well," he replied, "if I did it I would be called a popularizer."

It's very tragic when some conventional economists are afraid to come out with a message to the people. And it's very much against old American opinions and traditions in science and economics. Always the great economists in our tradition have been people who have been prepared to simplify things and tell them to the people. And there, of course, is Galbraith — absolutely without restrictions, talking to the people in their terms. My old mathematics teacher, Gustav Castle, whom I succeeded in Sweden, used to say that the economist's work is not finished until he can get the maid to understand it. I agree that all of us should be prepared to speak the language of the people and Ken Galbraith, of course, is the glorious example of the man who is not frightened of being a "popularizer."

Of course America is quite out of balance, and Galbraith has seen this and stressed it more than anybody else. The railroads are in their present situation because automobiles have been subsidized. When I'm in New York, no one sends a letter by mail. They send a messenger. Galbraith has been courageous enough to say that America is deficient in public services — not only in welfare, but in making the state responsible for providing the right direction.

America, of course, is fundamentally a country of immigrants and their descendants, and it is split in all possible directions — ethnically, religiously, racially. I think Americans need not ethnic identity, but American identity — a solidarity with the nation.

Kenneth Galbraith comes in as a fresh wind against the old beliefs of the conventional economists and he's very much needed in America.

I admire my old friend and comrade-in-arms, Ken Galbraith, for the freedom and freshness of his thoughts and, of course, his unsurpassed mastery of presenting them. Through his writings over the years, he has been an effective countervailing force against the pretended wisdom of the politically biased sect of conventional economists, working with their closed models that exclude so much of reality. I shudder to think of the power of reactionary thinking in this country, often dressed up as "liberalism," if Galbraith's books would have been unwritten.

Gunnar Myrdal
March, 1977
Stockholm, Sweden

A
SAMPLING OF
GALBRAITH WIT

THE GREAT CRASH — 1929

Like most other liberal academicians, I had been a thoughtful observer of the methods of the Wisconsin Titus Oates. Two had always seemed to me worth adopting by anyone attacked. The first was to avoid defense of one's self and instead assault the accuser. The second was to avoid any suspicion, however remote, of personal modesty.

I have never adhered to the view that Wall Street is uniquely evil, just as I have never found it possible to accept with complete confidence the alternative view, rather more palatable in sound financial circles, that it is uniquely wise.

Courage is required of the man who, when things are good, says so.

This is a world inhabited not by people who have to be persuaded to believe but by people who want an excuse to believe.

. . . the time had come, as in all periods of speculation, when men sought not to be persuaded of the reality of things but to find excuses for escaping into the new world of fantasy.

By affirming solemnly that prosperity will continue, it is believed, one can help insure that prosperity will in fact continue. Especially among businessmen the faith in the efficiency of such incantation is very great.

Such is the genius of capitalism that where a real demand exists it does not go long unfilled.

One of the oldest puzzles of politics is who is to regulate the regulators. But an equally baffling problem, which has never received the attention it deserves, is who is to make wise those who are required to have wisdom.

The regulation of economic activity is without doubt the most inelegant and unrewarding of public endeavors.

If there must be madness something may be said for having it on a heroic scale.

Between human beings there is a type of intercourse which proceeds not from knowledge, or even from the lack of knowledge, but from failure to know what isn't known.

Wisdom, itself, is often an abstraction associated not with fact or reality but with the man who asserts it and the manner of its assertion.

. . . as often in our culture, it is far better to be wrong in a respectable way then to be right for the wrong reasons.

Of all the mysteries of the stock exchange there is none so impenetrable as why there should be a buyer for everyone who seeks to sell.

Our political life favors the extremes of speech; the man who is gifted in the arts of abuse is bound to be a notable, if not always a great figure.

A banker need not be popular; indeed, a good banker in a healthy capitalist society should probably be much disliked.

The autumn of 1929 was, perhaps, the first occasion when men succeeded on a large scale in swindling themselves.

Two men jumped hand-in-hand from a high window in the Ritz. They had a joint account.

To the economist embezzlement is the most interesting of crimes.

Even though nothing of importance is said or done, men of importance cannot meet without the occasion seeming important.

One trouble with being wrong is that it robs the prophet of his audience when he most needs it to explain why.

Speculation on a large scale requires a pervasive sense of confidence and optimism and conviction that ordinary people were meant to be rich.

When people are least sure they are often most dogmatic.

. . . it is that very specific and personal misfortune awaits those who presume to believe that the future is revealed to them.

Long-run salvation by men of business has never been highly regarded if it means disturbance of orderly life and convenience in the present. So inaction will be advocated in the present even though it means deep trouble in the future. Here, at least equally with communism, lies the threat to capitalism. It is what causes men who know that things are going quite wrong to say that things are fundamentally sound.

AMERICAN CAPITALISM

. . . one of the most important and difficult of the responsibilities of the economist is to resist the authority of the accepted.

Good times may last out this year and next, but obviously we are going to have a smash one of these days.

It is a simple matter of arithmetic that change *may* be costly to the man who has something: it cannot be so to the man who has nothing.

Man cannot live without an economic theology — without some rationalization of the abstract and seemingly inchoate arrangements which provide him with his livelihood.

Indeed, for most Americans free competition, so called, has for long been a political rather than an economic concept.

No union leader ever presents himself as anything but a spokesman for the boys.

Prestige in business is equally associated with power.

Power obviously presents awkward problems for a community which abhors its existence, disavows its possession, but values its exercise.

In a state of bliss, there is no need for a Ministry of Bliss.

To resist progress is to perish. If there is only a handful of producers, there is a chance that none will assume the initiative. There is at least the possibility that all will prefer and concur in choosing profitable and comfortable stagnation.

In the American liberal tradition, a finding that private economic power exists has been tantamount to a demand that it be suppressed.

Pessimism in our time is infinitely more respectable than optimism; the man who foresees peace, prosperity, and a decline in juvenile delinquency is a negligent and vacuous fellow.

The man who foresees trouble — except perhaps on the stock market — has a gift of insight which insures that he will become a radio commentator, an editor of *Time* or go to Congress.

There is no more pleasant fiction than that technical change is the product of the matchless ingenuity of the small man forced by competition to employ his wits to better his neighbor.

There is a deeply held belief, the Puritan antecedents of which are clear, that if a wealthy man admits even to himself that he can afford a measure of recklessness in his expenditures, an angry God will strike him dead — or certainly take away his money.

In one way or another the vendor has always had to cry his wares; the modern techniques that are brought to the service of his particular task may be no more costly or no more raucous than those that have been used throughout time.

In one way or another nearly all of the great American fortunes are based on the present or past possession of monopoly power.

In principle the American is controlled, livelihood and soul, by the large corporation; in practice he seems not to be completely enslaved.

The more commonplace but more important tactic in the exercise of countervailing power consists, merely, in keeping the seller in a state of uncertainty as to the intentions of a buyer who is indispensable to him.

It is by our experience, not our fears, that we should be guided.

Like the executioners during the French Revolution, they have offered the guillotine as a cure for the headache. This is not the best frame of mind in which to seek improvement in what is certain to continue.

There is nothing an economist should fear so much as applause, and I believe I am reasonably secure.

It is sufficiently candid to keep the American businessman constantly alarmed about the ideas of economists but sufficiently conservative to make the alarm unwarranted.

THE AFFLUENT SOCIETY

In economics, it is often professionally better to be associated with highly respectable error than uncertainly established truth.

In a world where everyone is poor, there is nothing very remarkable about poverty. It becomes remarkable, and also less forgivable, in a community where the great majority of people are well-to-do.

. . . beyond doubt, wealth is the relentless enemy of understanding.

. . . the bland lead the bland.

The affluent country which conducts its affairs in accordance with rules of another and poorer age also forgoes opportunities.

To a very large extent, of course, we associate truth with convenience.

The enemy of the conventional wisdom is n t ideas but the march of events.

Only posterity is unkind to the man of conventional wisdom, and all posterity does is bury him in a blanket of neglect.

Ideas are inherently conservative. They yield not to the attack of other ideas but to the massive onslaught of circumstances with which they cannot contend.

But many had always perished for one reason or another. Now some were flourishing. This was what counted.

The race for increased efficiency required that the loser should lose.

. . . Veblen dramatized, as no one before or since, the spectacle of inequality. The rich and successful were divorced from any serious economic function and denied the dignity of even a serious indignant attack. They became, instead, a subject for detached, bemused and even contemptuous observation.

Might it be that Marx faced facts while others sought the dubious shelter of wishful thinking?

. . . few things are more evident in modern social history than the decline of interest in inequality as an economic issue.

As the rich have become more numerous, they have inevitably become a debased currency.

Over the centuries, those who have been blessed with wealth have developed many ingenious and persuasive justifications for their good fortune.

In the conventional wisdom of conservatives, the modern search for security is billed as the greatest single threat to economic progress.

Precisely because he lives a careful life, the executive is moved to identify himself with the dashing entrepreneur of economic literature.

While unemployment compensation is better than nothing, a job is better than either.

The most impressive increases in output in the history of both the United States and other western countries have occurred since men began to concern themselves with reducing the risks of the competitive system.

Why is that as production has increased in modern times concern for production seems also to have increased?

We view the production of some of the most frivolous goods with pride. We regard the production of some of the most significant and civilizing services with regret.

Nothing in economics so quickly marks an individual as incompetently trained as a disposition to remark on the legitimacy of the desire for more food and the frivolity of the desire for a more elaborate automobile.

Production only fills a void that it has itself created.

It is a far, far better thing to have a firm anchor in nonsense than to put out on the troubled seas of thought.

When the speaker himself enjoys it, it ceases to be a vested interest and becomes a hard-won reward.

A businessman who reads *Business Week* is lost to fame. One who reads Proust is marked for greatness.

Can the bill collector be the central figure in the good society?

The individual has an instinct for good living that should be encouraged. . . .

Through most of man's history, the counterpart of war, civil disorder, famine or other cosmic disaster has been inflation.

In the political spectrum of modern economic policy, monetary measures are the instrument of conservatives. The weapon of liberals is fiscal policy.

Just as there must be balance in what a community produces, so there must also be balance in what the community consumes.

The greater the wealth, the thicker will be the dirt.

An austere community is free from temptation. It can be austere in its public services. Not so a rich one.

Over much of the world, there is a rough and not accidental correlation between the strength of indigenous communist parties or the frequency of revolution and the persistence of inflation.

. . . men of high position are allowed, by a special act of grace, to accommodate their reasoning to the answer they need. Logic is only required in those of lesser rank.

Our liberties are now menaced by the conformity exacted by the large corporation and its impulse to create, for its own purposes, the organization man.

Investment in human beings is, *prima facie,* as important as investment in material capital.

. . . the rate of technical progress in American industry in recent decades would have been markedly slower had it not been for military inspired and for this reason publically supported research.

The nontheological quality which most distinguishes men from horses is the desire, in addition to these attributes of material and psychic well-being, to know, understand and reason.

Education . . . is a double-edged sword for the affluent society.

Emancipation of the mind is a no less worthy enterprise than emancipation of the body.

Social philosophy, far more than nature, abhors a vacuum.

The income men derive from producing things of slight consequence is of great consequence.

It is the good fortune of a rich country that like a rich man, it has the luxury of choice. But it cannot avoid choosing.

The economy is geared to the least urgent set of human values. It would be far more secure if it were based on the whole range of need.

Once the decision was taken to make education universal and compulsory, it ceased to be a marketable commodity.

. . . high tax rates are justifiable for military purposes but considered immoral and confiscatory if used for civilian purposes.

Poverty is self-perpetuating because the poorest communities are poorest in the services which would eliminate it.

The limiting factor is not knowledge of what can be done. Overwhelmingly, it is a shortage of money.

Few things enlarge the liberty of the individual more substantially than to grant him a measure of control over the amount of his income.

We are able to dispense with the labor of those who have reached retiring age because the goods they add are a low order of urgency, whereas a poor society must extract the last ounce of labor effort from all.

Nearly all societies at nearly all times have had a leisure class — a class of persons who were exempt from toil.

The New Class is not exclusive. While virtually no one leaves it, thousands join it every year. Overwhelmingly, the qualification is education.

A society has one higher task than to consider its goals, to reflect on its pursuit of happiness and harmony and its success in expelling pain, tension, sorrow and the ubiquitous curse of ignorance. It must also, so far as this may be possible, insure its own survival.

. . . the basic demand on America will be on its resources of ability, intelligence and education.

THE NEW INDUSTRIAL STATE

Those who say that what is so seen cannot be proven are, in effect, saying that nothing can be proven. They are using a pseudo-scientific syllogism to avert attention from reality.

Those who serve in the industrial system are rarely poor; those who are not members often are.

A corporation, contemplating an automobile of revised aspect, must be able to persuade people to buy it. It is equally important that people be able to do so.

The imperatives of technology and organization, not the images of ideology, are what determine the shape of economic society.

. . . we are becoming the servants in thought, as in action, of the machine we have created to serve us.

Modern liberalism carefully emphasizes tact rather than clarity of speech.

The denial that we do any planning has helped to conceal the fact of such control (individual behavior) even from those who are controlled.

Much of what the firm regards as planning consists in minimizing or getting rid of risks.

The option of eliminating a market is an important source of power for controlling it.

The fully planned economy, so far from being unpopular, is warmly regarded by those who know it best.

By all but the pathologically romantic, it is now recognized that this is not the age of the small man.

. . . the enemy of the market is not ideology but the engineer.

The individual serves the industrial system not by supplying it with savings and the resulting capital; he serves it by consuming its products.

In the assumption that power belongs as a matter of course to capital, all economists are Marxists.

Beneath the mantled cross [during the Crusades] beat hearts soundly attuned to the value of real estate.

If a man adds little and can easily be replaced, he has small power and small bargaining power.

Power goes to the factor which is hardest to obtain or hardest to replace.

The entrepreneur — individualistic, restless, with vision, guile and courage — has been the economists only hero.

One can do worse than think of a business organization as a hierarchy of committees.

Men who believe themselves deeply engaged in private thought are usually doing nothing.

Group decision, unless acted upon by another group, tends to be absolute.

A vivid image of what *should* exist acts as a surrogate for reality. Pursuit of the image then prevents pursuit of the reality.

By taking decisions away from individuals and locating them deeply within the technostructure, technology and planning thus remove them from the influence of outsiders.

As stockholders cease to have influence . . . efforts are made to disguise this nullity.

The annual meeting of the large American corporation is, perhaps, our most elaborate exercise in popular illusion.

The assertion of competitive individualism by the corporate executive, to the extent that it is still encountered, is ceremonial, traditional or a manifestation of personal vanity and capacity for self-delusion.

Between being in and out of political office the difference is not slight. It is total.

Socialism has come to mean government by socialists who have learned that socialism, as anciently understood, is impractical.

The market has only one message for the business firm. That is the promise of more money.

The essence of free enterprise is to go after profit in any way that is consistent with its own survival.

In our culture few things give more pleasure than the sight of men caught in embarrassments of their own manufacture.

. . . in the past, many notably avaricious men have thought it well to protest their fealty to a higher morality than making money.

. . . the executive cannot afford to have it thought that his commitment to the goals of the corporation is less than complete or that he is at all indifferent to his opportunity to shape these goals. To suggest that he subordinates these latter motives to his response to pay would be to confess that he is an inferior executive.

That one need never look beyond the love of money for explanation of human behavior is one of the most jealously guarded simplifications of our anthropology.

What is marketable in a textbook is what is commonly believed or what is commonly believed to be believed.

"Who are you with?" Until this is known, the individual is a cipher.

To the desire of the individual to mold the world to his goals, a thoughtful Providence has added the illusion of a great ability to do so.

Truth is never strengthened by exaggeration.

Modern economic belief is the servant, in substantial measure, of the society which nurtures it.

We discriminate against those who, as a result of numbers and weakness, must use crude or overt methods to control their markets and in favor of those who, because of achieved size and power, are under no such compulsion.

The further a man is removed from physical need the more open he is to persuasion — or management — as to what he buys.

The industrial system is profoundly dependent on commercial television and could not exist in its present form without it.

Advertising by making goods important makes the industrial system important. And therewith it helps to sustain the social importance and prestige that attach to the technostructure.

Like private consumption, any new public service quickly becomes a part of the accustomed standard of living.

Men of conservative temperament have long suspected that one thing leads to another.

Only the soft-minded could suppose that government, by regulation, could thwart the primal instinct for self-enrichment.

In almost any view the unions are less militant in attitude and less powerful in politics than in earlier times.

Shared privation is easier to bear than individual privation.

Pecuniary power expresses itself in highly unsubtle form; it offers financial reward for conformity or threatens financial damage for dissent.

The financier and the union leader are dwindling influences in the society. They are honored more for their past eminence than for their present power.

But no man who believes in liberty can accept a world that is forever half slave and half free.

Indeed it may be laid down as a rule of foreign relations that the lower the probability that advice will be taken, the more firmly it will be proffered.

Yet it remains that the Cold War has elements of a self-fulfilling prophecy for it has cultivated the reciprocal mistrust which it assumes.

To excel, or to hope to excel, is sufficient to justify the contest.

For knowledge of the forces by which one is constrained is the first step toward freedom.

Artists do not come in teams.

Art is one manifestation of order. And it is the first casualty of disorder.

Men who speak much of liberty should allow and even encourage it.

The price that the industrial system must pay for the education of *its* people and the conduct of *its* research is the support of general enlightenment.

Those who complain that they have been censored in the United States usually turn out, on examination, to have had nothing much to say.

Those one would least trust to decide man's fate are invariably the first to pronounce upon it.

One does not wonder where one is going if one is already there.

Vanity is a great force for intellectual modernization.

The two questions most asked about an economic system are whether it serves man's physical needs and whether it is consistent with his liberty.

But it can be laid down as a rule that those who speak most of liberty are least inclined to use it.

The danger to liberty lies in the subordination of belief to the needs of the industrial system.

We must remind ourselves that specialization is a scientific convenience, not a scientific virtue.

Even personal liberty is best defended and spiritual salvation best pursued on a full stomach. In a poor society, economics is not all of life but, as a practical matter, it is most of it.

To many it will always seem better to have measurable progress toward the wrong goals than unmeasurable and hence uncertain progress toward the right ones.

Knowledge for the intellectual is what skill is for the artisan and capital for the businessman.

ECONOMICS AND THE PUBLIC PURPOSE

For better or for worse I am a reformer and not a revolutionist.

Left to themselves, economic forces do not work out for the best except perhaps for the powerful.

The best economic system is the one that supplies the most of what people most want.

Who would pay more than the going price if he could get all he wanted at the going price?

The conversion of women into a crypto-servant class was an economic accomplishment of the first importance.

The servant role of women is critical for the expansion of consumption in the modern economy.

In fact the modern household does not allow expression of individual personality and preference. It requires extensive subordination of preference by one member or another.

No innovation of importance originates with the individual farmer. Were it not for the government and the farm equipment and chemical firms, agriculture would be technologically stagnant.

The excessively independent man is regularly defended in an organization as 'something of an artist.'

. . . the artistic superiority of the small firm will often allow of its survival in competition with the large organization.

The technostructure [of the large corporation] embraces and uses the engineer and the scientist; it cannot embrace the artist.

Only the more modest religious offices share the artist's belief that merit is inversely related to compensaticn.

The number of artists produced cannot, however, exceed the number of people with intrinsic talent.

The large corporation is the recipient of little social praise. The small entrepreneur, in contrast, is all but universally admired.

The power of management is not flaunted. Rather it is subject to elaborate disguise.

. . . a modestly inadequate man will seem a genius among men of more determined mediocrity.

. . . economics, as always, is a tapestry in which each part must be in harmony with the rest.

It is inconceivable that the public could be universally exploited without being aware of it.

The first step in reform, it follows, is to win emancipation of belief.

. . . the human mind has a retrieving resistance to authority.

. . . the woman, as the administrator, should have the decisive voice on the style of life, for she shoulders the main burden.

. . . it will be generally agreed that women are not less stupid than men and that the intelligence available to the technostructure is, at any time, limited.

Those who get the largest pay have the most pleasant jobs.

In contrast those who do the most unpleasant and soul-destroying jobs get the least pay.

The large weapons firms are already socialized except in name. . . .

In economics there are few absolutes.

. . . those who have found more comfort than they knew in the fact that economists teach and discuss the wrong problems or none at all.

NOTES

CHAPTER 1

1. John Kenneth Galbraith, *The Age of Uncertainty* (Boston: Houghton Mifflin Co., 1977), p. 77.
2. David McLellan, *Karl Marx: His Life and Thought* (New York: Harper & Row, 1973), p. 14.
3. Ibid., p. 56.
4. David McLellan, ed., *Karl Marx: Early Texts* (Oxford: Blackwell, 1972), p. 129.
5. Ibid., p. 217.
6. Galbraith, *Age of Uncertainty*, p. 91.
7. Karl Marx, *The Communist Manifesto*, in Karl Marx and Friedrich Engels, *Selected Works*, Vol. 1 (New York, Pathfinder Press of New York, 1962), pp. 108–37.
8. Galbraith, *Age of Uncertainty*, p. 96.
9. McLellan, *Early Texts*, pp. 268–9.
10. Karl Marx, *Capital: A Critique of Political Economy*, Vol. 1 (Chicago: Charles H. Kerr & Co., 1926), pp. 836–7.
11. McLellan, *Early Texts*, pp. 365–6.
12. Galbraith, *Age of Uncertainty*, p. 57.
13. Ibid., p. 60.
14. Ibid.

CHAPTER 2

1. R. F. Harrod, *The Life of John Maynard Keynes* (London: Macmillan & Co., 1951), p. 121.
2. Ibid., p. 256.
3. Galbraith, *Age of Uncertainty*, p. 207.
4. Arthur M. Schlesinger, Jr., *The Crisis of the Old Order* (Boston: Houghton Mifflin Co., 1957), p. 231.
5. Galbraith, *Age of Uncertainty*, p. 213.

6. Harrod, *John Maynard Keynes*, p. 447.
7. Robert Lekachman, *The Age of Keynes* (New York: Random House, 1966), p. 123.
8. Ibid.
9. Galbraith, *Age of Uncertainty*, p. 218.
10. Ibid., p. 222.
11. Ibid., p. 223.
12. Ibid., p. 224.

CHAPTER 3

1. John Kenneth Galbraith, *The Affluent Society* (Boston: Houghton Mifflin Co., 1971), pp. 240–1.
2. Ibid., p. 250.
3. Ibid., p. 257.
4. Ibid., pp. 302–3.
5. Ibid., p. 308.
6. Galbraith, *Age of Uncertainty*, p. 67.
7. Ibid.
8. Ibid., p. 71.
9. Ibid.
10. Ibid., p. 75.

CHAPTER 4

1. John Kenneth Galbraith, *Economics and the Public Purpose* (Boston: Houghton Mifflin Co., 1973), p. x.
2. Galbraith, *Affluent Society*, p. 294.
3. Ibid.
4. Ibid., p. 6.
5. Ibid., p. 7.
6. Ibid., p. 8.
7. Ibid., p. 18.

CHAPTER 5

1. Galbraith, *Affluent Society*, p. 224.
2. Ibid., p. 229.
3. Ibid., p. 227.
4. Ibid., p. 231.
5. Ibid., p. 232.
6. Ibid., p. 300.
7. Galbraith, *Public Purpose*, p. xiii.

CHAPTER 6

1. Galbraith, *Public Purpose*, p. 30.
2. Ibid.

3. John Kenneth Galbraith, *The New Industrial State* (Boston: Houghton Mifflin Co., 1971), p. 148.
4. Ibid., p. 156.
5. Ibid., p. 161.
6. Galbraith, *Affluent Society*, pp. 92–3.
7. Galbraith, *Public Purpose*, p. 44.
8. Ibid.
9. Galbraith, *Affluent Society*, p. 152.
10. Galbraith, *New Industrial State*, p. 206.
11. Ibid., p. 211.
12. Ibid., p. 213.
13. Ibid.
14. Galbraith, *Public Purpose*, p. 236.
15. Ibid., p. 237.

CHAPTER 7

1. Galbraith, *Public Purpose*, p. 64.
2. Ibid., p. 66.

CHAPTER 8

1. Galbraith, *Affluent Society*, p. 181.
2. John Kenneth Galbraith, *Money: Whence It Came, Where It Went* (Boston: Houghton Mifflin Co., 1975), p. 155.
3. Galbraith, *Affluent Society*, pp. 191–2.
4. Galbraith, *Money*, p. 290.

CHAPTER 9

1. Galbraith, *New Industrial State*, p. i.
2. Ibid., p. 21.
3. Ibid., p. 30.
4. Ibid., p. 61.
5. Ibid., p. 63.
6. Ibid., p. 81.
7. Galbraith, *Money*, p. 5.
8. Galbraith, *New Industrial State*, p. 176.
9. Galbraith, *Public Purpose*, p. 75.
10. Ibid., p. 259.
11. Ibid., p. 261.
12. Ibid., p. 262.
13. Galbraith, *New Industrial State*, p. 331.

CHAPTER 10

1. John Kenneth Galbraith, *Ambassador's Journal* (Boston: Houghton Mifflin Co., 1969), p. 42.

2.   Ibid., pp. 44–5.
3.   Ibid., p. 46.
4.   Ibid., p. 52.
5.   Ibid.
6.   Ibid., p. 54.
7.   Ibid., p. 63.
8.   Ibid., p. 69.
9.   Ibid.
10.   Ibid., p. 89.
11.   Ibid.
12.   Ibid.
13.   Ibid., pp. 89–90.
14.   Ibid., p. 107.
15.   Ibid., p. 127.
16.   Ibid., p. 132.
17.   Ibid., p. 135.
18.   Ibid., p. 136.
19.   Ibid., p. 154.
20.   Ibid., p. 156.
21.   Ibid., p. 187.
22.   Ibid., p. 205.
23.   Ibid., p. 210.
24.   Ibid., p. 235.
25.   Ibid., p. 248.
26.   Ibid., p. 252.
27.   Ibid., p. 256.
28.   Ibid., p. 266.
29.   Ibid., pp. 267–8.
30.   Ibid., p. 317.
31.   Ibid., pp. 342–3.
32.   Ibid., p. 344.
33.   Ibid., p. 431.
34.   Ibid., p. 433.
35.   Ibid.
36.   Ibid., p. 447.
37.   Ibid., p. 464.
38.   Ibid., p. 473.
39.   Ibid., p. 474.
40.   Ibid., p. 475.
41.   Ibid., p. 510.
42.   Ibid., p. 519.
43.   Ibid., p. 560.
44.   John Kenneth Galbraith, *The Triumph* (Boston: Houghton Mifflin Co., 1968), p. 48.
45.   Ibid., p. 57.

46.   John Kenneth Galbraith, *A China Passage* (Boston: Houghton Mifflin Co., 1973), pp. 17–8.
47.   Ibid., p. 19.
48.   Ibid., p. 23.
49.   Ibid.
50.   Ibid., p. 27.
51.   Ibid., p. 119.
52.   Ibid., p. 34.
53.   Ibid., p. 44.
54.   Ibid., p. 52.
55.   Ibid., p. 61.
56.   Ibid., p. 75.
57.   Ibid., p. 98.
58.   Ibid.
59.   Ibid., p. 101.
60.   Ibid., p. 136.
61.   Ibid., p. 137.
62.   Ibid.
63.   Ibid.
64.   Ibid., p. 138.
65.   Galbraith, *Age of Uncertainty*, p. 243.
66.   Ibid., p. 245.
67.   Ibid., p. 246.
68.   Ibid.
69.   Ibid., p. 248.
70.   Ibid.
71.   Ibid., p. 256.

CHAPTER 11

1.   Galbraith, *Ambassador's Journal*, p. 17.
2.   Ibid.
3.   Ibid., p. 588.
4.   Ibid.
5.   Ibid., p. 629.
6.   Ibid., pp. 629–30.
7.   Ibid., p. 632.
8.   Ibid.

CHAPTER 15

1.   Galbraith, *Age of Uncertainty*, p. 136.
2.   Ibid., p. 138.
3.   Ibid.
4.   Ibid., p. 133.
5.   Ibid., p. 142.

6.   Galbraith, *Age of Uncertainty,* p. 142.
7.   Ibid., p. 22.
8.   Adam Smith, *Wealth of Nations,* Vol. 1 (London: Methuen & Co., 1950), p. 412.
9.   Ibid., p. 144.
10. Adam Smith, *Wealth of Nations,* Vol. 2 (London: Methuen & Co., 1950), p. 264.
11. Ibid., pp. 264–5.
12. John Rae, *Life of Adam Smith* (New York: Augustus M. Kelley, 1965), pp. 290–1.
13. Galbraith, *Age of Uncertainty,* p. 32.
14. Ibid., p. 36.
15. Ibid., p. 37.
16. Dudley Edwards, *The Great Famine* (Dublin: Brown & Nolan, 1956), p. 257.
17. Galbraith, *Age of Uncertainty,* p. 40.
18. Herbert Spencer, *The Study of Sociology* (New York: D. Appleton & Co., 1891), p. 438.
19. Herbert Spencer, *Social Statics* (New York: D. Appleton & Co., 1865), p. 413.
20. Galbraith, *Age of Uncertainty,* p. 46.
21. Richard Hofstadter, *Social Darwinism in American Thought 1860–1915* (Philadelphia: University of Pennsylvania Press, 1945), p. 44.
22. Galbraith, *Age of Uncertainty,* p. 55.

CHAPTER 16
1.   Galbraith, *Ambassador's Journal,* p. 598.

BIBLIOGRAPHY

American Capitalism. Boston: Houghton Mifflin, 1952, rev. ed. 1956.
The premise here is that the industrial corporations, now more powerful than ever and less subject to the competition of the marketplace, are controlled by a new mechanism called "countervailing power."

A Theory of Price Control. Cambridge, Mass.: Harvard University Press, 1952.
An account of Galbraith's experience as deputy administrator of the Office of Price Administration during WWII; an early articulation of his views on controls which have dominated his economic philosophy to the present time.

The Great Crash: 1929. Boston: Houghton Mifflin, 1954 (3rd ed. 1972).
Describes the events leading up to the crash of 1929, the mood of the time, the crash itself, and its implications for the future.

Economics and the Art of Controversy. New Brunswick, N.J.: Rutgers University Press, 1955.
In a bold analysis of some current battlefields of economic controversy, this essay advances a thought provoking rationale for disagreement among Americans on matters of prime economic importance; i.e., trade unions vs. private employers, the welfare state, etc.

The Affluent Society. Boston: Houghton Mifflin, 1958, revised 1969 and 1976.
The book which firmly established Galbraith as one of America's leading thinkers in the related fields of economics, sociology, and politics. The main thesis is that an affluent society over-produces and over-consumes private goods of little consequence while, at the same time, it refuses to spend money on public services of great consequence, such as education, health, the environment, or the elimination of poverty.

267

The Liberal Hour. Boston: Houghton Mifflin, 1960.
Discusses pertinent issues ranging from U.S. economic competition with Russia to the public images of U.S. politicians.

Economic Development in Perspective. Cambridge, Mass.: Harvard University Press, 1962.
A series of lectures dealing with poverty, choice of an economic system, planning, education, etc.

The Scotch. Boston: Houghton Mifflin, 1964.
This book tells of the Scotch in Canada and their countryside as it was in the author's youth. It is Galbraith's autobiography of his early years.

Economic Development. Cambridge, Mass.: Harvard University Press, 1964.
A revised and enlarged edition of *Economic Development in Perspective*.

The New Industrial State. Boston: Houghton Mifflin, 1967, second edition revised 1971, third edition 1978.
The case presented here is that classical economics (where the consumer and the citizen are sovereign) is incorrect and that the real power lies in the hands of the technostructures; e.g., the great industrial bureaucracies.

How To Get Out of Vietnam. *The New York Times*, NAL, 1967.
A carefully reasoned tough-minded plan for U.S. action to solve its dilemma in Southeast Asia.

The Triumph. Boston: Houghton Mifflin, 1968.
A novel about rebellion in an undistinguished and sleepy Latin American republic, and a lampoon against the U.S. State Department.

Indian Painting. Boston: Houghton Mifflin, 1968, co-authored with Randhawa, Mojinder S.
A critical and historical analysis of classical Indian painting; with illustrations.

How to Control the Military. New York: Doubleday, 1969.
A succinct primer on the military-industrial complex: how it developed, how it wields power, and how it can be controlled.

Ambassador's Journal. Boston: Houghton Mifflin, 1969.
A diary of John Kenneth Galbraith's tour of duty as Ambassador to India. Galbraith here discusses his early attempt to keep the U.S. from involvement in Vietnam, candid comments on many famous political individuals of the sixties, and his role in the India-China border dispute; a major book on Galbraith's role and influence during the Kennedy years.

Who Needs the Democrats. New York: Doubleday, 1970.
This book discusses the reasons for the successful years of the Democratic Party and how each of these turned into failure:

— Keynesian economics
— The promise of the welfare state
— The alliance with the trade unions
— Progress toward racial equality
— Foreign policy that reflected what he calls the "super power mystique"

Economics, Peace and Laughter. Boston: Houghton Mifflin, 1971.
Essays on economics, politics, and famous friends and enemies.

Economics and the Public Purpose. Boston: Houghton Mifflin, 1973.
Galbraith explores the world system of the small entrepreneur, the planning system of the large firms, the state as an instrument of the planning system, and how the economic-political system can be reformed.

A China Passage. Boston: Houghton Mifflin, 1973.
Galbraith recounts his visit to mainland China in 1972 with his two predecessor presidents of the American Economic Association, Professors Wassily Leontief of Harvard and James Tobin of Yale.

Money: Whence It Came, Where It Went. Boston: Houghton Mifflin, 1975.
A broad treatment tracing the history of money from the period of the kings of Lydia to the present.

The Age of Uncertainty. Boston: Houghton Mifflin, 1977.
Textual version of Galbraith's BBC-TV series of the same title. An entertaining and illuminating historical treatment of economics in Europe and North America from the time of Adam Smith to the present, with sage insights into our future.